BRITAIN'S MAIN-LINE RAILWAYS

Edited by P. B. Whitehouse

NEW ENGLISH LIBRARY
TIMES MIRROR

Volume Editor: P. B. Whitehouse
General Editor: E. L. Cornwell
Picture Editors: Patricia E. Hornsey

Copyright © New English Library 1977

First published in this format by New English Library,
Barnard's Inn, Holborn, London EC1N 2JR in 1977.

Printed in Italy by Stabilimento Grafico Editoriale
Fratelli Spada S.p.A. Ciampino (Roma)

4500 33422

1 (previous page) GWR 0-4-2T No 1466 on the Wallingford
branch. *M Pope*

2 Driving wheel of Bulleid Pacific *Okehampton*. *M Pope*

3 (following page) Nameplate and driving wheel of Stanier
Pacific *Princess Elizabeth*. *R Bastin*

2

CONTENTS

INTRODUCTION

The year 1975 saw the passing of a century and a half of passenger train operations by steam. The Stockton and Darlington Railway of Henry Pease proved to the world that the Stephensonian steam locomotive was the only practical prime mover, though in truth the Middleton Railway in Leeds and Trevithick before that had been forerunners in the race. But it was the Liverpool and Manchester and Grand Junction lines which really placed steam traction on the map and the names of the great engineers in the history books; George Stephenson, Robert Stephenson, Locke, Bury, Brunel and Gooch, all now house-hold names. With the engineers and the railways came the inevitable amalgamations, the Railway Mania and finally the building, stage by stage, in earnest competition, of the great trunk lines which still exist today. It is interesting to note that it is the early railways joining the major towns which still remain, whilst their younger sisters, built with a desire to tap what was left of the traffic, have disappeared under relentless economic pressure and the change brought about by the invention of the internal combustion engine.

The lines engineered by the Stephensons, Locke and Brunel — Liverpool to Manchester, Liverpool to Birmingham, Birmingham to London and London to Bristol, are still vital arteries for both passenger and freight, where inter-city trains roll behind purring electrics and snarling diesels. The later line of the Watkin empire, the Manchester Sheffield and Lincolnshire Railway's extension to London, ambitiously styled the Great Central, has gone and the last main line to Scotland, the Midland, is in danger. Duplication of routes can no longer stand up against the motor car and lorry, the improved roads and the motorways.

Britain's railways, great and small, found themselves in dire trouble after the first World War, and by 1923 all were grouped into four main companies: the London, Midland and Scottish, the London and North Eastern, the Great Western and the Southern. A few minor — very minor — lines escaped the net, but most were absorbed into one or other of the Big Four. World War II saw to it that even this situation was no longer tenable, and after twenty-five years of tribulations, competition and economic problems, the Four were welded into one under nationalisation; the lame ducks were to be fed by the British tax-payer for his convenience.

With the help of carefully chosen pictures, mostly in colour, this book tells this story of the four main lines, their evolution, their public and private faces, train operation, signalling, locomotive and coach development over a hundred and twenty-five years, with the emphasis on the period from 1923 to 1948. Though little of the text may be new to the enthusiast, the pictures, brought together in this context, are evocative of an exciting period of railway development. Today, with a modern railway system that is constantly in need of cash transfusions but nevertheless provides essential services appropriate to the times, it is easy to forget that railways were once built not only to provide public transport, but also to bring a profit to their shareholders — and good profits too for many years. These early days provided little in the way of competition except for the horse, and, just as the great trunk lines of Canada and America opened up those huge countries, so it was with Britain in Victoria's reign. The story of the Big Four is one of big change which the companies could not digest, partly through the constraints put on them. For instance, freight charges were set by the book, leaving road transport to undercut these at will. Yet for the enthusiast they were interesting though somewhat sad years; interesting because of the tremendous variety of locomotive power, the charming branch lines, and the introduction of new and larger engines; and sad because all these were slowly to disappear. There was excitement too, for the 1920s saw the coming of the Kings and Castles, the A3 Pacifics and the Nelsons; the 1930s was the streamline era with the LMS and LNER competing in the routes to Scotland. Fares were cheap, too. One old penny per mile third class (now second class) was the going rate and one could find even cheaper excursion rates; for instance six shillings and six pence (32p) took you from Birmingham to London and back, and on a weekend the Birmingham to Glasgow return fare was just under one pound. These, too, were the days of the travelling Post Office vans, with their set-down and pick-up gear to ensure swift deliveries, the slip coach was still in vogue and the idea of a streamlined diesel rail car (the Great Western's of course) novel.

The Big Four have now passed into history and even the bric-a-brac of the old-type railway system is being swept away relentlessly. That period was still one of solidarity, of the steam engine, semaphore signals, cavernous stations and the railway horse to help with the shunting. It is worthy of remembrance.

EARLY DAYS

The Railway Mania

OFTEN ENOUGH an innovator has at first to contend with popular scepticism or even opposition. Then he has his way and the dust settles for a while, and his old opponents and the public at large hold their peace and observe. Then, if the innovation succeeds and especially if it makes money, very often there is a sudden awesome rush as everybody joins the party, the ancient scoffers often leading the field. So it was with railways. During the 1830s the first parts of the main-line inter-city network began to be laid down in Britain, and by 1841 you could travel by train from London to Brighton, Southampton, Bristol, and Birmingham, while branching or extending from the London & Birmingham Railway were lines to Liverpool and Manchester, Leeds, Derby, and York.

These railways had not been in business for more than a few years, but they rapidly proved two things to the whole country. First of all, they gave a very useful and convenient service for passengers and freight, which was of great advantage also to the districts served in opening up new markets for their produce. Secondly, the railway companies were profitable, and paid a very reasonable return on the money invested in them.

By 1841 there were some 1,500 miles of railway in operation in Britain. For the next couple of years there was rapid but fairly steady growth. The government had kept some control over the development of new schemes both by careful debate in Parliament and by requiring them to be approved in draft by a Commission set up for the purpose, which had to consider both the public need for any new railway and also its effect on existing lines. But the Commission was short-lived and was abolished in 1845 out of a feeling that railway promoters knew their own business best, while at the same time a vast rush of new Bills overwhelmed the government machinery. All of a sudden the public caught on to the idea of a national railway grid, which 'Punch' ridiculed by publishing a satirical map of the future, apparently insanely complex,

British railway network which, fifty years later, had come to look fairly accurate. One of the biggest laughs had been the idea of railways in the Isle of Man.

But as so often when politicians' and economists' fashion prompts action, greed also appeared. Many of the schemes of 1845 were ill-considered and not a few were downright fraudulent. For a while it was possible to put one's name down as a subscriber to a railway scheme, receiving shares for a nominal payment, which one could then resell at a substantial profit, so eager was the throng of investors with spare cash; and of course the sharks gathered. A day was named by which all plans for new line to be considered by the 1845/6 Parliament had to be submitted, and a near-riot followed, with special trains and stage-coaches bringing promoters from all parts with their boxes of papers and rolls of plans. Porters struggled to close the doors of the Board of Trade offices against the pressure of the crowd. It was a brief, mad, spell; a few weeks later some smooth gentlemen had done extremely well out of it, and rather more had done very badly.

In the usual British manner after things have gone spectacularly wrong, the Government carried on exactly as before. During 1844 and 1845 Parliament had laid down a broad legal framework for the railway system, which remained unaltered for the rest of the century. A department of the Board of Trade was set up with powers to regulate matters of railway safety; certain minimum standards of service were laid down, including a requirement that each line should run at least one train a day, at an average overall speed of at least 12mph, carrying passengers at a fare not above a penny a mile; and the state was given power to control or reduce the charges of any company which paid unreasonably large dividends. As an aid to its efforts, Parliament for the first time codified basic Company law and laid down standard legal obligations on the railways, avoiding the need to discuss the administrative matter over again with every fresh

scheme. But apart from these administrative provisions, 'laissez-faire' ruled. The state did not concern itself with the detail of where railways were to be built and imposed no plan or strategy. Provided it took its chance, survived the debate, and raised enough money, any project was as good as any other. There was no second Railway Mania because the public had learnt its lesson.

And in spite of the upheaval, railway construction proceeded apace. By 1850 there were some 6,500 miles of line open, and the railway map of Britain looked not unlike today's main-line network. There were some gaps, but not many. The most apparent was the lack of a railway across South Wales, which was not ready until 1852. Twenty years from the opening of the Liverpool & Manchester, therefore, the national railway system was established throughout; later construction was a matter of filling in gaps.

4 Crest of the Stockton & Darlington, the world's first public steam railway, opened in 1825.

5 Excavating the deep cutting at Olive Mount on the Liverpool and Manchester Railway.

6 Euston station in the early days of the London & Birmingham Railway.

7 1837 lithograph showing a rural scene at Cowran on the Newcastle & Carlisle Railway. *All British Transport Museum/ B Sharpe*

8 Having laid its track since the 1830s to a gauge of 7ft, the Great Western Railway began to embark, from the mid-1860s, on the huge task of reducing it to the standard gauge of 4ft 8½in, as in this picture. This was not finally completed until 1892. *Ian Allan Library*

Development of Passenger Services to 1900

IN THE LATTER PART of the nineteenth century some of the principal British railway companies had become convinced that speed had no special virtues and that to achieve fast runs required an unwarrantable consumption of locomotive coal. The South Eastern Railway definitely forbade speeds in excess of 60mph in the rule book. Even where companies were in direct rivalry, the one with the longer route very often dictated the time. The small engine policy initiated by Bury on the London & Birmingham and weak underline bridgework that prevented mechanical engineers from building bigger machines made it easy to justify moderate speeds, because thrashing of inadequate locomotives inevitably led to an eruption of live cinders from the chimney and an excessive coal bill.

Pinchpenny restrictions did not apply to the Great Northern, which as a latecomer to London felt its competitive position must be maintained by a reputation for fast travel. This gave edge to its shorter mileage to towns east of the Pennines and even justified expresses over its roundabout route to Manchester over the Manchester, Sheffield & Lincolnshire Railway from Retford. This Manchester service began in 1883, with 100-ton trains which covered the 105½ miles from Grantham to Kings Cross in 124 and later 117 minutes. In 1880 there were also Leeds expresses from London in 3¾ hours. Maxima of over 70mph were common with the Stirling 8ft singles.

On the Great Western, which had been at pains in earlier years to show the speed capabilities of its 7ft gauge, the trains that averaged much more than 40mph were few and far between; dilatory schedules were made worse by the 10-minute compulsory refreshment stop at Swindon, which was eventually eliminated in 1895 by buying out the lessees, whose rights extended to 1940. In the eighteen-eighties there were two trains that averaged nearly 46mph between London and Exeter, but on the South Wales line the Irish Boat express to Milford could claim only 35mph. The great awakening came after the retirement of G N Tyrell as superintendent of the line. Whereas in 1887 there were five morning trains from Paddington only one of which could be called express, by the end of the century there were 11 trains in the same period, of which eight qualified.

High speeds by a few holiday trains began towards the end of the century; the present direct 107½ mile route to Bournemouth opened in 1888 with a train taking 147 minutes; in 1898 a 2hr 5min non-stop became one of the fastest bookings in the country. The Great Eastern Cromer expresses in 1897 ran non-stop from Liverpool Street to North Walsham, 131 miles at 49mph. The North Eastern, which had thought 30mph a good average for its Scar-

9 Taking water at Parkside station on the Liverpool & Manchester. *British Transport Museum/B Sharpe*

10 Robert Stephenson's A-type long-boiler locomotive of 1846-7 for use on the London & Birmingham. *Edito Service*

9

borough trains, called for 50mph running from York to the sea from 1898.

Whereas on the London & North Western in 1889 the train called by popular acclaim the 'Wild Irishman' averaged only just over 40mph to Holyhead, the Midland had a Scottish train which averaged 52mph from St Pancras to Leicester and 48mph through the Pennines from Skipton to Carlisle. In the 'nineties the leaven of the 1888 and 1895 races to Scotland worked on many services, resulting in faster runs, dining cars, corridor trains and some curious through carriage workings. Although Bradshaw was often dubbed a work of fiction, it is safe to say that Britain made a better showing than most of Europe for speed and frequency and certainly better than most of the USA, where 25mph was often about the top average.

11 Liverpool & Manchester train crossing over the Bridgewater Canal. *British Transport Museum/B Sharpe*

12 William Powell Frith's painting of Paddington station in the 1850s. The original hung for many years at Hanover station in Germany. *DB Film Archiv*

13 Hamilton Ellis painting of an 1838 posting saloon on the Great Western.

Train Services 1900 to Grouping

IN BRITAIN the first quarter of the twentieth century was a period of proliferation of cross-country facilities; in Europe and America it heralded a period of grand luxury in train travel. The Midland Railway provided a summer train from Leeds to Windermere (really Lakeside) reached by way of the Yorkshire Clapham Junction and Arnside over the Furness. After 1893 the Midland also helped the Midland & South Western Junction to run through coaches from Southampton to Sheffield, Bradford, and other northern towns. For many years the quickest way from London to Cheltenham in the afternoon was from Waterloo to Andover and then by the MSW south-north express. It cost no more than the direct route; private enterprise railways charged for the most part between places and not by mileage, so that a return ticket from London to Inverness could be an open sesame to the main northern lines and to Scotland.

Many new services from the Midlands and North to the South Coast developed after 1906, when the Great Central used its Woodford-Banbury link for a Newcastle-Barry through train. The Great Northern ran trains through the Metropolitan Widened Lines to Bournemouth on the London & South Western; the West London Railway was used for such trains as the Sunny South Special from London & North Western stations to the London, Brighton & South Coast Railway, Birkenhead to Dover via the GWR. Reading and the South Eastern was another of many innovations strengthened from the 'nineties with a Paris connection.

The Great Western did away with its speed inhibitions with a Royal special that covered 135½ miles in the first two hours on the way to Plymouth, and after the short cut via Westbury opened, the Plymouth non-stop ran in four hours seven minutes after July 21, 1906, the 225½ miles being for some years the world's longest non-stop run. During the years to 1914 the North Eastern trip from Darlington to York at 61.5mph was the fastest booking in the British Empire.

There was a marked recession in facilities through the war of 1914-18 and others disappeared after grouping, such as Great Eastern trains into St Pancras, which ended in 1922. From 1921, however, a new facility was the Aberdeen-Penzance through coach, and Grouping brought new connections such as Waterloo-Dorking North and London Bridge to Guildford, via Effingham.

Just before the war of 1914 Pullman extended from the Southern lines and the Metropolitan Railway to Caledonian and Great Eastern services. In the USA Pullman sleepers, diners, parlour cars, drawing room cars and observation cars were seen everywhere. The Compagnie Internationale des Wagons Lits et des Grands Express Européens was not so universal in Europe; but its influence in building up through sleeping car services and dining car and hotel facilities was enormous. The Orient express of 1883 was supplemented by the Berlin-Orient in 1900 and one via the Simplon after 1906, just to pick a very famous route. Before 1914 Wagon-Lits extended to Vladivostock, through North Africa to Egypt and could claim to be the way of princes. With the development of air and car transport after 1919 the railway had become the way of common man.

14 Lance Calkin's study 'Third Class', from the *Graphic* of 4 December 1904.

FOUR MAIN LINES

London, Midland and Scottish Railway

THE LONDON MIDLAND and Scottish Railway was the largest of the four main line companies to come out of the grouping of railways in Britain in 1923. Its main constituents were the London & North Western Railway and Caledonian Railway, forming the West Coast route to Scotland, and the Midland Railway, which, as well as having an excellent cross-country service from Leeds to Bristol, also provided a rival trunk route to Scotland in association with the Glasgow & South Western Railway. Other medium sized lines thrown into the pot included the Highland Railway, running from Perth to Inverness and then farther north, and the North Stafford Railway in the bustling smoky Potteries and North Midlands. Technically, the Lancashire & Yorkshire Railway based on Manchester did not come into the 1923 amalgamation, as it had already joined forces with the London & North

Western in 1922. Oddly, the LMS acquired (through the Midland) the London, Tilbury & Southend Railway which, by logic, ought really to have gone to the easterly based London & North Eastern Railway. The LMS also shared the ownership of two joint lines — the Midland and Great Northern (with the London & North Eastern Railway) and the Somerset & Dorset (with the Southern Railway). In addition it took over railways in Ireland, including the extensive Northern Counties Committee system and the Dundalk, Newry & Greenore Railway. All in all it formed a very impressive organisation.

To go back a little farther in history, the LMS can perhaps claim descent from one of the earliest of railways,

15 Aquatints by J Shaw showing passenger and freight trains at work on the Liverpool & Manchester.
British Transport Museum/B Sharpe

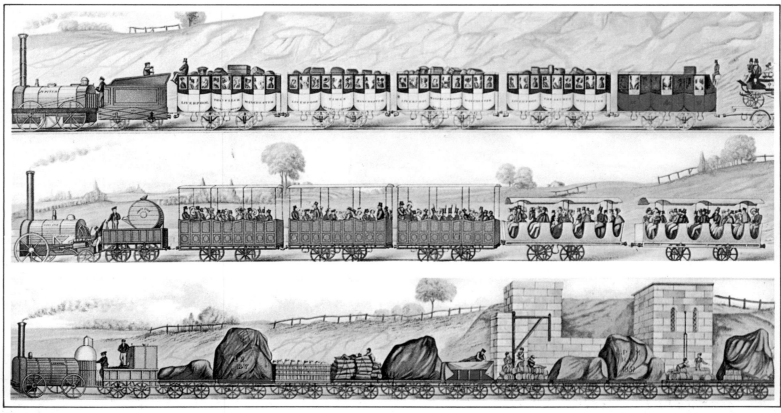

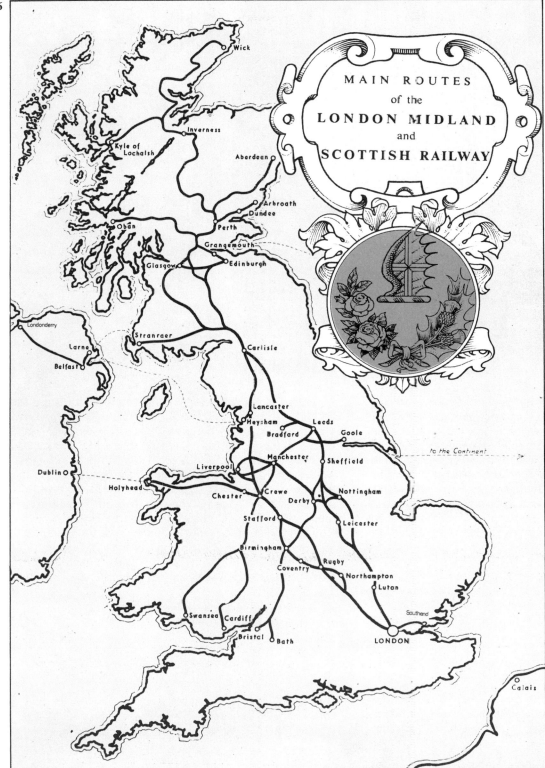

16 Map of the LMS main routes in 1923, with crests of some of
the major constituents.

the Kilmarnock & Troon Railway, which opened in 1810 and had steam locomotive trials as early as 1817. The Kilmarnock & Troon came into the consortium as part of the route of the Glasgow & South Western (opened 1840 to Ayr). The G&SW was one of three Scottish railways of the LMS which together totalled 2,200 miles at grouping. Of the other two, the 896-mile Caledonian started operation in 1845, and the Highland was formed of several small constituents in 1865, including the Inverness & Nairn which opened in 1855. The Highland brought in the line over Drumochter pass, with a summit of 1,484ft the highest main line in Britain.

Of the English constituents, the Liverpool & Manchester was perhaps the most important; it opened in September 1830 as the world's first railway with all steam locomotive operation. The L&M joined with the Grand Junction Railway (1838) in 1845, and the pair linked with the Manchester & Birmingham and London & Birmingham in 1846 to form the London & North Western Railway. The LNWR absorbed the Chester & Holyhead in 1858 (inheriting the Conway and Britannia tubular wrought-iron bridges) and several other smaller lines during the next 10 years.

The Midland Railway was formed in 1844 by the amalgamation of the joint York & North Midland (1839) and the Midland Counties (1839) with the Birmingham & Derby Railway (1839). It took in the Leicester & Swannington (1832), the Bristol & Gloucester in 1846, and other smaller lines, and opened to London St Pancras in 1868, though some Midland trains already operated to London over Great Northern Lines.

The other LMS major constituent, the Lancashire & Yorkshire Railway, started in 1846 with the amalgamation of the Manchester & Leeds (1841) and the Manchester & Bolton (1838) and matured a year later by merging with

17 Curzon Street station, originally the Birmingham terminus of the London & Birmingham and now used as a goods depot. *J Adams*

17

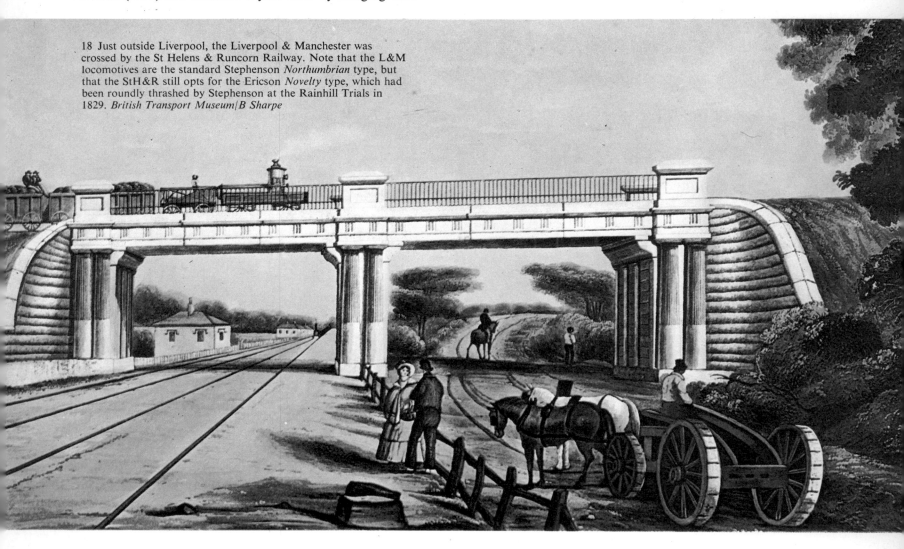

18 Just outside Liverpool, the Liverpool & Manchester was crossed by the St Helens & Runcorn Railway. Note that the L&M locomotives are the standard Stephenson *Northumbrian* type, but that the StH&R still opts for the Ericson *Novelty* type, which had been roundly thrashed by Stephenson at the Rainhill Trials in 1829. *British Transport Museum/B Sharpe*

19 The western entrance to Shugborough tunnel on the Trent Valley Railway in about 1846.

20 Hamilton Ellis painting of a train on the Leicester & Swannington Railway in 1835. The locomotive, *Samson*, was the first ever to carry a steam whistle.

21 Early print of the Britannia Bridge over the Menai Straits on the Chester & Holyhead Railway, designed by Robert Stephenson and opened to traffic in 1850.

22 (facing page) F Moore painting of a McConnell 2-2-2 in the red livery of the Southern Division of the LNWR.
All British Transport Museum/B Sharpe

five other railways. Other constituents included the Furness Railway, the North Staffordshire Railway and the North London Railway.

On formation at the beginning of 1923, the London Midland & Scottish Railway was indeed an impressive organisation. It had a total single-track length, including sidings, of almost 19,000 miles and a main line 729 miles long from London to Wick (and the most northerly British station at Thurso). It operated in 32 of the 40 English counties and until 1939 had a staff bigger than the British Army. At one time the LMS in fact was the largest joint stock corporation in the world. Not an unmixed blessing was its inheritance of 10,316 steam locomotives, of nearly 400 different designs!

Somewhat naturally the early years of the LMS were a period of rather slow consolidation, for it was no easy task to forge erstwhile rival lines and strong personalities into one strong unit. Certainly at the beginning, the railway tended to operate in Divisions based roughly on the territories of its principal constituents and it is doubtful whether the general public really noticed much difference for some considerable time. It even took around six or seven years for some of the old distinctive liveries to disappear.

The main line of the LMS was the North Western route to Scotland, running from London Euston via Rugby, Crewe, Preston and Carlisle (where it joined the Caledonian) to Glasgow and Edinburgh. Branching off the trunk line were heavily trafficked routes to Manchester, Liverpool, North Wales (for Holyhead and Dublin) and a great loop from Rugby to Stafford, taking in Coventry, Birmingham and the industrial Black Country. Trains over these sections had always been among the elite of the old L&NWR company and continued to be so of the new; many of them became the famous named expresses of the inter-war years. They included the Royal Scot (London to Glasgow) the Comet (London to Liverpool) the Mancunian, the Mid-day Scot, the Welshman, and later the Coronation Scot.

23

24

25

26

23 LNWR Ramsbottom 2-2-2 *Princess Royal*, built at Crewe in 1859 and rebuilt in 1876. It regularly hauled the 10am Scotch Express between Euston and Crewe at an average speed of 57mph during the races to Edinburgh in 1888. *A Wood collection*

24 The famous Precedent class 2-4-0 *Charles Dickens*, which reputedly covered two million miles in the twenty years following its construction in 1882. *Ian Allan Library*

25 A pair of the ubiquitous LNWR 'Cauliflower' 0-6-0s at Keswick in May 1950. *P Ransome-Wallis*

26 Superheated LNWR 4-4-0 No 2495 *Bassethound* with a heavy load near Kenton in the early years of the century.

27 Accident at the west end of Standedge tunnel in 1904. The engine was travelling chimney first and swung completely about after derailment. *A Wood collection*

27

28

28 A Webb 2-4-2T at Cambridge with a train for Bletchley. *Colourviews Ltd*

29 The Webb 'Coal Engines' cost about £500 each (minus tenders) when built at Crewe from 1873 – compare with the current £24 million price-tag on a Jumbo jet! *British Rail*

30 The then-enormous Webb three-cylinder compound No 2053 *Greater Britain*, photographed ex-works at Crewe. *British Rail*

31

32

33

31 Terence Cuneo's painting of *Queen of the Belgians* at Birmingham New Street in the 1930s. *Colourviews Ltd*

32 LNWR ferry *Hibernia* leaving Dublin North Wall for Holyhead. *A Wood collection*

33 LNWR horse and cart with a load of empty fish boxes. *A Wood collection*

34 *Hibernia* as modified in 1920, leaving Dun Laoghaire on the Irish Mail service in late 1948. *W Guiver*

34

35 A Midland Railway Johnson 4-2-2 of 1900. This was the last class of singles for the Midland and they had 4000 gallon bogie tenders for long runs. *Colourviews Ltd*

36 Kirtley 2-4-0 No 158A as preserved today at Butterley. *J Adams*

The Midland Division, not to be outdone, produced the Thames-Clyde Express from London to Glasgow via Leeds and the Settle-Carlisle line, and the Devonian running across country from Leeds to Birmingham, Bristol, and on to South Devon via the Great Western. Scottish services were good on the old Caledonian line between Glasgow and Edinburgh, and up to Perth, but on the Highland and Glasgow & South Western section, where most of the track was single, it was the service provided and not the speed, which mattered. High speed in any case, did not become the hallmark of even star expresses until the late 1930s.

In a way the progress of the LMS in the early years after formation was very much like that of any modern company take-over or merger. Of economic necessity, it became a slimming down, a centralising and standardising operation. By 1930, limbs in the shape of unremunerative branch lines began to be lopped, and the shape of things to come, mirrored in the motor car, bus and lorry, became slowly apparent, over thirty branches closing to passengers in that year alone.

On the mechanical side matters were also somewhat complicated, with the huge collection of locomotives of varying age and efficiency, not to mention the differences of mechanical engineering and running policies. The London & North Western, for example, thought nothing of hanging 450 tons behind one of the George V class 4-4-0s, whereas the Midland would have provided two engines of similar classification for such a load. It was the Midland which dominated the LMS and nowhere more than in the mechanical and running departments. Gradually the weak and the non-standard went to the scrapheap (usually the smaller company's engines) and a stop-gap policy of continuing to build what was considered the best of the old

companies' engines lasted for a while, though in the main it meant Midland designs.

It became obvious that steps would need to be taken to obtain an LMS-built express engine suitable for the heavier trains and as the star of the Great Western was rising high in the locomotive world, the company borrowed a Castle class locomotive in 1926 and ran it over the LNWR route where it easily mastered the heaviest loads set for it to haul. The experiment confirmed the LMS running department's prognosis that a good 4-6-0 would fill the bill. So, to get over the immediate problem quickly, the company borrowed a set of Lord Nelson drawings from the Southern Railway for overall guidance, and arranged for the North British Locomotive Company to build fifty of the three-cylinder Royal Scot class.

The first of the new engines emerged in 1927 and the class proved to be a reasonable stop-gap until the next step in the process of consolidation and rationalisation began. That was the importation from the Great Western Railway of the second-in-command at Swindon Works, Mr William Stanier (later Sir William) to be the LMS Chief Mechanical Engineer. Stanier immediately began a programme of standardisation of locomotives and rolling stock, introducing his own efficient designs and quickly reducing the numbers of pre-grouping locomotives. Among his famous classes were the Princess Royal and Coronation classes of Pacific wheel formation, the latter being some of the finest express engines to be designed and operated in Britain. Stanier also introduced a three-cylinder mixed-traffic 4-6-0 in the Jubilee class, and hundreds of the ubiquitous two-cylinder mixed-traffic 4-6-0s and their tank engine counterparts.

Freight was worked generally by a large class of ex-

37 Midland Railway poster circa 1900, showing that the Midland
(broad red lines) served more areas of the country than any
other single railway. The LNWR was a close second.
British Transport Museum/B Sharpe

37

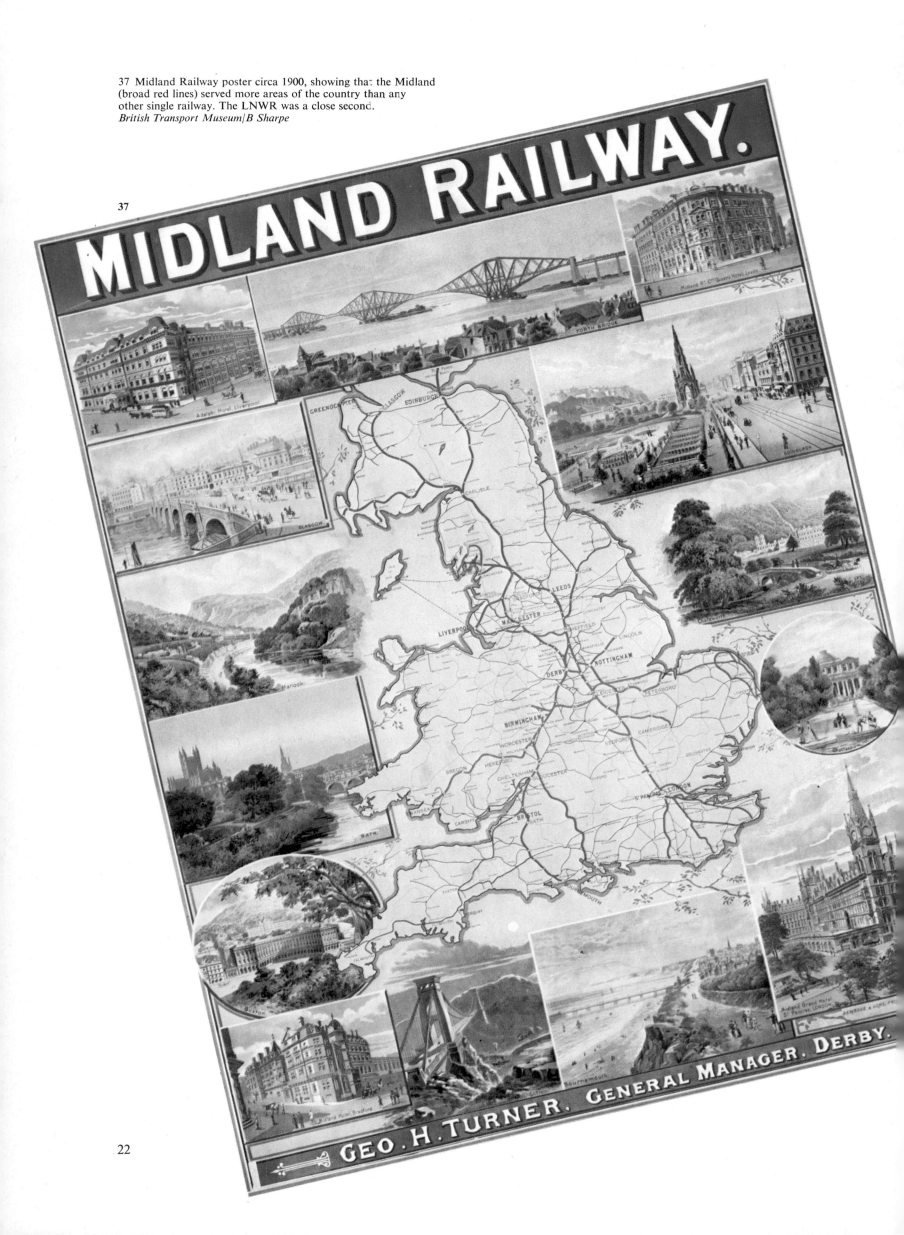

LNWR 0-8-0s and Midland 0-6-0s of varying power definitions. Later Stanier brought in his well-known 8F class 2-8-0 for freight work. In all, over 600 of the 8Fs were built, as they were ordered by the Ministry of Supply for wartime service; some ended their days in Palestine, Egypt, Iraq and Persia, but most were eventually brought home. One was seen still working in Istanbul in 1966. They were built in far-flung works, including Brighton on the Southern, Darlington and Doncaster on the North Eastern, and even at Swindon, their designer's Alma Mater.

The LMS operated an excellent service of suburban trains based on the larger towns, and the pattern with those followed that of the main line in that gradually standardised 2-6-2 and 2-6-4 tank engines replaced the heterogeneous collection of small tank engines from the pre-grouping lines. To the end however, some of the small engines were kept to work certain branch and push-pull shuttle services, which lasted well into nationalisation. The Stanier 2-6-4 tanks could be found anywhere from Tilbury to Bangor or Birmingham to Glasgow.

Cross-country routes were slower in modernising, but as motive power was improved so were the services, and by 1935 such lines as the Somerset & Dorset, and the single-track main lines of the Glasgow & South Western, and the Highland, began to hear the sound of Stanier's deep-toned hooter instead of the shrill whistle of the older engines.

Rationalisation was also carried out with force in LMS workshop practice. Small works, such as that at Lochgorm

(Inverness) on the Highland, and at St Rollox (Glasgow) on the Caledonian, were downgraded for repairs only, and locomotive building was carried on solely at Crewe and Derby—with outside help from the private locomotive builders when necessary. The North Western carriage works at Wolverton and the Midland works at Derby produced the new coaches. A start was also made on the vacuum fitting of wagons for higher-speed freight services, and large concentration and hump yards, such as that at Toton, were built and put into operation.

The first ten years to 1933 were those of formation, and the following period to 1939, and the war, saw the emergence of a new pattern for the future. There were two important factors: the first was the general overall financial position, which demanded efficiency and economy and second was road competition, which was an enemy stronger than had been thought possible by those used to thinking in terms of the railways as a transport monopoly. Diesels for shunting were introduced in 1934 and orders were placed for more the next year; mechanisation in the form of coaling and ash-lifting plants was installed in running sheds; the 'mechanical horse' with its trailer was brought into use for railway road services; and over in Ireland petrol railcars were introduced on the jointly owned County Donegal Railway.

Freight revenue, especially from coal traffic, was still good—it was the passenger traffic which had to be kept and improved if possible. By 1935 the East Coast rivals, the LNER, had inaugurated the Silver Jubilee, a very fast

38 The classic Midland design, Compound 4-4-0 No 1000, now preserved in the National Railway Museum, York, and occasionally used on main-line specials. *J Adams*

39 The original Johnson compound 4-4-0, built at Derby in 1901. *Ian Allan Library*

40 F Moore painting of Compound No 1013 with a train of typically Midland clerestory-roofed stock.
Locomotive Publishing Co

38

39

40

service between London and the Tyneside, running at 100mph using streamlined locomotives, and speed became a publicity feature of some importance. The year 1936 found the LMS making experimental runs with its Pacific No 6201 *Princess Elizabeth* from Euston to Glasgow and back, and by 1937 the Coronation Scot had been introduced complete with streamlined locomotive; it was in truth the Mid-Day Scot on a faster schedule. What is now known as Inter-City traffic was also speeded up and well publicised with improvements to schedules, particularly between London and Liverpool, and London and Manchester.

The London to Birmingham services, though loading to heavier trains, remained on the two-hour timing originated by the old North Western. It was only ever improved by a few minutes until electrification of the route in 1967. Although for publicity purposes the crack trains were the Scottish expresses, the Midland division did well enough for the businessman, and the London to Nottingham, Derby and Leeds trains were well filled, as were the Bristol to

42 Pullman car No 8, built in 1874, had 18 first-class and 32 second-class seats.

41 Official MR postcard of 1908 showing the company's dining cars. *A Wood collection*

Birmingham and the Birmingham to Leeds expresses. Average speeds were not high, being generally under 50mph start to stop. Holiday resorts in Lancashire (such as Blackpool) were extremely well served, as were the principal holiday resorts in North Wales, particularly Llandudno.

The LMS was well to the fore in its signalling programme, replacing the familiar lower-quadrant arms of the old companies with the American-looking fail-safe upper-quadrant arms. Multi-aspect colour-light signalling was also introduced, and the company was the first in Britain to concentrate on that side of safety in high speed running.

Like its three competitors, the LMS invested in other means of transport, taking a considerable interest for example, in the large Midland Red bus company among others, and operating shipping services mainly inherited from the London & North Western and Midland companies, sailing from Wales and Western Scotland to Ireland. They included the Holyhead-Dublin, Heysham-Belfast, and Stranraer-Larne boats and there was also a service (later only freight) to Greenore just south of the Irish border. The Greenore route was the remnant of an attempt by the LNWR to obtain its own private foothold in Ireland, where it owned the short Dundalk, Newry & Greenore Railway, connecting with the Great Northern Railway of Ireland. It operated 5ft 3in-gauge replicas of ancient North Western 0-6-0 saddle tanks and six-wheeled coaches, painted in 'plum-and-spilt-milk' livery.

43

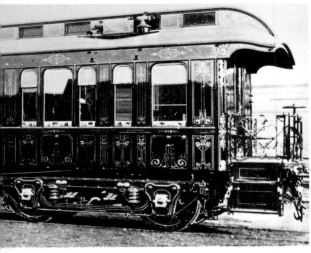

43 Midland-design 'Jinty' 0-6-0Ts banking on the Lickey incline. *H C Casserley*

44 The LNWR 2-2-2 *Cornwall* stands outside Crewe works after restoration. *J Adams*

In Ireland the LMS took over the Midland's Belfast & Northern Counties Railway, changing its name to the Northern Counties Committee. This organisation, based on Belfast, was built to the standard Irish gauge of 5ft 3in and served principal towns in the Six Counties with a good express service between Belfast and Londonderry. In LMS days its locomotives and stock were built at Derby and patterned very much on Derby designs. There were some 3ft-gauge lines merged into the NCC, including the Larne to Ballymena section which actually operated boat trains for a while. The company also owned a narrow-gauge line from Londonderry to Strabane which connected with the extensive County Donegal system, jointly owned with the GNR (I).

In the days of expansion the larger railway companies built themselves hotels and the constituents of the LMS were no exception to the rule. Most of the London mainline termini had hotels, as did the principal cities and towns, and without doubt they were of a very high standard for the period; today some of them, such as the Queen's in Birmingham, are sorely missed. The Queen's was a North Western hotel, and that company regarded itself regally, even using the word BESTOTEL as its telegraphic code, but the Midland had no such pretensions—its hotels, of equal standard, were named after the company. The Caledonian in Scotland pursued a similar policy. The smaller companies were also hotel owners, and one of the most memorable of them is the Station Hotel at Inverness, where surely some of the excellent plumbing and the huge comfortable baths were made in the works at Lochgorm! The Irish lines also had their establishments, including that at Greenore where one's bedroom looked over the Mountains of Mourne and the bathroom window opened on to the platforms and the sound of an old LNWR tank engine.

By the coming of the 1939-45 war, the LMS had established a pattern, but its last eight years, mainly in times of austerity, exceedingly heavy traffic and minimum maintenance, left their mark, though there is little doubt that Stanier's policy of standardisation must have paid off many times. In fairness it must be stated that it was during the war period (1943) that the first of the Royal Scots was rebuilt, turning a reasonable engine into probably one of the most successful and efficient 4-6-0s to have run on any railway in Britain. The LMS performed its duty to the nation and emerged with plans for the future, which were carried on into nationalisation, one of them being the changeover to diesel motive power. It also provided the men who were certainly to influence steam's remaining years in Britain, and a large part of the thinking behind the modern systems of signalling.

To conclude, the LMS of all the four Main Lines was probably the greatest pointer to the way the railway system of Britain would go in the future. It pulled a conglomeration of smaller organisations, all with their personalities and idiosyncrasies, into a homogeneous whole, more efficient but less personal, and it provided a transport system which, though far from perfect, was an example to many others in Europe and overseas. Sadly it was never a maker of money for its shareholders, for it passed its ordinary dividends altogether after only five years, and certain preference dividends in three. Even so, it was not by any means the worst of the four—that doubtful honour goes to the LNER.

45 An LYR 0-6-0 fitted with rotatable chimney during World War I to create anti-aircraft smoke-screens. *E S Cox*

46 LYR 2-4-2T No 1008, preserved at Tyseley. *P B Whitehouse*

47 Two LYR veterans preserved on the Worth Valley Railway: 0-4-0ST 'Pug' No 51218 and 'Ironclad' 0-6-0 No 957. *J Marshall*

45

46

47

48

48 LT&SR 4-4-2T No 80 *Thundersley* as preserved at
Bressingham. *F V Archer*

49 Model of a Furness Railway 2-2-2WT. *B Monaghan*

50 LT&SR Whitelegg 4-6-4T No 2104. *Ian Allan Library*

49

50

51 During the 1950s BR (LMR) compartment stock sported carriage panels by Hamilton Ellis, such as this one showing a North Staffordshire Railway 4-4-2T at Stone station.

52 North Staffordshire Railway 2-4-0 No 14 on the turntable at Stoke. *Ian Allan Library*

53 (overleaf) One of the many fine LMS posters of the 1920s. *British Transport Museum/B Sharpe*

LMS   THE PERM

REL

ANENT WAY

YING

54 The Caledonian Railway's famous 4-6-0 *Cardean* in charge of the 'Corridor' on Beattock bank, from an F Moore painting published as an LPC postcard.

55 One of the few pre-grouping designs to benefit from repainting in standard BR livery were the class 72 4-4-2s of the Caledonian Railway. *J Adams*

56 The unique Caledonian 4-2-2 of 1886, built by Neilson & Co in 1886 specifically for high-speed running with the west coast Scottish expresses. It is seen here at Carstairs in 1965. *J M Boyes*

57 and 59 Highland Railway No 103 was the very first 4-6-0 in the British Isles. It was designed by David Jones for goods work and, though it never carried this specific livery in service, has now been preserved at the Glasgow Museum of Transport. *J Adams*

58 These Jones 4-4-0s, of which the first appeared in 1874, carried the characteristic Highland Railway louvred chimneys. *E S Cox*

60 A Glasgow & South Western Railway 0-6-0T with outside cylinders, preserved at the Museum of Transport in Glasgow.

61 LMS taper-boiler Royal Scot class 4-6-0 No 6113 *Cameronian* passing Colwyn Bay with a very light second portion of the up Irish Mail. *E D Bruton*

62 A Royal Scot built in 1929 with an experimental high-pressure boiler; after a fatal explosion the engine was substantially modified and became the prototype of the rebuilt Royal Scots with taper boilers. *British Rail*

63 Two eras of LMS motive power on a Birmingham train passing Berkhamsted in 1953: 4-4-0 Compound No 41090 pilots a Stanier Jubilee class 4-6-0. *British Rail*

64 Painting by Hamilton Ellis of Blair Atholl station in LMS days, with ex-Highland 4-4-0 and River class 4-6-0 engines.

58

60

59

61

62

63

Blair in 1930
C. Hamilton Ellis

65

66

65 Jubilee 4-6-0 No 5593, now restored to LMS livery and based at Tyseley. *J Adams*

66 One of the great workhorses of the LMS, the 'Crab' 2-6-0s betrayed a very strong Lancashire & Yorkshire influence. They were spread very widely over the LMS, and many gravitated to the Ayrshire coalfield, such as this particular example seen at Falkland Junction. *D Cross*

67 Crewe works fitted one Jubilee-type boiler with a double chimney, and over the years it appeared on several engines of this class, lattery No 45742 *Connaught*. It finally ended up on No 45596 *Bahamas*, and when this engine was withdrawn it was preserved with the double chimney, though it never carried both LMS red and double chimney in service. *M Pope*

(Facing page). Stanier Pacifics of the LMS: (68 and 70) examples of the Princess class and (69) the later Coronation class. *M Pope*

67

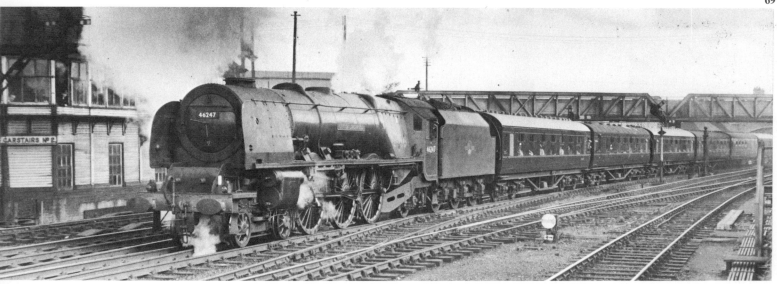

71 The standard LMS heavy freight engine was the 8F 2-8-0, one of which is seen climbing away from Chinley to Chapel-en-le-Frith in February 1968. *D Huntriss*

72 An LMS class 5 with an up goods at Thrimby in July 1966.
R Bastin

73 An early LMS diesel-mechanical shunter. *British Rail*

74 The Coronation Scot on Bushey troughs behind streamlined
Coronation class 4-6-2 No 6222 *Queen Mary*.

75 Painting by John Wigston showing streamlined Coronations
in both red and blue liveries.

74

72

73

75

76

76 No 10000 was the very first British main-line diesel, a 1600hp
machine built in 1947 by the LMS. *British Rail*

77 No 10000 moved around the country a good deal in its 17-year
career, and here it is leaving Southampton with a Waterloo-
Bournemouth train in 1953. *Ian Allan Library*

78 LMS official photograph of streamlined Coronation No 6235
City of Birmingham. *Ian Allan Library*

77

78

London and North Eastern Railway

IT CAN BE SAID with some truth that the London & North Eastern Railway had its roots with George Stephenson and the world's first public railway. Certainly its largest, wealthiest, and most influential constituent company—the North Eastern—evolved from the Stockton & Darlington, which opened in 1825. The North Eastern had a virtual monopoly in the North and East Ridings of Yorkshire, the counties of Durham and Northumberland, and running powers right through North British territory to Edinburgh, with tentacles as far west as Cumberland and Westmorland. In 1922 it gobbled up its rival, the Hull & Barnsley, and finished up with a track mileage of 5,407.

The next largest company was the Great Northern abutting and south of the North Eastern; the two lines, with the help of the North British over the border, formed the East Coast route to Scotland. The Great Northern did not come into being until 1846 and from the start set Yorkshire as its target. Kings Cross was its London terminus from 1852, and at amalgamation its mileage was 3,124.

The other two English constituent 'greats' were the Great Central (2,698 miles) and the Great Eastern (2,637 miles). The former was a descendant of the Manchester, Sheffield and Lincolnshire, which was part of the Watkin 'empire'—Watkin was also chairman of the Metropolitan and the South Eastern Railways. This was the final fling in Sir Edward's determination to have a line of railway from Manchester to the Channel coast. The line's name was changed to the Great Central once the MS&L extension southwards to its new London terminus at Marylebone was completed in 1899. The Great Eastern began life as the Eastern Counties Railway in 1836 and merged with four others to form the new railway in 1862. It shared with the Midland Railway the distinction of being the first to admit third-class passengers to all its trains and had the honour also of being a Royal line, serving Sandringham, which was reached from London via the terminus at Liverpool Street. Neither of these two 'greats' was ever wealthy.

In Scotland the LNER absorbed the North British, (2,675 miles) the Caledonian's deadly rival, plus the last 'great' the Great North of Scotland, a once terrible railway (526 miles). The North British was the largest railway in Scotland and ran its trains over two of Britain's more famous bridges, those of the Forth and Tay. It started off as the Edinburgh & Dalkeith Railway, a horse-worked line of 1826, originally built to 4ft 6in gauge but widened to the standard 4ft 8½ in in 1846. The board of the NBR held its first meeting in 1844 and construction of the railway proper began in that year. It was based on Edinburgh, and its Waverley station in that city has always been one of Scotland's finest. During its later days the Great North of Scotland (which dated from 1852) was a prim little railway based on Aberdeen, whose General station it shared with the Caledonian. The Great North, like the Great Eastern was a 'royal' line in that its branch from Aberdeen to Ballater served Balmoral.

The LNER participated in Joint lines, the two largest of which were the Cheshire Lines Committee (partly in Lancashire) and the Midland and Great Northern. Both were joint with the LMS. The former possessed its own passenger stock but the motive power was LNER (Great Central) while the permanent way came under the LMS. The M&GN was a self-contained railway which owned its own locomotives, coaches and wagons, based on Melton Constable. The locomotives were for many years painted a distinctive yellow ochre and had a marked Derby parentage.

In some ways the final evolution of the LNER confirmed a long-standing arrangement of alliances which had become known as the East Coast route, rivalling the equally well-known West Coast route activated by the London & North Western and Caledonian Railways. The East Coast companies, the Great Northern, North Eastern and North British, although not always the happiest of bedfellows, provided a fast service from London to Edinburgh. The addition of the Great Central, Great Eastern and Great North of Scotland companies, all of them poorer relations, was complementary. Fortunately there was no unpleasantness in the merging of the LNER's constituents, though the North Eastern was almost certainly the most wealthy and consequently the strongest.

So, LNER expresses ran from London Kings Cross to York, Newcastle and Edinburgh, London Liverpool Street to Norwich and the East Coast, and London Marylebone to Manchester via Rugby and Leicester. In Scotland the North British section provided an excellent service between Glasgow and Edinburgh and Edinburgh to Aberdeen. Other lines of some importance included those between Manchester, Sheffield and Lincoln, Doncaster and Leeds, Newcastle and Carlisle, Aberdeen, Keith and Elgin, and that magnificently scenic route, the West Highland to Fort

79

80

Central Station, Newcastle-upon-Tyne

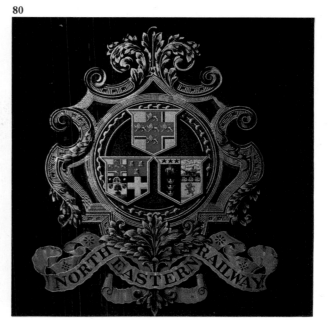

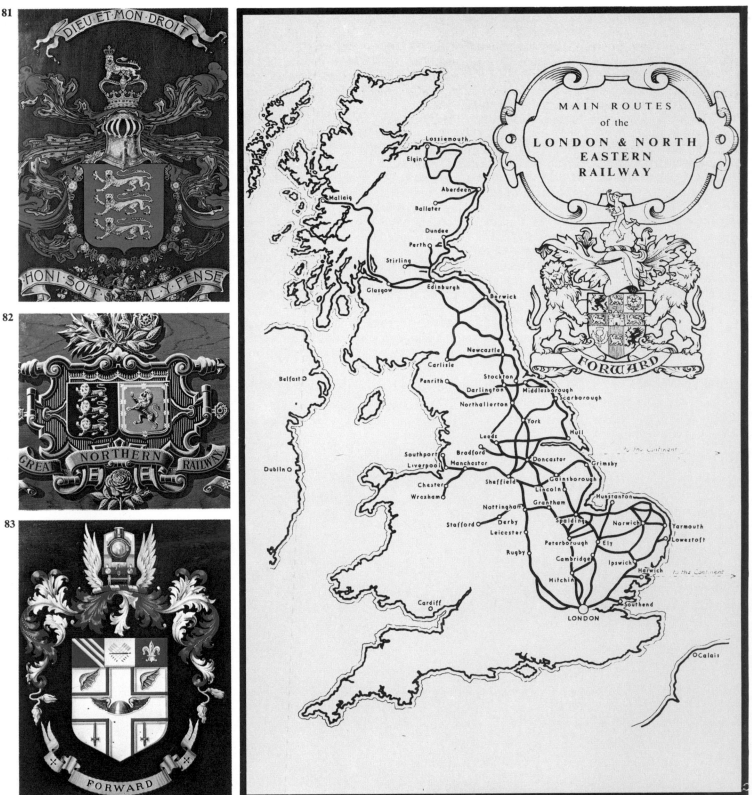

82

83

William, extending to Mallaig for Skye.

In 1925 the new company was the host for the Railway Centenary celebrations, when exhibits ranging from the ancient Hetton Colliery locomotive built in 1822 to an A1 Gresley Pacific, a Southern King Arthur and, above all, a Great Western Castle ran over the Stockton & Darlington route in the presence of Royalty. The same year also saw the famous locomotive exchanges between the LNER and the Great Western, when Gresley's Pacifics were tried against Collett's Castles.

Over the years, most of the fast running on the LNER was over the East Coast route, mainly on the old Great Northern section, and many of the trains were of special interest in that they were made up of Pullman stock. There were the Harrogate Pullman, the West Riding Pullman, the Yorkshire Pullman and above all the famous Queen of

79 Newcastle Central station in 1905, as portrayed on a Denholm Brash postcard.

80-3 Crests of the LNER's principal constituents.

84 The LNER's main routes at grouping.

Scots Pullman. All were luxury trains subject to supplementary fares, but they were very popular.

Competition between the West and East Coast routes began to intensify by 1928 when the LMS, with its new Royal Scot class locomotives began to run non-stop between London and Carlisle. In retaliation the LNER brought in the new Flying Scotsman, inaugurating the longest non-stop run in the world, 393 miles, between London and Edinburgh.

It was made possible by the use of Gresley's now well-known corridor tender which enabled locomotive crews to change over en route. By 1935 streamlining had come into vogue with the Silver Jubilee train which brough Newcastle within a four-hour journey of London. So successful was this train that a further flyer, the Coronation, began to run in 1937. The Coronation was able to wrest the then speed record from the Great Western's Cheltenham Flyer by being booked to run between Kings Cross and York at an average speed of 71.9 miles per hour — Edinburgh, the next stop, was reached in six hours from London. By the following year a third streamlined train was in operation — the West Riding Limited running from Kings Cross to Bradford with a timing not equalled until 1966 with modern 3,300hp Deltic diesels.

Other main line services were also of a high standard and included such names as the Scarborough Flyer and the East Anglian. Expresses were speeded up between London and Manchester on the Great Central section and to Cambridge on the Great Northern and Great Eastern lines. One of the more important improvements was that between Edinburgh and Aberdeen, where fast trains connected with the down Flying Scotsman and up Coronation expresses.

As on all other railways, LNER services suffered a severe downward trend during the 1939-45 war. Trains such as the Flying Scotsman still ran but only in name — it took almost nine hours to reach Edinburgh. Trains were slower and heavier — loads of 25 coaches being not uncommon. It was very much a case of 'Is your journey really necessary?' and especially at night time, travel was no joke. The war probably saved a large number of LNER branch lines from the axe, for, with petrol rationing, the road competition which had grown increasingly heavy since 1930 became almost non-existent, but it was only a temporary respite. The LNER had itself invested in certain road undertakings by the early 1930s.

From the motive power point of view the LNER was particularly fortunate in having the services of Mr (later

85 Lithograph after J W Carmichael of the oblique bridge over
the River Gelt on the Newcastle & Carlisle Railway.
British Transport Museum/B Sharpe

86 and 87 The Forth bridge, shown shortly after opening in 1890
(*Illustrated London News*) and as it is today. (*R Bastin*).

88 Great Northern Railway Sturrock engine of 1866 with
condensing equipment designed to reduce exhaust when working
through from Kings Cross on the Metropolitan underground lines
to the City. *Ian Allan Library*

89 Probably the best known of all the Great Northern engines,
the Stirling Singles were built over a period of years from the
1870s and handled the top east coast trains until the advent of
larger engines at the turn of the century. *B Jackson collection*

Sir) Nigel Gresley, whose locomotives became world famous. Gresley's policy was to use the best of the old, supplemented by his own designs, and there is little doubt that it paid dividends. Of all British express engines in the early days of the Grouping (many would say for all time) his A3 class Pacifics named after racehorses and of course the evergreen A1 *Flying Scotsman* were not only the most handsome, but also the epitome of what was best in express steam locomotives. The Great Western Castles beat them on their own ground in 1925, but even that lesson was absorbed and acted upon.

In 1925 the LNER obtained a 2-8-8-2 Garratt articulated engine, built to Gresley's design by Beyer Peacock & Co. It was the most powerful steam engine ever to be built for use in Britain and was constructed for work on the formidable seven-mile Worsborough incline on the old Great Central route from Wath to Lancashire via the Woodhead tunnel.

Gresley was a firm advocate of three-cylinder propulsion and his engines of this type ranged from the K3 class 2-6-0 through the large O2 class freight 2-8-0s to the A1, A3 and later the A4 streamlined Pacifics. By 1935, test runs had been carried out with the A3s to investigate the possibilities of steam in comparison with the German streamlined diesel, the Flying Hamburger. Somewhat naturally the Germans had publicised the Hamburger well and questions had been asked. Gresley claimed that he

90

90 Stirling 4-2-2 and 2-2-2 locomotives heading the Flying Scotsman in 1900. *Ian Allan Library*

91

92

93

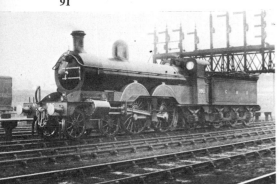

91-3 The Ivatt Atlantics replaced the Stirling Singles on GNR expresses in the early 1900s. The prototype was No 990 *Henry Oakley* seen (left) shortly after construction in 1898, (centre) removed from York Museum to pilot the later – and larger – No 251 on a special train on Holloway bank in 1953 and (right) as preserved at the old York Railway Museum. Nos 990 and 251 have since moved across to the new National Railway Museum.
Respectively Ian Allan Library, P B Whitehouse and Picturepoint

94 Despite the success of the Atlantics, Ivatt was still building 4-2-2s in 1900-1. They were fitted with inside cylinders and inside bearings on the bogie and driving wheels, but were the last class of singles to be built for a British railway. *Colourviews Ltd*

94

ON LOCH LOMOND.

95 Joint GNR/NER/NBR poster of the late 1890s. *British Transport Museum/B Sharpe*

96 Dining in the restaurant car of the Flying Scotsman in 1900.
K Westcott Jones collection

97 The GNR Atlantics were succeeded by Gresley's even larger Pacifics. The first was No 1470 *Great Northern*, built in 1922.
Ian Allan Library

98 A class C1 Ivatt Atlantic leaving Kings Cross with a Leeds train in 1925.
B Stephenson collection

could do better with steam, using British coal rather than imported fuel oil. Encouraged by the LNER Chief General Manager and the board, Gresley went ahead with the design of the A4 Pacific, which many consider to be his masterpiece; the first engine was named *Silver Link* in honour of King George V's Silver Jubilee in 1935. On trial runs the new engine twice reached the record speed of 112½ mph. By 1938, 35 A4s had been built and were in regular service; of them No 4468 *Mallard* on a further test run attained the world speed record for steam of 126mph.

But it was not only for his Pacifics that Gresley has been recognised by historians. He also designed numerous locomotives capable of the whole range of duties required by his company, of which probably the star was the V2 2-6-2, named Green Arrows after the first of the class. The company adopted a big engine policy which certainly paid dividends, particularly during the war years when loads were prodigious. Other notable classes included the B17 4-6-0 for use on the Great Central and East Anglian routes and an excellent range of 2-6-4 tanks. The largest

passenger engine class was the P2 of which the first engine, No 2001 *Cock o' the North,* incorporated certain features of the Chapelon designs and was tested in France on the plant at Vitry.

Nor were the older classes forgotten. The ex-Great Eastern B12 class 4-6-0s, once the star turns of the Liverpool Street to Norwich expresses, were sent to Keith and Elgin to work the Great North of Scotland expresses, which they did until well after nationalisation of the railways. New Director class 4-4-0s were built and also sent to Scotland, while the older engines of their class performed well on the Great Central main line until ousted by the B17s in the later 1930s. Pre-grouping classes were retained for many secondary branch-line duties, including wheel arrangements such as the 2-4-0 which disappeared on the other main lines much earlier — several of these engines were running in East Anglia well into the 1950s.

After Gresley's death in 1942, first Thompson and then Peppercorn took over the reins, the former rebuilding and modifying several of his old CME's designs. Two cylinders

99 The last class of Crewe-type 2-2-2s to be built were these Manchester, Sheffield & Lincolnshire engines of 1882-3. *British Rail*

100-2 The Great Central was not opened throughout until 1899 and thus had far more modern power in the early years of the century than most other companies. Shown left is the Robinson 4-6-0 express engine of 1912, No 423 *Sir Sam Fay.* Centre right is an F Moore painting of a 1911 4-6-2T leaving Marylebone, whilst bottom right is an oil-fired example of the same class. *All Ian Allan Library*

103 (overleaf) Hamilton Ellis painting of a North Eastern Railway Scarborough-Leeds express near Castle Howard in the early 1900s. The engine is Fletcher 2-4-0 No 329 of 1875 and the coaches typify the archaic vehicles used on this line until well into the century. The second vehicle is an old Pullman sleeping car with its berths removed and catering facilities substituted.

were now to be the rule. Notable among the conversions was the K4 class 2-6-0 built for the West Highland line, from which came the very capable two-cylinder K1. A most successful class introduced as early as 1942 was the B1 4-6-0, a general purpose locomotive comparable to the LMS Class 5 and the Great Western Hall. Most LNER engines were either built at the old Great Northern works at Doncaster or the North Eastern shops at Darlington.

Although the LNER had not been diesel-minded, it had turned its thoughts towards electrification. It inherited the Tyneside electric trains from the North Eastern and joined with the LMS in the electrification of the joint Manchester South Junction and Altrincham line. In London the company worked with the London Passenger Transport Board in the electrification of some of its suburban routes. The most comprehensive plan, however, was the proposed Manchester to Sheffield electrification, but it could not be completed until the long Woodhead tunnel was rebuilt, and the project was not finished until after nationalisation.

104 A J72 0-6-0T repainted in North Eastern green for station pilot work at Newcastle Central. *J Adams*

105 The North Eastern entrusted its heaviest freight workings to three classes of 0-8-0s. This painting by Victor Welch shows a class T2 engine working high-capacity coal wagons up to Anfield Plain in pre-grouping days. *Courtesy David & Charles Ltd*

106 Most of the freight on the LNER's constituents was entrusted to 0-6-0 tender engines. Some of the Scottish engines, such as this Holmes design from the North British, lasted until the close of steam working in Scotland at the end of 1966. The septuagenarian No 65345, in fact, was photographed shunting at Seafield colliery in March 1967, several months after its official withdrawal. *D Cross*

Like its competitors, the LNER had maritime interests, in fact not only did it own a considerable shipping fleet, but also the largest number of docks and harbours of any of the railway companies. Most were on the Tyne, Tees and Humber, though to travellers Harwich was no doubt the best known. There were also extensive installations in Scotland at Methil in Fife, with smaller docks at Burntisland and Bo'ness. Passenger steamships to the Continent left Grimsby for Hamburg, Harwich for Holland, and Hull for Germany, France and Belgium. Parkeston Quay at Harwich also served the Belgian port of Zeebrugge with a train ferry service inaugurated in 1924, and was the port for a regular nightly ferry service to the Hook of Holland. In Scotland the company also operated a delightful fleet of ex-North British Railway paddle steamers, named after Walter Scott's novels.

Hotels were profitable investments and the LNER inherited a large number from the constituent companies. Among the most notable were those at Liverpool Street

(the Great Eastern) and at Edinburgh (the North British). The Great Central built a huge edifice at Marylebone (now the headquarters of British Railways Board), the Great Northern appeared at Kings Cross, and most provincial towns of size had their railway hostelry if served by the LNER and the Great Northern in particular.

The LNER (though it was not alone) realised a little late that other forms of transport, particularly the road, were thorns in the side which could only fester and needed drastic treatment. With the other three companies it put a great deal of effort into the 'Square Deal' campaign in the nineteen-thirties when it was argued, with some justice, that legal restrictions put on the railways in the days of their monopoly were unfair. The complaint applied particularly to the old basis of freight charging, which was roughly to equate the charge with the service rendered and that in turn depended on the value of the article moved. So road transport often got a high-rated job of carrying full cases by slightly undercutting the published rail rate.

Nothing however, was to happen until the Transport Act of 1953, by which time it was too late.

In the end, times and the war made it necessary that either the railways were given a massive subsidy in one form or another or they should be nationalised outright. The latter course was chosen and the LNER disappeared, except in nostalgia and history, on December 31, 1947. Unfortunately, from its shareholders point of view it had not been a great success — in fact the LNER had the worst record of the Big Four companies. Not one of its several series of dated or first or second preference shares was regularly paid, or in full, and its ordinary preference shareholders had nothing after 1930. Money was always tight-and it is to the company's credit that it was able to perform so well under the circumstances. It had a first-class line of railway officers, and one of its memorials must be that many of them reached high, and indeed the highest, ranks in the new British Railways organisation.

107 2-4-2T No 1099 was one of the considerable number of small passenger tanks which worked Great Eastern Railway suburban services in the London area.

108 A class J15 0-6-0 preserved by the Midland & Great Northern Joint Preservation Society at Sheringham. *V C K Allen*

109 Distinctive North Eastern Railway station architecture at Hexham, Northumberland. *G Robson*

110 An ex-Great Eastern B12 4-6-0 which has lain semi-derelict at Sheringham for many years awaiting restoration. *S A Fenn*

111 (inset) A GER Holden mixed-traffic 2-4-0, 100 of which were built between 1891 and 1902.

112 North Eastern Railway officers' inspection saloon built in 1902 and now preserved at Didcot.

109

112

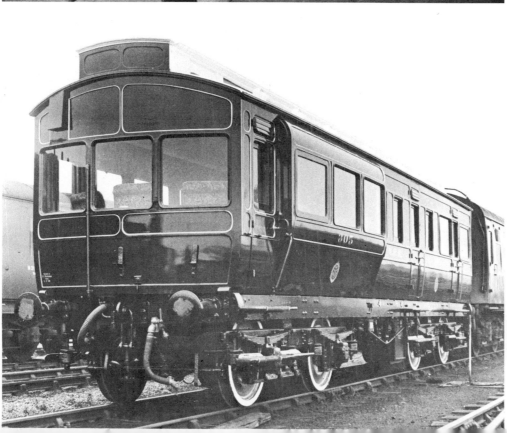

113

114

115

113 LNER class A3 Pacific *Flying Scotsman* on an enthusiasts' special crossing Lockwood viaduct in June 1969. *R Bastin*

114 A North Eastern Atlantic rebuilt by the LNER in 1931 with tender articulated with the locomotive's frame. *British Rail*

115 Remains of a North British Railway Wheatley 4-4-0 recovered from the river after the Tay Bridge disaster in December 1879.

116 and 117 In the early 1960s this NBR Glen class 4-4-0 was brought out of retirement and used on special trains. It can now be seen in the Glasgow Museum of Transport.
Respectively M Pope and T Dority

117

116

118

119

120

121

122

123

124

125

118 Preserved LNER Gresley A4 No 4498 *Sir Nigel Gresley*.
P B Whitehouse

119, 120 and 121 Details of record-breaking Gresley A4 *Mallard*.
J Benton-Harris

123 The streamlined West Riding Limited leaving Kings Cross
in the 1930s. *B Jackson*

122, 124 and 125 Kitchen and first-class accommodation on the
1935 Silver Jubilee train. *British Transport Museum*

126 A4 Pacific No 60034 *Lord Faringdon* with an Aberdeen-
Glasgow train near Stonehaven in September 1965. *R Bastin*

127 Preserved Thompson B1 class 4-6-0 No 1306 at Steamtown,
Carnforth. *R W A Swain*

128 Preserved LNER Pacifics *Bittern* and *Blue Peter* in store at
York in 1968. *J M Boyes*

129 (overleaf) Terence Cuneo's painting of LNER class K4 2-6-0
The Great Marquess inside Tyseley roundhouse flanked by GWR
Castle class 4-6-0s. *Colourviews Ltd*

127

128

TERENCE CUNEO
APRIL 1957

Great Western Railway

OF THE FOUR British railway companies to emerge from the Grouping of 1923, the Great Western was unique. It was the only line to absorb others, to keep its own territories and networks inviolate, and to retain its original identity. These facts are probably the main reason for the adulation which the GWR has received for the past fifty years. It absorbed thirty-two smaller railway companies embracing practically all the Welsh railways and the whole of the railway-owned docks in South Wales. At the Grouping it had 8,000 miles of track, 1,500 stations and halts, over 3,900 locomotives and over 10,000 coaches, and during the last years before Grouping the total number of engine miles run was 86,309,020. A great deal has been said and written about the 'Great Western Tradition', the saying and writing depending to some degree on whether one considered the concern to be 'God's Wonderful Railway' or the 'Great Way Round'. But, there is no doubt at all that there *was* a tradition and it *was* a magnificent railway — stubborn to the end in that even during the early days after nationalisation it could still be thought that there were five Regions of British Railways and the Great Western Railway.

So, the Great Western was different; indeed, it was different from the very beginning in that it was built to the unusual gauge of 7ft. This was due to the imaginative thinking of its first great engineer, Isambard Kingdom Brunel (Mr Brunel Junior, as the Annals of Bristol describe him). The selection of that young man and its momentous consequences was made by Bristol men in the year 1832, the year of the Great Western's birth, and by 1835 the decision was made to construct the line to the 7ft gauge. Those were early days, and although George Stephenson was advocating one gauge for all railways laid down in Britain, Brunel so convinced his board of the superiority of his proposals that he won the day.

Bristol later had some cause to regret the decision, for much of the city's trade was with the Midlands, and the use of the broad gauge meant railway frontier points with other companies at places such as Worcester, Warwick and, in particular, Gloucester. In fact, so bad did matters become that the delays in transhipment forced merchants to send their wares for foreign lands via London or Liverpool, where no such problem arose.

By 1846 the Government had put the Gauge Act through

130 Principal routes and stations of the Great Western Railway.
P B Whitehouse

131 and 132 Crest and shield of the GWR.

133 Painting of the Cornish Riviera Express commissioned from G H Davies by the *Illustrated London News* in 1929.

parliament forbidding anything but the standard 4ft 8½in for use on any new railways. The Great Western then had 270 miles of broad-gauge line; it reached from London to Bristol and on to Exeter. Further extensions took it to Penzance, Haverfordwest, Shrewsbury, Hereford, and Salisbury. Mixed-gauge tracks were laid from Oxford through Birmingham to Wolverhampton. By 1859 the maximum mileage of the broad gauge had been reached, and slowly the standard gauge took over. Brunel himself died the same year at the early age of fifty-three, only months after the Prince Consort had opened his magnificent bridge over the Tamar at Saltash.

In the early days of railways there were great opportunities, and in 1837 Brunel had taken on a young man of 21 as his Locomotive Engineer — Daniel Gooch, who was to serve the company for fifty-two years, ending up as Sir Daniel and its Chairman. By 1846 Gooch had designed and built at the new works at Swindon the magnificent express engine aptly named *Great Western,* which was to be the prototype of the class which served the company during the whole of the broad-gauge era.

It was Gooch who steered the company through the years of change — he, more than any other man helped to bring Brunel's dream of the broad gauge to fruition and almost completion. For speed and comfort as well as power no standard-gauge engine of 1850 could approach those of the Great Western, but Gooch realised that the

ultimate success and perhaps salvation of the company depended on co-operation with standard-gauge concerns, such as the Midland and the London & North Western, which connected with his own railway. He remained convinced that the broad gauge was the better system, but common sense prevailed. Gooch died in 1889 when his own eight-foot-single-driver locomotives were still taking the expresses out of London. Three years after his death the very last broad-gauge train left Paddington for Penanze and an era was over.

The Edwardian years were those of development and consolidation. The Great Western was primarily a railway of the West of England, the Midlands and South Wales, and its mileage in the London area was small compared with the others. It was a line which served the less-developed parts of the country, where it was the main employer, albeit a disciplined but benevolent one. Among its staff the soft burr of Devonshire, Wiltshire and Gloucestershire mixed with the broader Black Country dialect and the Welsh lilt. It built up a loyalty which politics could not break — it was the Great Way to the West and to Wales — so its publicity organisation told the world as far back as 1905.

By 1910 the wind of change had begun to blow strongly and the railway began to implement a huge modernisation plan, organised as a two-fold operation. The first was the new lines which were planned and built to straighten out

the old Great Way Round and effectively to compete with the Midland from Bristol to Birmingham and later the London & North Western from London to Birmingham. The long-awaited straightening of the line to South Wales via Badminton was also completed. The second was in the locomotive department, and was perhaps the more radical. It certainly affected Great Western locomotive designs and classes for the rest of its existence; it also influenced considerably locomotive design and practice in Britain for at least thirty years. .

During the later years of the nineteenth century, the whole of the locomotive design, construction, maintenance and running had been under the charge of William Dean, with senior assistant George Jackson Churchward as second in command. Dean's health had not been good and during his last years Churchward had virtually assumed control, with the full authority of the GWR locomotive committee of the board of directors. During that period Churchward laid down the foundations of the locomotive policy to be followed, and which *was* followed for a quarter of a century and more. It was a radical departure from precedent, but it worked. Some of the basic thinking was American.

The new policy was to produce a boiler design which was extremely sound and capable of being reproduced in a considerable range of standard capacities, and thus to lead to a general standardisation of locomotive stock. Once the new boiler (which was coned) was settled, Churchward

turned his thoughts to the re-design of the front end, developing principally an internal streamlining designed to pass the necessary large volumes of steam freely through the valves and cylinders. It involved a new arrangement of valve motion which proved most effective and by 1902 the first of the big 4-6-0 express passenger engines had been built at Swindon and put to work.

Churchward next began a scheme for replacing the many and varied classes of older engines by modern locomotives of as few different types as possible. Between 1903 and 1911 the programme was completed and nine new standard classes were constructed and put into use. They included a two-cylinder 4-6-0 (Saint class), a 4-4-0 (County class), a 2-6-0 (43XX class), a 2-8-0 (28XX class), a 4-4-2 tank (22XX class), two classes of 2-6-2 tank (31XX and the small-wheeled 45XX), a 2-8-0 tank (42XX class) and a four-cylinder 4-6-0 (Star class), which formed the basis of all Great Western motive power for the future.

The Grouping had little effect on the Great Western locomotive scene, apart from the absorption of engines from the various Welsh lines. The older and smaller classes of Welsh engines were rapidly withdrawn; the more-modern and efficient locomotives were equipped with standard GWR boilers and boiler fittings. The Midland & South Western Junction Railway, also absorbed by the GWR, had its locomotives treated similarly.

Shortly before the Grouping, G J Churchward retired, having left his mark on Swindon for all time. He was

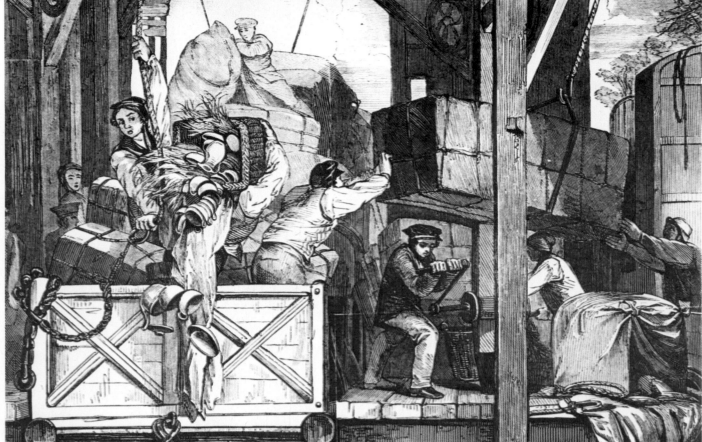

134 and 136-8 Crests of GWR constituent companies.

135 J C Bourne lithograph of the GWR goods shed at Bristol in 1842. *British Transport Museum/B Sharpe*

139 An impression of the chaos caused by the necessity to trans-ship goods between the standard-gauge Midland and the broad-gauge GWR at Gloucester, from the *Illustrated London News* of 6 June 1846.

140 A broad-gauge GWR train running over the mixed-gauge track installed prior to full conversion to standard gauge. *British Rail*

141 Roll of honour of GWR casualties in the 1914-18 war. *J R Batts*

succeeded by C B Collett, who continued in his footsteps, providing the famous Castles (which were really modernised and modified Stars) Halls (which were smaller-wheeled Saints) and hundreds of little 0-6-0 pannier tanks which were developments of Dean's old 0-6-0s of the 23XX class. Other new classes and improvements on the old included the 51XX 2-6-2 tanks, the taper-boilered 0-6-0s of the 22XX class and the South Wales 0-6-2 tanks of the 56XX class.

So successful were the Castles that both the LMS and the LNER borrowed examples for test running in the 1920s, the results going a long way towards changing the course of locomotive development on both railways. The Castle had appeared in 1923 and in 1927 the first King was completed at Swindon. Not that any deficiency had been found in the Castle class, but an extra-powerful machine was required to deal with the heaviest West of England and Birmingham trains. At the time of building the King was the most-powerful locomotive in Britain. Both Castles and Kings were finished in the ornate livery of green and polished brass so beloved of the Great Western over the years.

By 1941 Collett had been succeeded by F W Hawksworth, who introduced the two-cylinder County class 4-6-0s, with boiler pressure of 280lb per square inch, which carried the Great Western banner high into the post-war era. Conditions had deteriorated considerably during the war, and the Counties were unable to show their

142

142 Cuneo painting of the Royal Albert bridge, Saltash, commissioned by British Railways to mark the bridge's centenary in 1959. *British Rail*

143 Crumlin viaduct, South Wales, the biggest metal lattice bridge in the world when completed in 1857. *British Rail*

146 Memorial to the founder engineer of the GWR adjacent to the former Birmingham Snow Hill station. *J R Batts*

143

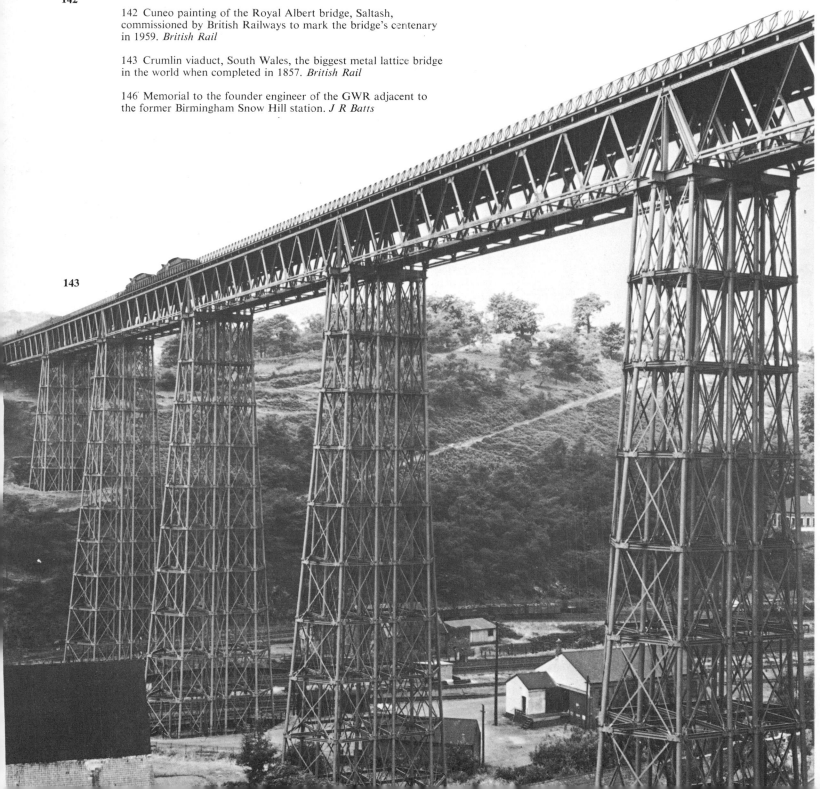

prowess as well as might have been hoped. Other innovations made after the war included the conversion of some Halls and other classes to oil burning, but because of difficulties with the then almighty dollar and the need to use home-produced fuel, this was not continued. Another was the experimentation with gas-turbine locomotives. Two engines, roughly of the power classification of the Castles, were built and passed into the era of nationalisation; the experiment was not conclusive.

The Great Western was one of the first of Britain's railways to introduce a system of automatic train control (the North Eastern also had an automatic warning alarm). The system introduced by the GWR as early as 1905 was simple, enterprising and safe. It was the precursor of the automatic warning device at present used on British Railways and it went a long way towards ensuring that the Great Western was one of the safest lines in the country. The primary object of the system was to give audible warning to a driver when his train was approaching a distant signal in the on position, and in the event of it being disregarded, automatically to apply the brakes to ensure that the train pulled up before the home signal was reached. Another distinctive audible indication was given in the cab when the distant signal was off.

The Great Western was always noted for fast running and as early as 1848 broad-gauge trains were booked over certain sections at an average speed of nearly 57 miles per hour. Some of the well-known named trains included the Flying Dutchman, at 11.45 from Paddington to the South West, and the Zulu, at 15.00 from Paddington to reach Exeter in 4¼ hours. By 1904 Plymouth was reached non-stop from Paddington with long stretches booked at over 60mph. The year 1906 saw the opening of the shortened route via Castle Cary, and slip coaches for Taunton and Exeter were put on the down trains. Over the years, slip coaches were a regular feature of Great Western express running and they did not finally pass out of use until the end of the 1950s. The run from Swindon to Paddington was for a long time the fastest booked start-to-stop run in the British Isles.

There is one special run which must be mentioned — the record-breaking journey made by the Ocean Mail train from Plymouth to London in May 1904. The train from Plymouth to Bristol was made up of five eight-wheeled vans headed by locomotive No 3440 *City of Truro* and timed by that doyen recorder of the day, Mr Charles Rous-Marten (though some students of locomotive performance doubt the accuracy of his recording on that occasion).

144

144 Trainshed and tower of Brunel's perpendicular Gothic design for Bristol Temple Meads. *Clifford and Wendy Meadway*

145 Saltash station in the mid-nineteenth century, with curved masonry viaduct leading out to the Royal Albert bridge. *Clifford and Wendy Meadway*

145

During the descent of Whiteball bank the maximum speed reached, according to Rous-Marten, was 102.3mph, the highest recorded until the 112mph by the LNER A4 *Silver Link* in 1935.

Of all the Great Western expresses two stand out — the Cornish Riviera Limited and the Cheltenham Flyer. The former left Paddington at 10.30 each day until May 1, 1972, when it was retimed at 11.30. The Ten-Thirty Limited, as it was known on the railway, was one of Britain's most famous trains. South Wales to Newport, Cardiff and Swansea, and northwards to Banbury, Birmingham and Wolverhampton were all well served by fast and comfortable Great Western trains. Beyond Swansea to the west and Wolverhampton to the north, the expresses usually became semi-fast trains, as they did beyond Plymouth into Cornwall. Once the Bicester cut-off had been built, two-hour expresses vied with the North Western to Birmingham over a generally harder route, but it was the only really competitive main line the Great Western had. The line from Shrewsbury to Hereford was joint with the LNWR and some of its trains were also smartly timed.

146

Of the absorbed companies, trains of the Midland & South Western Junction from Cheltenham to Andover, those of the Cambrian from Machynlleth to Pwlhelli and Aberystwyth, and the little Wantage tram from Wantage Road to Wantage, all ambled. In South Wales the business was mainly freight, and coal at that, train after train running loaded down the valleys behind varieties of 0-6-2 tanks. There were Barry engines, Port Talbot engines, Rhymney engines and Cardiff engines, and out of the smoke and into the hills there were the Brecon and Merthyr engines. It was quite a collection.

The Great Western's hub for mechanical matters was Swindon, but even before the "Absorption" it had smaller out-stations, the principal ones in later years being at Wolverhampton, which dealt with the Northern division, and Caerphilly which looked after South Wales. The Cambrian's works were at Oswestry, which to the end dealt with most of the engines on that section.

From the point of view of way and works, the Great Western had a number of unique and interesting items. The Severn tunnel, with its huge beam pumping engines, was the longest underwater tunnel in the world, while Brunel's timber viaducts in Devon and Cornwall were, to say the least, extremely handsome, as was, and is, the Saltash bridge across the Tamar, and a similar though smaller structure over the Wye at Chepstowe. The Cambrian brought in that long timber viaduct over the Mawddach at Barmouth, ending with a steel swing structure hardly ever used, though it *was* swung for the making of a film *The Ghost Train* in the early 1930s.

Compared with the LMS and the LNER, the Great Western owned few hotels and even fewer ships.

147 and 148 Stephenson's 1837 *North Star*. It was originally built for the 5ft 6in gauge New Orleans Railway in America but was converted to 7ft gauge for the GWR. The engine in Swindon Railway Museum is a replica.
Respectively Edito Service and R C H Nash

Paddington, of course, had the Great Western Royal Hotel and Weymouth served the Channel Islands by Great Western ships. But like the LNER the company considered itself to be a 'royal' line, carrying the Crown — Royal funeral specials tended to start at Sandringham and end up at Windsor; special plaques and headlamps were kept for such sad occasions.

To conclude, there was one further thing that the Great Western did superbly well — it sold itself not only to the travelling public, but to the public at large. Its staff were smartly dressed, and one always *felt* that they were efficient, and the public relations department carefully fostered that image. This was especially so during the period between the wars when it seemed almost a crime to go to 'Glorious Devon' in any other way than by Great Western train — and if you were lucky enough to travel on the Cornish Riviera Limited, the Torbay Express or the Cornishman, then that really *was* something.

The Great Western produced books of engine classes, names and numbers, books on its glories such as the Ten-Thirty Limited, the Cheltenham Flyer and Locos of the Royal Road — all for a shilling, and really superb jig-saw puzzles of its trains, engines and the places of tourist interest it served — 150 pieces of plywood for two shillings and sixpence. Above all it produced the great thick handbooks on the areas it served, full to the brim with information and advertisements, called *Holiday Haunts*. Without doubt it was an enterprising railway and of the big four it was the Great Western which produced results for its shareholders — not as much as one might have liked, but it produced them, to the end.

149 One of the famous Dean singles, No 3031 *Achilles*. which were converted from broad to standard gauge. *British Rail*

150 Preserved GWR Dean Goods 0-6-0 No 2516. *R C H Nash*

151 A GWR hybrid – the Dukedog 4-4-0s were constructed from reusable parts of worn-out Duke and Bulldog engines. No 3217 is preserved on the Bluebell Railway in Sussex. *M J Esau*

152

153

154

155

152 Another notable GWR 4-4-0 was the City class, here represented by No 3437 *City of Gloucester*. *Ian Allan Library*

153 Saint class No 171 *Albion*, one of the first of a long line of GWR 4-6-0s.

154 Prototype 2-6-0 mixed-traffic engine produced mainly from standard GWR parts in 1911.

155 A production 2-6-0 in works grey livery for the official photograph. *Ian Allan Library*

156 2-6-0 No 5330 leaving Newton Abbot with a Plymouth-Paddington train in 1958. *D S Fish*

157 The larger GWR mixed-traffic engine, the Collett-designed Hall class. *B A Reeves*

158

159

160

161

158 2-6-0 No 6393 leaving Parsons tunnel, near Dawlish, with an express fish train in June 1949. *E D Bruton*

159 Later batches of 2-6-0s were given side-window cabs.

160 The GWR's *Pendennis Castle* stands alongside the LNER's *Flying Fox* during the 1925 Locomotive Exchanges.

161 In the 1930s No 5005 *Manorbier Castle* was fitted with a semi-streamlined front end. The experient was not a success. *J Adams*

162 Castle No 5058 *Earl of Clancarty* after arrival at Penzance with the Cornish Riviera Express in September 1952. *Leslie Overend Ltd*

163 King class No 6025 *King Henry III* on an up express at Dawlish in September 1955. *P Ransome-Wallis*

164 Up Cornish Riviera Express at Savernake in August 1952 behind No 6029 *King Edward VIII. G W Goslin*

165 A King on the Cambrian Coast Express – No 6016 *King Edward V* in Saunderton cutting. *M Pope*

166 Double chimney as fitted to the King and Castle classes. *M Pope*

167 No 6000 *King George V* hauling the Bulmer Pullmans through Sonning cutting in October 1971. The success of *KGV's* outings on the main line on such occasions finally persuaded British Rail to reinstate steam specials on their tracks. *V C K Allen*

162

163

164 165 166

167

168 *King George V* in action on BR. The locomotive is on loan to the Bulmer cider company at Hereford and can be seen working return to steam specials on the Newport-Shrewsbury route. *V C K Allen*

169 (inset) Nameplate and centre driving wheel of No 6005 *King George II. M Pope*

169

170 A King passing North Acton with a Birmingham-bound train of BR chocolate-and-cream stock. *M Pope*

171 2-6-2T No 4555, now based on the Dart Valley Railway, at Alveley colliery in September 1965. *P B Whitehouse*

172 Dart Valley train behind No 4555 crossing Nursery Pool bridge in October 1967. *J Adams*

176 (facing page) Though this 16XX class 0-6-0PT is a pure Hawksworth GWR design it was actually built at Swindon by British Railways after nationalisation. It is now preserved on the Dart Valley Railway. *C J Gammell*

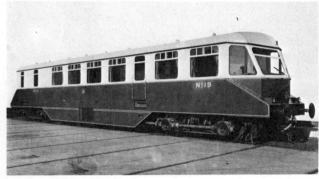

173 2-6-2T No 7 of the Vale of Rheidol Railway – the GWR's only narrow-gauge line – taking water at Aberffrwd in BR days. *M J Esau*

174 One of a fleet of streamlined diesel railcars introduced by the GWR in the 1940s. *British Rail*

175 GWR Ocean Saloon *Duchess of York*, used on Paddington-Plymouth boat trains. *J Adams*

Southern Railway

THE HISTORY of the Southern is bound up with the stories of the first 'public' railway in the world — the Surrey Iron Railway of 1803; the first railway to carry passengers by means of a locomotive — the Canterbury & Whitstable Railway of 1830; and the first railway into London — the London & Greenwich of 1836. It is true that the Stockton & Darlington line was opened as early as 1825 but all that company's passenger coaches were horse-drawn until 1833, and although the Liverpool & Manchester is sometimes thought of as being the first major public railway to use steam haulage, the *Invicta* of the Canterbury & Whitstable started running about five months earlier.

The main constituents to form the Southern in 1923 were the London & South Western, the London, Brighton & South Coast, the South Eastern, and the London, Chatham & Dover Railways — the two last-named coming under the banner of the South Eastern & Chatham Railway Companies Managing Committee. Other lines to be drawn into the new organisation included those in the Isle of Wight (the Freshwater, Yarmouth & Newport, the Isle of Wight and Isle of Wight Central Railways). The Southern also shared the Somerset & Dorset Joint Railway with the London Midland & Scottish Railway. In addition there was a unique and delightful narrow gauge line, the Lynton & Barnstaple, which came in under special parliamentary powers.

These railway companies covered virtually all Southern England and spread well into the South West. The London & South Western was the largest, with a total route running line of 1,019 miles, of which 324 miles was single track. It sprang from the London & Southampton Railway of 1837 whose contractor was the famous Thomas Brassey. The next in size was the South Eastern & Chatham Committee's line comprising the South Eastern and London, Chatham & Dover Railways. It had a total route running line of 638 miles and its ancestry is traceable back to the Canterbury & Whitstable. The London Brighton & South Coast was the smallest of the 'Big Three' having a route running line of 457 miles, its beginnings going back to the London & Croydon Railway opened in 1839. The Southern Railway's historian Dendy Marshall tells us that the company inherited in total 2,178 miles of first running track, 4,175 miles of total track (running line) and 1,205 miles of siding. There were 2,281 locomotives, 7,500 coaches and 36,749 wagons, as well as 41 steamboats and 11 hotels.

The Southern was very much a passenger line; it dealt with vast numbers of commuters in the London area as well as holidaymakers, cross-Channel and ocean-going travellers. It spread its commuter belt wider and wider, encouraging suburban growth down to Margate, Ramsgate, Brighton and Sevenoaks. It advertised and encouraged its seaside resorts from Kent to North Cornwall. Its cross-Channel steamers plied from Dover or Folkestone to Calais or Boulogne, Newhaven to Dieppe, and Southampton to Cherbourg, Le Havre and St Malo. There was also a Channel Islands service. Train ferries crossed over from Dover to Dunkerque, and Southampton docks was built up into the vast Ocean terminal, rivalling and then eclipsing Liverpool for the Atlantic passenger trade.

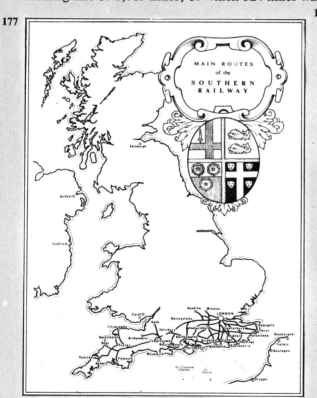

177

178

179

180

177 Principal routes of the Southern Railway in 1923.

178 The final version of the Southern's coat of arms, which appeared shortly before nationalisation in 1948. *Ian Allan Library*

179 Two distinctive features of the Brighton section of the Southern – the ornate mouth of Clayton tunnel (the house is still lived in) and the Brighton Belle electric Pullman train. *J C Morgan*

180 The Southern Railway was unique in its operation of a cross-Channel ferry taking passengers overnight from London to Paris. Here is the Night Ferry, made up of special *Wagons-Lits* vehicles suited to the British loading gauge at Victoria. *P B Whitehouse*

The
DEVON BELLE

Fridays. Saturdays. Sundays and Mondays in each direction

dep 12.0 noon	Waterloo	arr 5.20 p.m
arr 3.16 p.m	Sidmouth Jct.	dep 2.3 p.m
arr 3.36 p.m	Exeter Ctl.	dep 1.40 pm
arr 5.32 pm	Ilfracombe	dep 12. 0 noon
arr 5.36 pm	Plymouth Friary	dep 11.30 a.m

NEW!

ALL-PULLMAN TRAIN TO THE WEST OF ENGLAND
with Observation Car

SOUTHERN RAILWAY & PULLMAN CAR COMPANY

181

181 1930s Southern poster by M Secrétan for the Devon Belle
Pullman. *British Transport Museum/B Sharpe*

The Southern Railway's expresses, apart from those serving Devon and Cornwall, were comparatively short-distance ones. The South Eastern & Chatham's termini at Charing Cross and Cannon Street were the starting points for the Kent Coast trains running via Chatham or Ashford, and the South Eastern's westerly route, into Hastings via Tonbridge. Victoria served the lines to Brighton, Newhaven, Hastings, Bexhill and Eastbourne, and trains from Waterloo ran to Southampton, Bournemouth, Salisbury, Exeter, North Devon and North Cornwall. Portsmouth and the Isle of Wight trains ran over both the old LBSC and LSW sections from Victoria and Waterloo. Pullman cars ran regularly on the Golden Arrow (Victoria to Dover) the Southern Belle (also from Victoria) and the Atlantic Coast Express. The latter was the Southern's longest express journey and the train carried portions which were shed beyond Exeter for Plymouth, Bude, Padstow, Barnstaple, Ilfracombe and Torrington. Through trains ran regularly to its connecting northerly neighbours, the old LBSCR's Sunny South express route to the LMS, and trains from Bournemouth or Margate to Birkenhead via Reading and Birmingham on the Great Western. Bath and the Midlands were reached

from Bournemouth via Templecombe and the Somerset & Dorset line.

Barnstaple was the junction for the 1ft 11½in-gauge railway to Lynton, which was closed by the Southern in September 1935. It was one of the most delightful journeys that could be made, and had it survived the 1939-45 war there is little doubt that it could have become one of Britain's finest tourist railways. The locomotives were, in the main, Manning Wardle 2-6-2 tanks with lovely river names like *Exe, Taw* and *Yeo,* all of 1897 vintage, assisted by an American Baldwin-built 2-4-2 tank, *Lyn,* also of 1897. The Southern obtained a third 2-6-2 tank, *Lew,* and it was the only engine to survive the line's demise, having been, it is said, sold out of service to Brazil. It has never yet been traced and remains one of the interesting speculations of narrow-gauge railway lore.

The Isle of Wight lines were retained by the Southern and although Ryde and Portsmouth were the principal pierheads, ferries also ran to Freshwater (from Lymington) and Cowes (from Portsmouth). The train service from Ryde to Shanklin and Ventnor was as busy in the summer as the single line could take. By the early 1930s, most of the old Isle of Wight companies' engines

182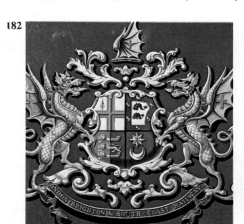

183

185

184

184 Maunsell 2-6-0 with long valve travel, introduced on the SECR in 1917. *Ian Allan Library*

186

187

had gone and the traffic was worked by imported tank engines from the mainland. There were ex-LSWR 02 class 0-4-4 tanks, with enlarged bunkers (which worked most of the trains), ex-LBSCR 0-6-0 Terrier tanks (mostly on the 'branch' trains) and two ex-LBSCR E1 class 0-6-2 tanks for freight. All carried names of towns or villages on the island.

Electrification of the Southern suburban lines made considerable headway immediately after the Grouping. They ran out to Rochester, Chatham and Gillingham on the South Eastern section, spread during the decade over much of the LBSCR (Central section) and took in the South Western's remaining steam suburban services out of Waterloo, as well as the Portsmouth line. The London & South Western had already carried out an electrification project in 1915, trains running out of Waterloo to East Putney, Shepperton and Hampton Court. This followed the lead set by the London Brighton & South Coast, which had put in an overhead system as early as 1905, having in all about 62 miles of electrified track out to Crystal Palace and West Norwood. The Southern followed the South Western's principle of third-rail direct current whereas the LBSC favoured overhead-line and alternating current.

The Southern's first chief mechanical engineer was R. E. L. Maunsell, who came from the SE&CR; he inherited a collection of somewhat ancient engines from each of the constituent companies. They were augmented by further 2-6-0 engines of the SE&CR N class, the ill-fated River class 2-6-4 tanks, some L1 4-4-0s based on the SE&C's L class, and more 2-6-0s of U, U1 and N1 classes. In 1925 the

186 Wainwright SECR 0-6-0 No 592 at Sheffield Park on the Bluebell Railway awaiting attention. *C J Gammell*

187 Another Bluebell engine, LBSCR 'Terrier' No 55 *Stepney*. *P B Whitehouse*

famous King Arthur class was born at Eastleigh works; they were based on the LSWR Urie H15 4-6-0 and were an immediate success. This was perhaps the most famous Southern Railway class and until final withdrawal almost forty years later the King Arthurs were used on express work. During their heyday they hauled virtually every important fast train, including the Continental services, the Atlantic Coast Express and the Southern Belle (the predecessor of the electric Brighton Belle).

Between 1926 and 1929 an even more powerful 4-6-0 class was tried out — the Lord Nelson, a four-cylinder design whose eight beats per revolution of the wheels sounded rather odd to the uninitiated. When originally built, the Lord Nelson was the most powerful locomotive in the country and drawings of it were borrowed by the LMS when contemplating its Royal Scot class. In 1930 Maunsell produced the most powerful 4-4-0 in Europe — the Schools class; the new engines were put to work on the South Eastern main lines, including that to Hastings which had been worked until then mainly by the old L class 4-4-0s.

Maunsell retired in 1937 and was succeeded by O. V. Bulleid, whose designs were revolutionary to a degree. His first class (Merchant Navy) came out in 1941 at a period when wartime restrictions on the building of express engines were in force; the restriction was avoided by terming the engine a mixed-traffic type — because the driving wheels were only 6ft 2in in diameter! The Merchant Navys were the Southern's first Pacifics and they boasted a form of streamlined casing, chain-driven

radial valve gear (peculiar to their designer), disc wheels and electric lighting. They were followed by two classes of a lightweight version, the West Country and Battle of Britain classes. After nationalisation of the railways all the Merchant Navy engines and a large number of the light Pacifics were rebuilt with orthodox valve gear and had their streamlined casings removed. They ran over the Bournemouth line until the end of steam in 1967. Probably the most controversial of all Bulleid's designs was the Leader class running on two six-wheel power bogies. Although ten were ordered, only one engine was ever completed. Southern engines were built at Ashford (SE&CR), Brighton (LB&SCR) and Eastleigh (LSWR) works.

Partly because of the Southern's determination to electrify and partly because existing locomotives were still able to perform their duties on secondary and shunting services, a largish number of pre-grouping engines lasted well into nationalisation — some almost to the end. Of them, the SE&CR's efficient 4-4-0 D1 and E1 rebuilds remained hard at work on the Eastern section — especially to Margate and Ramsgate — until electrification at the end of the 1950s, and Drummond's T9 class 4-4-0s took the subdivided Atlantic Coast Express to Plymouth, Bude and Padstow. Drummond's 0-0-4 tanks of Class M7 lasted as long as most of the push-and-pull services in Devon or the shunters at Waterloo were required. Two ancient London & South Western classes had particularly long lives — the old Beattie 2-4-0 well tanks which worked the Wenford Bridge line out of Wadebridge, and the Adams 4-4-2 tanks

79

190

188 'Terrier' No 32678 at Havant in August 1962. *J B Snell*

189 Billinton class E4 0-6-2T No 473, built for the LBSCR in 1898 and now preserved on the Bluebell Railway. *P B Whitehouse*

190 An LBSCR class B4 4-4-0 fitted by Marsh with a Phoenix superheater.

191 The last Hayling Island train at Havant in November 1963, hauled by 'Terrier' No 32636. The first vehicle is an experimental Southern resin glass-fibre bodied compartment coach. *C J Gammell*

192 The LBSCR took delivery of the first of these 4-4-2Ts in 1908. No 91 was the last of the class to be built in 1912. *Ian Allan Library*

193 (facing page) SECR Wainwright class P 0-6-0T No 27 taking water at Sheffield Park on the Bluebell Railway. *A D Deayton*

191

192

which ran from Axminster to Lyme Regis over a hilly and twisting road where they needed to double-head on a load of three coaches. Other classes working almost to the end of steam included the N15 class 4-6-0s, the O2 0-4-4 tanks on the Isle of Wight, and the Maunsell Moguls.

Like its competitors, the Southern was a ship- and dock-owning company. The ships were cross-Channel steamers (some owned jointly with French Railways) and were generally in service on the short sea route to France. Two larger vessels, the *Dinard* and the *St Briac,* were put to work on the overnight Southampton-St Malo run. Other steamers ran from Weymouth and Southampton to the Channel Islands, Dover to Ostend, and Gravesend to Rotterdam; there was also a ferry service to the Isle of Wight. Passengers from London could travel to Paris via the Night Ferry from Dover, and in 1939 the Southern introduced a new ship, the *Invicta,* for the luxury Golden Arrow service from London to Paris. No fewer than twelve of the Southern's ships became casualties during the 1939-45 war.

Of all its docks, Southampton was the most valuable and certainly the most famous — it has a remarkable double high tide — the second high water occurring only two hours after the first, with only a slight fall in between. The docks were inaugurated by the London & South Western Railway and were developed by the Southern into the country's premier Atlantic terminal. Other docks owned by the company included Dover, Folkestone and Newhaven for the Channel crossings, and Ryde in the Isle of Wight.

The Southern system, in general, was badly hit by the war, as a large proportion of its Channel holiday resorts were prohibited areas. It made tremendous efforts during the retreat from Dunkerque, and in the events prior to the D-day landings; it was not only a target for marauding aircraft, buzz-bombs and rockets, but the Dover district also suffered constant shelling.

The two years between 1945 and the end in 1947 were ones of austerity, but in 1945-6 some cross-Channel services were restored; the same year saw the luxurious Golden Arrow/*Invicta* service re-opened and Pullman restaurant cars back on some trains. In 1947, a hundred engines were converted to oil burning and the all-Pullman Devon Belle came into operation, bringing an appearance of normality again. Once more the Southern turned its attention towards leisure and holidays instead of just troops and commuters. New plans were brought forward and old ones taken from cupboards and dusted, mostly for further electrification, and when the new Railway Executive was formed to administer Britain's newly nationalised railways, it was the Southern's general manager, Sir Eustace Missenden, who became its chairman.

The Southern came second to the Great Western in its returns to its shareholders, having always paid a preference dividend — though not necessarily at the promised rate. It had the best record of all the four group companies for forward-looking improvements, especially in the ambitious electrification schemes, and the docks at Southampton which have long proved a great asset to the nation. Because it was very much a passenger line and served most of south London's long-suffering suburbanites, who were (and still are) crammed like sardines in peak-hour trains, the Southern never had the popular image of the Great Western. It helped to push and develop suburbia in its crowded electric services and consequently had its share of public stone-throwing, but like the tubes it became an essential part of the pattern of London and outer-London life.

But as well as suburban and commuter electrics, it had the more leisurely hop-pickers' train, ramblers' trains, race-goers' trains, boat trains, and even opera trains; it used Pullmans to give comfort to the well-off and the overseas visitor and can be said to have served every facet of life from Royalty en route to Ascot to the day tripper on Margate excursions. However, the pattern changed very quickly and apart from its holiday trains and Continental traffic (which tended to be seasonal anyway) the Southern became more and more a railway whose future lay in the none-too-profitable job of taking the willing but ungrateful public from home to work and back, five days a week. Had it not been for the excellent planning of its management in bringing forward the electrification works, then road traffic congestion in and out of London would have become so bad that the thought is hardly bearable. It is worth remembering.

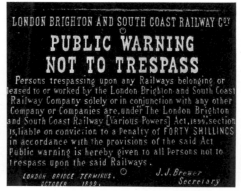

194 A 'Terrier' crossing Langstone bridge with a Hayling Island-Havant train. *Alison Esau*

195 An LBSCR express 4-4-2T of 1914. After the Brighton and Eastbourne lines were electrified there was no suitable work for these fine engines, so they were rebuilt as 4-6-0 tender engines. The erstwhile *Charles C Macrae* thus became No 2327 *Trevithick*. *Ian Allan Library*

196 LBSCR trespass notice.

197 F Moore/LPC postcard showing an LBSCR class H1 Atlantic at Victoria. *Ian Allan Library*

198 An LSWR penny platform ticket machine once used at the British Transport Museum, Clapham.

199 Adams LSWR class 02 0-4-4T No 26 *Whitwell* at Newport, Isle of Wight. *M J Esau*

200 One of the Isle of Wight 02s has been preserved at Haven Street by the Wight Locomotive Society. *G M Kichenside*

201 Schools class No 926 *Repton* at Eastleigh awaiting shipment to Steamtown, Vermont, for preservation. *Colourviews Ltd*

202 Nameplate and driving wheel of a Schools class 4-4-0. *D N Jamieson*

203 A Maunsell King Arthur 4-6-0 on the Southern Belle Pullman train. *A Wood collection*

204 Line-up of Southern motive power at Nine Elms shed in August 1942. *Ian Allan Library*

205 The LNER's *Mallard* stands alongside a Southern King Arthur at Nine Elms during the 1948 Locomotive Exchanges. *Ian Allan Library*

198

199

200

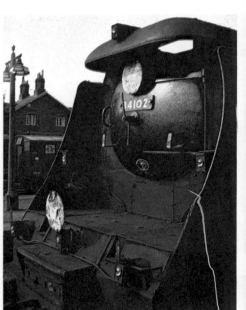

206

208

209

206 Rebuilt Bulleid Merchant Navy class 4-6-2 No 35027 *Port Line* takes the southbound Pines Express out of Oxford in January 1966. *D Huntriss*

207 Rebuilt Merchant Navy No 35028 *Clan Line* on a Waterloo-Salisbury train at Wimbledon Park in June 1967. *C J Gammell*

208 Bulleid West Country class Pacific No 34023 *Blackmore Vale*. Seen here on the Longmoor Military Railway, it has now found a home on the Bluebell Railway. *M Pope*

209 The last of the unrebuilt Bulleid Pacifics was No 34102 *Lapford;* the unorthodox shape of the front end can clearly be seen here. *A H Ellis*

207

210

211

210 A rare picture of the only operational Bulleid Leader class 0-6-6-0T running trials in 1949. The fireman worked inside the casing, alongside the transversely-mounted boiler, while the driver occupied one of the two cabs at either end. This twin-bogie, six-cylinder locomotive showed much promise, but BR were perhaps rather alarmed at such a revolutionary concept and, after Bulleid's retirement, No 36001 and the two other unused engines were quietly broken up. *The Times*

211 No 33035, one of Bulleid's austerely functional Q1 0-6-0s from the war years, on a Dover train at Folkestone Warren in 1961. *M Pope*

TRACKS TO THE NORTH

The Last Main Line into London

IT MIGHT WELL have been thought, after the Midland Railway had broken out of its provincial limitations in 1868 and made its way, against strong opposition from its neighbours, into its own palatial London terminus at St Pancras, that nothing of the kind would be likely to happen again. However, there were other important railways in the North of England, although two of them showed no disposition to follow the Midland example. The North Eastern Railway for instance, secure in its profitable corner, was content with an alliance with the Great Northern Railway to provide communication with London; the Lancashire & Yorkshire Railway, also, had excellent relations with the London & North Western Railway for the same purpose.

But there was another railway spread across the North Midlands from Liverpool and Manchester to Sheffield and Grimsby that was far from satisfied with its merely provincial status, and that was the Manchester, Sheffield & Lincolnshire Railway; three decades after the Midland reached London, the MSLR achieved the same goal and opened what was in fact to be the last main line into London.

The nucleus of the MSLR was the Manchester & Sheffield Railway, which after four years spent in construction, including the difficult task of penetrating the Pennine barrier with the three-mile Woodhead tunnel (the

longest in Britain to that date), was opened throughout in December 1845. Two years later, through the amalgamation of the MSR with the Sheffield & Lincolnshire and the Great Grimsby & Sheffield Junction railways, and the Great Grimsby docks, the Manchester, Sheffield & Lincolnshire Railway came into being. For the next half century its history was to be one of constant making and breaking of alliances, and of warfare with and without the London & North Western, the Midland and the Great Northern railways as allies. The stormy history of the line was largely bound up with the régime of Edward Watkin, who at the age of 35 went to the MSLR as general manager in 1854. He had had experience on the London & North Western Railway under Captain Huish, who had the reputation of being the most wily and unscrupulous railway general manager of his time, and whose methods Watkin was to copy before long.

In those days the only route from London to York and the north was from Euston and by the LNWR to Rugby, where the Midland took the trains over and worked them north-eastward through Leicester, Derby and Normanton. The LNWR was therefore strongly opposed to the Great Northern Railway, which in 1846 had obtained parliamentary powers for a new main line out of London that would provide a more direct route to York. Watkin, continuing the Euston tradition, did all he could to hamper

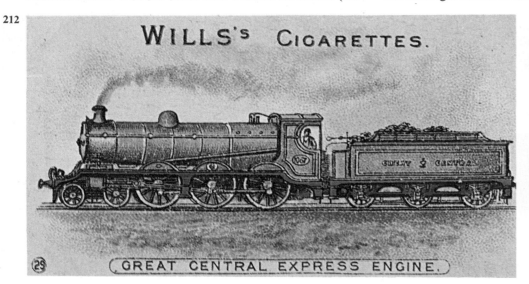

212 Wills cigarette-card representation of a Great Central 4-6-0 passenger engine.

213 Heraldic device of the Manchester South Junction and Altrincham Railway, in which the GC was a partner. *British Transport Museum/B Sharpe*

214 Ex-Great Central 4-4-2 on a Liverpool-Manchester express near Flixton in June 1939. *A R Prince*

215 A BR class 9F 2-10-0 with a freight train at Nottingham
Victoria in 1964. Steam passenger trains continued on the GC
main line between this station and Marylebone until the mid-
1960s, a year or so before the station was closed. *J Cupit*

216 A rare Robinson compound Atlantic on Charwelton
water troughs on the GC main line. *B K Cooper*

the GNR, which nevertheless completed its line by 1850.

In his harrying campaign, Huish had organised what
became known as the Euston Square Confederacy, in
which he enlisted the support of the Midland, the
Lancashire & Yorkshire and the Manchester, Sheffield &
Lincolnshire companies, all of which were opposed to the
hapless Great Northern. The alliance was later extended
into what was called the Octuple Agreement, in which
eight railways were concerned; it, in fact, included the
Great Northern and was intended to provide for pooling
the receipts from all traffic between London and stations
north of York, but in reality turned out to be a device of
the confederates to do all they could to divert traffic from
the Great Northern.

The next years saw all kinds of moves and counter-
moves, and then in 1857 an astonishing thing happened.
Watkin suddenly broke away from the Euston group and
entered into a Fifty Years Agreement with the GNR, which
Parliament ratified, against fierce LNWR opposition, in
1858. Without delay the GNR and MSLR began a
passenger service between Kings Cross and Manchester in
direct competition with that of the LNWR from Euston.
Morning and evening expresses began to operate on five-
hour schedules between Kings Cross and Manchester,
which, despite a journey of 202½ miles compared with the
189 miles of the LNWR route, and the tremendous climb
to Woodhead tunnel, came within 20 minutes of the best
LNWR time.

By virtue of running powers, the MSLR ran to and from
the LNWR London Road station at Manchester, where the
former's staff and passengers were subjected to every
possible harassment by the LNWR men. The latter even
tried taking into custody some of the passengers off the
MSLR trains; however, one of those so molested happened
to be a lawyer, who proved such a prickly customer to
handle that the LNWR abandoned its obstructive
practices.

By 1884 the service between Kings Cross and
Manchester had become the fastest of all over the Great
Northern main line, and the most outstanding for speed in
the country. The expresses were covering the 105½ miles
between Kings Cross and Grantham in 115 to 117 minutes;
at Grantham MSLR engines replaced those of the GNR
and ran 56 miles on to Sheffield in 61 to 63 minutes, giving
Sheffield a service to and from London in about three
hours, and only 55 to 59 minutes was spent over the
heavily graded 41½ miles between Sheffield and
Manchester. So the GN-MSL allies were practically
equalling the best LNWR times, and with punctual
running and comfortable rolling stock were proving very
serious competitors.

Meantime there had been other controversial
happenings. The thrusting Midland Railway, strenuously
opposed by the London & North Western, had succeeded
by 1867 in pushing its tentacles into Manchester and was
casting about to find a terminus in that city. The answer

was provided by the Manchester, Sheffield & Lincolnshire, which by then had its own independent platforms at London Road; so the MSLR offered hospitality to the Midland, with temporary access over its own lines, and thereby infuriated both the hostile LNWR and its own GNR allies. No wonder Watkin and the Manchester, Sheffield & Lincolnshire earned the nickname of the railway flirt! So, from the opening of St Pancras terminus, the Midland began its own London-Manchester express service.

But Watkin had far greater ambitions, the realisation of which eventually was to earn the fiercest of opposition by all his former enemies and allies alike. They were for the Manchester Sheffield & Lincolnshire Railway to break out of its provincial boundaries, and like the Midland, to make its own independent way into London. Moreover, he had visions of an empire extending from Manchester to the Continent of Europe, for he had interests in the projected Channel tunnel. In preparation for the necessary link he engineered a seat for himself on the boards of both the Metropolitan and the South Eastern railways; he later became chairman of both companies.

Because of opposition, various Bills for lines to extend the MSLR southwards were rejected by Parliament, but at last, in 1889, an Act was passed which made possible the first move. It was for a line from Chesterfield to Annesley, just north of Nottingham. Then, in 1891, the fateful decision was reached. Parliament sanctioned a brand-new main line from Annesley through Nottingham, Leicester and Rugby to a junction with the Metropolitan Railway at Quainton Road; from there, Metropolitan tracks would be used to Harrow and new lines, to be built by the Metropolitan from there on to Canfield Place, whence the MSL would continue into a new terminus at Marylebone. The Great Northern, Midland, and London & North Western railways were all now likely to be affected by new competition, and the violence of their opposition can well be imagined. The Great Northern was bought off by the plan for a joint MSL and GN station in the heart of Nottingham, and running powers over the new line between there and Sheffield.

Very costly engineering work was involved. The site for Nottingham Victoria station involved a massive excavation in the heart of the city; that at Leicester required a lengthy viaduct and much destruction of property. In Nottingham the new line was to cross the Midland station, and the Midland demanded a clear span of 170ft over all its platforms and tracks. There were to be many massive viaducts, the first at Bulwell, north of Nottingham; one over the Midland Nottingham station; a four-track construction over the River Trent; at Rugby a long one across the Avon valley, with 600ft of steel spans across the London & North Western main line; and the Valley crossings at Helmdon and Brackley demanding lengthy masonry viaducts, the latter with 22 arches and a maximum height of 180ft. There were also many tunnels, including Catesby, between Rugby and Woodford, 1¾ miles long.

The approach to Marylebone terminus involved some difficult engineering, especially where the line had to emerge from two tunnels under Hillgrove Crescent and rise sufficiently to clear the London & North Western main line at South Hampstead without disturbing the buildings above. There was a fearful outcry from entirely another quarter when it was realised that cut-and-cover tunnelling would be needed under part of the sacrosanct Lord's cricket ground, and endless negotiations were needed before a satisfactory compromise was reached. Massive compensation was also demanded by wealthy residents in St Johns Wood who considered that their peace would be disturbed by the passage of trains.

The new main line was engineered for speed, with no gradient throughout its length steeper than 1 in 176, the approaches, however, were a different matter. From Staveley Town to Heath southbound trains had to climb six miles at 1 in 100, followed by 11 miles down at 1 in 132 (with one short break) from Kirkby into Nottingham. Then, after reaching Metropolitan track at Quainton Road, there were six miles up at 1 in 117 from Aylesbury through the Chilterns, and six miles down at 1 in 105 from Amersham to Rickmansworth. Finally, there were the sharp descents from Harrow (two miles mostly at 1 in 91), and for 2½ miles from Brondesbury almost into the terminus, in part as steep as 1 in 95, making a difficult start for down trains.

In one respect the new main line was unique. All its stations were laid out as islands, with the running lines curved round them but at such long radii as not to demand any speed restriction. Nottingham Victoria had two island platforms 1,300ft long, and Leicester a single 1,240ft island; in both cases there were terminal bay platforms at the two ends.

In 1897, because of extending activities, the MSLR had assumed the imposing title of Great Central Railway. So it was as the Great Central that it began operating freight traffic over the London extension in the summer of 1898, and dispatched the first passenger train from Marylebone terminus on March 15, 1899. Another important development was set on foot by the Great Central and Great Western Railways with parliamentary powers obtained jointly in 1899. The Great Central wanted a line with easier gradients than those of the Metropolitan over which to work their freight trains into London, even at the expense of distance, and the Great Western wanted a shorter route from London to Birmingham, even at the expense of steeper gradients.

So the two companies built a joint line from Northolt, reached by a GCR spur from Neasden and a GWR spur from Old Oak Common, through High Wycombe and Princes Risborough to Ashendon Junction, where they parted company, the GCR with a short link to Grendon Underwood, and the GWR with a longer stretch to Aynho Junction, south of Banbury. The new Great Central freight route, used also by a few passenger trains, was 4½ miles longer than via Aylesbury, but had no gradient steeper than 1 in 164, and that only in short lengths. The joint line was opened in 1906, and another valuable development for the Great Central, brought into use in 1900, was an eight-mile link between Woodford on the GCR and Banbury on the GWR Birmingham-Oxford main line, which gave the Great Central a new route to the south and west.

Having at last made its way into London, the Great Central had the difficult task of trying to create a passenger business in competition with long-established rivals. Regular travellers do not readily change their habits, and one particular handicap of the GCR was that for its first eight years, until the Baker Street & Waterloo tube was extended to Edgware Road, Marylebone was the only London terminus without an underground connection. At first, too, speed over the new line had to be restricted until all the cuttings and embankments, some of considerable size, had settled down. Soon, however, and especially after the redoubtable Sam Fay became general manager in 1902, a remarkable train service had come into operation, backed by the claim 'Every express train vestibuled and with buffet car attached'.

By 1905, Marylebone's day started with fast newspaper trains to Sheffield at 02.45 and 07.05, followed by passenger expresses for Manchester at 08.45, for Bradford at 10.00, for Manchester again at 12.15 and (a very fast train) 13.40. But the star turn was the 15.25, which did not call at either Leicester or Nottingham and for the first time provided a non-stop express from London to Sheffield,

taking 177 minutes for the 164¾ miles. Manchester was reached at 19.15, in three hours 50 minutes from London, a time which compared favourably with the fastest Midland and London & North Western schedules at that time. Further Nottingham and Manchester trains were followed by a very fast 18.20 to Bradford.

Altogether there were 16 daily mainline departures from London, 4 of them to Leicester only, but 12 going on to Sheffield and then continuing either to Manchester or Bradford. Nine of the trains included a restaurant car. To and from Sheffield the competition with both the Midland and the Great Northern railways was severe. In 1904 the Midland experimented with a non-stop run over its 158¼ miles to Sheffield in 182 minutes; in 1905 the Great Northern put on an evening non-stop express at 18.10 from Kings Cross in 170 minutes for its 161½ miles, to compete with the 18.20 from Marylebone. But the service between London and Sheffield was being overdone and before long all three companies introduced intermediate stops into their fastest schedules or withdrew some trains, particularly the Great Central, whose lavish service was not proving the hoped-for attraction.

But one Great Central express was destined to become both permanent and popular, and that was the 15.25 from Marylebone to Manchester; although never officially titled, it became known as the Sheffield Special. It first appeared in the Great Central timetable in 1903, a year after Sam Fay's accession to power, and, with the help of water troughs at Charwelton and Killamarsh, became Sheffield's first non-stop service from London. By 1904, it was timed at 177 minutes, further reduced by 1905 to 170 minutes, equal to the Great Northern's new non-stop time. The GN train's time was soon increased by intermediate stops, leaving the GC's Sheffield Special to settle down to a non-stop time of 177 minutes, which continued up to the outbreak of war in 1914.

By that time the train had grown from its original three coaches to a four-coach formation, plus a coach which was slipped at Leicester. The Pollitt 4-4-0 engines initially used had been replaced first by Robinson's Atlantics — among the most graceful locomotives ever to run on British metals

— and then, just before the war, by the first of Robinson's capable Director 4-4-0s, which were to monopolise the working from that time onwards. At Sheffield, a second slip brake was attached, to be slipped at Penistone with a through coach from Bournemouth to Bradford; the main train then stopped at Guide Bridge, and worked round the Levenshulme loop into Manchester Central in order to make a Cheshire Lines connection to Liverpool. At that time the start from Marylebone had become 15.15 and the Manchester arrival 19.25.

The Sheffield Special continued to run during the war, most unusually retaining its restaurant car and also continuing at speeds only slightly inferior to those of peacetime. The slips were discontinued (and never reappeared), so from that time on the train stopped at Leicester, Nottingham and Penistone.

Between the wars, the Sheffield Special settled down to a 15.20 departure from Marylebone and covered the 103 mies to Leicester in 109 minutes; then followed 25 minutes for the 23½ miles to Nottingham, and 48 minutes for the heavily graded 38¼ miles on to Sheffield, reached in 186 minutes from London. The load to that point was normally seven coaches of 243 tons weight, including a through LMS coach for Bradford, detached at Penistone. With stops there and at Guide Bridge, Manchester Central was reached at 19.45. The Director 4-4-0 worked the entire 212 miles from Marylebone to Manchester, and it is doubtful if ever before or since a 4-4-0 locomotive has been faced with so arduous a task. It has been calculated that on the journey the train had to be lifted on adverse gradients through a total of no less than 2,900ft! The task was not eased until, in London & North Eastern days, Gresley's three-cylinder B17 4-6-0s arrived to replace the hard-worked Directors.

After the 1939-45 war, the Sheffield Special never reappeared in the timetable. Not only that; who would have conceived it possible that 25 years later, the Great Central main line that had been built in the face of such fierce opposition and at such tremendous cost over almost the whole of its length would have gone out of existence altogether, after a life of no more than 70 years?

217 Peak class diesel-electric locomotive No D70 on a Plymouth-Sheffield train at Chesterfield in July 1971. *V Bamford*

The Midland Route to Scotland

WHEN TRAVELLING from London to Scotland, one is inclined to think only of two routes, the West Coast route from Euston and the East Coast route from Kings Cross. But for many years there was a third rail service popular enough to provide considerable competition for the two lines and that was the Midland route. Indeed, in its heyday, up to the 1914-18 war, the Midland in winter ran three day expresses and three night trains from London St Pancras to Scotland; in summer there were no fewer than five by day and three by night, just as many as either of its rivals. In the latter part of the 1914-18 war, the only morning train from London to Glasgow was from St Pancras. Yet today nothing remains of that once lavish service other than the one-and-only Thames-Clyde Express by day, and a single night train on which sleeping cars are attached only when the train reaches Nottingham.

Although varied from time to time over the years, the Thames-Clyde service travels an historical route. In the earliest days of railways, two years after the opening of the Liverpool & Manchester Railway, a 16-mile line was completed between Leicester and Swannington. The new line formed the nucleus of a railway system which eventually was to extend to 1,519 route-miles in England and 265 miles in Ireland of its own, with a further 1,354 miles of leased and joint lines, to make the Midland Railway the third largest system in the British Isles. For a time the Leicester & Swannington remained isolated. However, during 1839 and 1840 the Midland Counties line was being opened from Rugby (connecting there with the London & Birmingham Railway) to Leicester and Trent, where it branched into lines serving Derby and Nottingham. At the same time the North Midland Railway was being completed from Derby by way of Masborough and Normanton to Leeds, as was also the Birmingham &

218

219

220

218 Page from the *Graphic* of 21 November 1874, illustrating the Pullman facilities that had just been introduced by the Midland. *Illustrated London News*

Derby line linking the same two towns through Tamworth and Burton. In 1844 the several railways converging on Derby joined forces to form the Midland Railway, which absorbed the Leicester & Swannington a year later.

Soon the restless Midland Railway was spreading its wings in all directions — to Bristol in the south, Lincoln in the east, Swansea in the west and Manchester in the north. But at the company's headquarters at Derby, eyes were on the greatest project of all, and that was to have a Midland line into London. In the 1850s, therefore, Parliamentary powers were obtained to build a line southwards from Leicester through Kettering to Bedford, and thence to a junction with the newly opened Great Northern Railway, over which running powers would be exercised into Kings Cross. Thus Midland trains for the first time made their way into London in 1858. But the arrangement led to hopeless congestion over the final 32 miles, with the GNR most certainly not giving the Midland trains preference; as a result the final task to continue the Midland main line through St Albans into a terminus at St Pancras, next door to Kings Cross, was undertaken. In 1868 Midland trains started entering their own London station, with its opulent hotel and magnificent Gothic frontage.

Meanwhile, at the northern end of its system, the Midland had extended from Leeds to Skipton, from where it was working an independent line, nicknamed the Little North Western, to Lancaster and Carnforth. From Lancashire's Clapham Junction the line threw off a branch north-westwards to Ingleton, where it made an end-on junction with a branch of the London & North Western Railway coming south from Low Gill, on the West Coast main line. For a time this route provided a service to Scotland for Midland passengers, but there were no through trains and through passengers received anything but friendly treatment from the LNWR; often they had lengthy waits in Spartan conditions at the windswept junction of Low Gill, in the heart of the Westmorland fells.

Again the Midland set out to obtain independence, and authority was sought for its own line from Settle Junction, just north of Hellifield, to Carlisle. The necessary powers were obtained in 1865, but after having faced the enormous cost of its London extension, the Midland company hesitated before embarking on what, with its many tunnels and viaducts, was going to be another very costly enterprise. Under pressure, however, from the two Scottish railways which were to be the Midland's partners north of the Border — the Glasgow & South Western and

the North British — work on the Settle-Carlisle line was begun in 1869, and in 1876 the first Midland trains ran on their own metals throughout from London St Pancras to Carlisle, and then over the partners' lines to both Glasgow St Enoch and Edinburgh Waverley. Both routes were a few miles longer than those of the rival West and East Coast routes, but the comfort of the Midland trains and the scenic attraction of the Midland line were soon winning passengers from the competitors.

At the time of the so-called Race to Edinburgh in 1888, and Race to Aberdeen in 1895, when East and West Coast routes vied hotly with their respective London-Scotland services, it was commonly reported that nervous passengers deliberately chose the Midland route for their Scottish journeys, thereby hoping for greater safety; passengers were obviously unaware that on the sharp ups and downs of the Midland route their maximum speeds might be higher than those of the racing East and West Coast trains! Midland competition was taken seriously by the East and West Coast companies. In 1901 the Midland announced a modest acceleration of its 09.30 train from St Pancras — predecessor of the Thames-Clyde Express — which would enable it to reach Edinburgh Waverley 10 minutes ahead of the 10.00 Flying Scotsman; the East Coast promptly staged a fast run with the Scotsman to bring it into Edinburgh first. The newspapers immediately scented another 'race' but nothing came of it.

One reason for the popularity of the Midland route has always been the exceptional comfort of its rolling stock. Two years before the Settle & Carlisle line completed the Midland route to Scotland, that company had introduced the first Pullman cars to run in Great Britain, and so on the very first journey in 1876 of what was to become the Thames-Clyde Express 51 years later, the train included in its formation some Pullman drawing-room cars, which continued in use for a number of years. Also, in 1875 the Midland had decided to provide third-class carriages in all its trains, which gave the Midland route a powerful advantage over the other two groups, whose principal day trains at that time carried first and second-class passengers only. Before long special rolling stock was being built to Midland standards for joint ownership of the English company and its Scottish partners; that for Glasgow trains

219 Informative poster advertising the attractions of the Midland route, reproduced in the *Illustrated London News* of 7 September 1907.

220 Poster for the GSWR, one of the Midland Railway's Scottish partners. *British Transport Museum/B Sharpe*

221 One of the forty Johnson 4-4-0s sent by the Midland to the Midland and Great Northern Joint Railway in 1894. This type was widely used on the Midland Scottish service. *Colourviews Ltd*

was lettered M&GSW (Midland & Glasgow & South Western) and that for Edinburgh trains M&NB (Midland and North British).

At the beginning of the century, and up to the outbreak of the 1914-1918 war, the Midland Scottish services had settled down to a fairly regular pattern. Through all but the summer months, the morning train which eventually was to become the Thames-Clyde Express left St Pancras at 09.30, and called at Leicester, Trent (with a connection from Nottingham) and Chesterfield, thence taking the straight line to Rotherham, avoiding Sheffield; the next stop was Leeds, with a reversal at Wellington station, and a further stop at Hellifield completed the Midland part of the journey, and brought the train into Carlisle by 15.50. There the Edinburgh section, with a through coach for Aberdeen, was detached; the main Glasgow train made stops at Dumfries and Kilmarnock and was due at Glasgow St Enoch station at 18.35.

In summer the Glasgow train ran independently from St Pancras at 09.45 and took the Sheffield loop, calling at that city instead of at Chesterfield; the other stops were unchanged. The up working was very similar; after leaving St Enoch at 09.20 the stops were the same, save that the express ran non-stop from Leeds to Trent; and another difference was that a coach was slipped at Kettering. St Pancras was reached at 18.30.

There were other Midland day trains from St Pancras to Glasgow, at 11.30 and 13.30; also, in the summer there was an 11.50, which was rather mendaciously advertised as making no stop south of the Border. Actually it made two, one at Shipley to change engines, after having made the longest non-stop run (206 miles) ever to appear in a Midland time-table, and then at Carlisle, which is well south of the Border, again for engine changing. Even so, the 11.50 was timed to complete the St Pancras-Glasgow run in 8¾ hours, compared with over 9 hours of the other day expresses.

At night there were sleeping-car expresses from St Pancras to Glasgow at 21.30 and midnight, supplemented in summer by a remarkable Highland Express at 19.10, which travelled via Edinburgh and conveyed through coaches and sleeping cars to Aberdeen, Inverness and Fort William. Such was the lavish nature of the Midland Anglo-Scottish service in the first decade of the century.

From 1902 operation over the Midland part of the route was greatly improved by the introduction of the first three-cylinder compound 4-4-0s, designed originally by S. W. Johnson, and built in improved form by his successor, R. M. Deeley, from 1905 onwards. Eventually, after the class had been expanded in London Midland & Scottish days to a total of no fewer than 245 engines, they were seen on Glasgow & South Western metals also, replacing the G&SW Manson 4-6-0s, a class of no great distinction, which until then had worked the trains between Carlisle and Glasgow.

From the gradient point of view the Midland route on the whole is more difficult than the West Coast route, and considerably more so than the East Coast. Between St Pancras and Leicester is a switchback of gradients, mostly at 1 in 176 to 200 as far as Bedford, but then with 1 in 119 and 1 in 120 inclinations over Sharnbrook summit and further sharpish climbs as far as Leicester. Between there and Leeds there are no hard grinds, but things are very different when Westmorland is reached. From Settle Junction there is a gruelling 1 in 100 ascent for 15 miles to Blea Moor tunnel, and in the opposite direction something very similar from Appleby to Ais Gill, where the line attains its maximum altitude of 1,167ft.

In Scotland, again, the Glasgow & South Western main line mounts to 616ft altitude at New Cumnock, and there are some stiff climbs between Kilmarnock and Glasgow, in part as steep as 1 in 70, to another level at Dunlop. Even

222 Class 5MT locomotives Nos 44871 and 44781 climbing towards Ais Gill summit in August 1968 with the last steam train operated by British Railways. *D Huntriss*

223 Blea Moor viaduct, on the Midland Settle-Carlisle line. *R Bastin*

224 Jubilee No 45711 *Courageous* blasts over Ais Gill summit with an Ayr-Leeds passenger train.

225 Jubilee No 45562 *Alberta* on a special train at Carlisle Citadel station in October 1967. *J Winkley*

with the Midland 4-4-0 compounds, loads were restricted to a maximum of 260 tons tare, and double-heading of the heavier trains was common. Incidentally, 10 miles south of Kilmarnock the G&SW line passes over Ballochmyle viaduct, of which the central 181ft arch was believed to be the biggest masonry span in the world.

After recovery from the effects of the 1914-1918 war, and the absorption of the Midland Railway into the London Midland & Scottish group, in a spate of LMS train naming in 1927, the morning train from St Pancras to Glasgow received the title Thames-Clyde Express. The Edinburgh portion had become a separate train, travelling via Nottingham, and was named the Thames-Forth Express. Just before the outbreak of the 1939-1945 war, the Thames-Clyde, now handled over Midland metals by the powerful Jubilee 4-6-0s of Stanier's design, had reached the fastest period of its steam-hauled history. On the down journey, the first stage of 72 miles from St Pancras to Kettering had to be covered in 71 minutes start to stop, and Leicester, 99 miles, was reached in 104 minutes. As Sheffield was served by the Thames-Forth Express, it was still avoided by the Thames-Clyde, which after stopping at Chesterfield continued to take the direct line to Rotherham, non-stop to Leeds, which was reached at 13.48.

After reversal at Leeds, the train acquired another Jubilee 4-6-0 for what had become a through locomotive working, and a tough one, over the 228½ miles to Glasgow. There were additional stops at Appleby south of the Border and at Annan and Mauchline (for connection to Ayr) in Scotland. Despite the extra halts, Glasgow St Enoch was reached by 18.38, in eight hours 38 minutes from St Pancras, the fastest time ever on the Midland route. In the up direction, after a start from Glasgow at 09.30, the Thames-Clyde reached Carlisle in time for Scottish passengers desiring a quick journey to London to change to the non-stop Royal Scot. From Leeds onwards a stop at Sheffield, which involved the subsequent stiff climb to Bradway tunnel, demanded extra time, but the Chesterfield stop was replaced by one at Trent, for the benefit of Nottingham passengers. So the up journey required five minutes under nine hours.

As to the train's composition, eight coaches normally sufficed for the through working, though one or two extra might be attached from St Pancras to Leeds going down, and coming up the train out of Glasgow included a composite-brake for Bristol, detached at Leeds, and another for Nottingham, which came off at Trent. The 1939-45 war brought great changes and eventually the 10.00 down was leaving St Pancras with a minimum of

nine coaches for Glasgow and four for Edinburgh, often with one or two extras. Also, its journey to Glasgow was extended to 444 miles by being routed via Nottingham, Trent and Derby to Chesterfield.

One remarkable feature of the re-routeing was that the down Thames-Clyde stopped at the up platform at Trent with the nose of the locomotive pointing south, while the up Thames-Clyde, travelling straight down the Trent Valley line from Chesterfield, stopped at the same platform before proceeding south to St Pancras! The northbound train on that route had the distinction of passing daily through more tunnels, 40 in all with a total length of about 15 miles, than any other train in Great Britain. By the end of the war the overall journey times were no less than 11 hours 32 minutes northwards and 11 hours 40 minutes southwards. By then rebuilt Royal Scot 4-6-0s had become available and their additional power was valuable working such loads, especially over the heavy grades between Leeds and Glasgow.

Restaurant cars had been withdrawn during the war, but were restored by October 1945. A year later the 10.00 down returned to the Leicester route and lost its through Edinburgh coaches; since the outbreak of war it had become the only day train from St Pancras to Glasgow and so it remained. For a time the separate Edinburgh morning train from St Pancras reappeared, and in 1949 both trains had their names restored, the 10.00 down as the Thames-Clyde Express, but the 09.15 changed from Thames-Forth to Waverley; the latter gave Nottingham a through service to Scotland once again. After some recovery in speed, a measure of deceleration had to follow in the early 1950s because of pitfall trouble between Trent and Leeds which necessitated severe speed restrictions.

By that time nationalisation had taken place and before long, because of changes in BR regional boundaries, the Thames-Clyde Express indulged in some hedge-hopping. Travelling north, at Chesterfield the train passed from the London Midland into the Eastern Region; then from Cudworth the North Eastern Region took charge as far as Skipton, where control passed once again to the London Midland Region onwards to Carlisle. Since then the North Eastern Region has been merged with the Eastern Region, and soon after these words are in print further regional changes are likely to have taken place.

In 1966, the Waverley Express was withdrawn and the Thames-Clyde was diverted through Nottingham, reversing there before proceeding northwards; similarly in the southbound direction. Farther north there has been another diversion to avoid the speed restrictions just mentioned; the train branches at Swinton, north of Rotherham, on to what formerly was the Swinton & Knottingley Joint Line as far as Moorthorpe, where it takes a spur down to the former Great Northern main line. This permits a stop at Wakefield, which is now made daily, and another new spur, from Gelderd Road junction, takes the train into the fine Leeds City station, which incorporates the old Midland Wellington station. There has also, of course, been the substitution of diesel for steam power, and the capable 1Co-Co1 Peak diesel-electric locomotives of 2,500hp now work the train throughout.

226 The Thames-Clyde express passing Langcliffe, Yorkshire, in March 1972. *J Winkley*

High Roads and Great Trains to Scotland

THERE HAS LONG been a Great North Road to Scotland but despite Dick Turpin's ride over its southern portion and the eloping couples who followed it to Scotch Corner before bearing left for Gretna Green, road traffic between London and Scotland was never heavy before the coming of the motor-car. Many people went by sea between London and Leith (Edinburgh) or Dundee or Aberdeen, and for years after the 1848 opening of the West Coast Euston to Glasgow and East Coast Kings Cross to Edinburgh railway routes, development of the steamship and the low fares charged kept many passengers on the sea routes.

It had been physically possible in the 1840s, shortly before the opening of the two main Anglo-Scottish routes, to travel between London and Edinburgh and Glasgow by train over a roundabout route from Euston via Rugby, York and thence the East Coast route via Newcastle, but 1848 saw the start of direct Anglo-Scottish train services. The third route, that from St Pancras to Glasgow and Edinburgh, was opened in 1876.

Thenceforth there were three main routes between the South and Scotland. They were the East Coast of the Great Northern Railway (to Shaftholme Junction, north of Doncaster), North Eastern Railway (to Berwick-on-Tweed) and North British Railway; the West Coast route of the London & North Western Railway to Carlisle and thence Caledonian Railway to Glasgow and Edinburgh via Carstairs; and the Midland Railway route via Leeds to Carlisle, whence trains ran over the Glasgow & South Western line via Dumfries to Glasgow and over the North British line to Edinburgh. The NBR part of the Midland itinerary was named the Waverley route in later years, because of associations with Sir Walter Scott.

Anglo-Scottish passenger services were slow in the early days. The first West Coast Euston-Glasgow express took 16 hours for the 400-odd miles, but the time was soon reduced to 12 hours, which was very creditable in view of the motive power of the time and of two summits — Shap in Westmorland and Beattock in Dumfriesshire — to be climbed, and it was one-quarter only of the time taken by road mailcoach. More powerful locomotives and improvements in braking and signalling brought about progressive reductions in journey times. By 1860 the railways were carrying most of the passenger traffic between England and Scotland. During the previous decade the Highlands had begun to attract tourists and field sportsmen — thanks largely to the royal venture of Balmoral. There is no record of the relative amounts of railborne and seaborne freight, but goods traffic was increasing by both West Coast and East Coast lines at the expense of sea routes, largely because the tempo of industry more particularly in Central Scotland, demanded quick deliveries.

A landmark in passenger travel was the introduction in June 1862 of the morning 10 o'clock East Coast express from Kings Cross to Edinburgh Waverley. It was first known as the Special Scotch Express, but far better known was its unofficial title Flying Scotsman. Exactly when this name was first used is not known, but it was not used officially in timetables and on coach destination boards until after the railway grouping in 1923 which merged the East Coast partners, the GNR, NER and NBR, into the London & North Eastern. For a short time during the 1914-18 war, the Flying Scotsman left Kings Cross at 09.30, but otherwise its northbound departure time has remained at 10.00 even during the 1939-45 war, when the train was considerably slowed down and made up to great length and weight. Third-class passengers were not carried

227 Locomotive Publishing Co (F Moore) representation of the Scotch express at Euston, *circa* 1905. *A Wood collection*

228 Pacific No 46200 *The Princess Royal* at Camden shed in 1962. *M Pope*

at first. Their admission in 1887 was a challenge to the LNWR and Caledonian, as by that time there was not so much passenger traffic that the operators of any route could afford to ignore their rivals. The opening of NER cut-off lines in the 1870s enabled the Scotsman's overall timings in both directions to be cut in 1876 to nine hours.

Competition touched off the first of the so-called Races to the North, in 1888. In July and August of that year the East Coast companies cut the Kings Cross to Edinburgh time from nine hours to seven hours 45 minutes and by stages lopped off another 18 minutes. Such speed was quite uneconomic, as it disturbed traffic working in many parts of the system. When the LNWR and CR cut the time

of the Scotsman's rival on the West Coast route, all parties soon agreed to a truce; this did not, however, stop them from engaging in London-Aberdeen races in 1895. One result was an agreement that the overall London-Edinburgh and London-Glasgow transits should be not less that 8¼ hours, which remained the unambitious norm for many years, even after the revival of faster running when the First World War ended, and the earlier introduction of the restaurant cars that made meal stops unnecessary.

In considering Anglo-Scottish routes, especially for passenger traffic, there is a tendency to exaggerate the importance of London. Much of the West Coast Scottish traffic was with Birmingham and other cities in the Midlands; Crewe and Lancashire cities, and York, Leeds and centres in the North-East generated considerable East Coast traffic; and a high proportion of the Midland's traffic with Scotland was from and to Bristol, Birmingham, Derby, and the West Riding of Yorkshire.

The Midland and its partners never tried to beat the East and West routes in schedules. The heavy gradients of the main line through the Pennines between Settle (north of Leeds) and Carlisle precluded timings comparable to those of the other routes, despite some fast running on both the Midland and the Glasgow & South Western. Nevertheless passenger and freight traffic over the Midland route steadily increased until 1914. The Midland specialised in passenger comfort. In the early years after reaching Carlisle, it experimented at some length with Pullman coaches; later, its own more conventional corridor coaches and sleeping and restaurant cars were some of the best designed in Britain and, indeed, the world, besides running over superbly laid and maintained track — though the LNWR's Euston-Crewe main line boasted track as good or better.

The first Anglo-Scottish sleeping cars were introduced in 1873 by the North British Railway between Edinburgh and Kings Cross. (Passengers supplied their own bedding.) They were forerunners of generations of sleeping-berth carriages, some, in their time, considered the most comfortable (for journeys of up to 12 hours or so) in the world. As with other British sleeping cars, the supplement charges have always been modest compared with overseas. Such was the rivalry between the three routes from London that for many years until 1914 there were nightly sleepers from Euston, Kings Cross and St Pancras to Inverness — ridiculous except at the height of summer; even after grouping there were sleepers by West and East Coast routes to Inverness. Sleeping-car passengers do not wish to arrive too early, so that the Anglo-Scottish night trains are not particularly fast. To reach Aberdeen, 523 miles, in 11 hours from Kings Cross by today's Night Aberdonian, however, demands sustained fast running, and 12 hours from Euston to Inverness, 567 miles, by the Royal Highlander is creditable even in these days of electric and diesel haulage. The last-mentioned train (named only since 1927) has always been fast and its forerunner, the eight o'clock evening express from Euston, achieved the fastest London-Aberdeen transit of two minutes over 8½ hours for 540 miles (by West Coast) in the 1895 race, but that was admittedly only a flash in the pan.

By and large, Anglo-Scottish day expresses have not been the fastest trains over the routes on which they run. On the straight and level route (part of the East Coast main line) of the NER between York and Darlington, immediately before the 1914-18 war, it was the Leeds to Edinburgh and Glasgow flyer, not the Flying Scotsman or any other London-Edinburgh express, that made the fastest running.

Until the railway grouping, all three lines to Scotland were worked by a variety of motive power, and the gradients on the West Coast and Midland routes taxed the ingenuity of locomotive designers and the skill of enginemen. There were some notable locomotive classes, many of which are also described or illustrated elsewhere in this book. Flying Scotsman, which became a very heavy train by the end of the century as bogie corridor coaches were brought into use, was hauled by engines ranging in the short space of 20 years from the famous antiquated and highly efficient Stirling 4-2-2 singles to Ivatt Atlantics. On the West Coast route south of Carlisle, the weird products of the LNWR designer Webb and the gallant little Precedent 2-4-0s of Ramsbottom gave way to Whale's Precursor 4-4-0s in roughly the same period. Early in the present century, Johnson's 4-2-2 singles were working Midland expresses but the Midland clung to a small-engine policy and its expresses were never hauled by anything bigger than Johnson and Deeley 4-4-0 compounds.

By 1914 Bowen-Cooke had brought out the Claughton 4-6-0s on the LNWR, and on the CR McIntosh's magnificent Cardean-class inside-cylinder 4-6-0s were working some of the West Coast day expresses between Carlisle and Glasgow. On the East Coast, the fastest passenger trains were headed by Ivatt Atlantics over the GNR and Worsdell and Raven Atlantics or Worsdell 4-4-0s over the NER; the NBR did not participate in express passenger working on the East Coast main line between Berwick and Edinburgh and NER engines ran through; but NBR Atlantics worked over the Waverley route between Carlisle and Edinburgh — and did magnificent work north of Edinburgh, over the Forth Bridge to Dundee and Aberdeen.

August 1914 was in some ways the heyday of Anglo-Scottish passenger services before grouping, although there had been some recent decline in punctuality on the Midland. Express passenger train weights had increased to 260 tons and more, but motive power had been developed to a point which enabled it to move the loads at speeds considerably higher than were demanded by the agreed 8½-hour schedules between Kings Cross and Edinburgh Waverley and Euston and Glasgow Central. Steam was supreme; only the NER was beginning to dream of electrifying — from York to Newcastle-on-Tyne. Diesel traction was in its infancy.

During the preceding 60 years, the weights of freight trains had been increasing with motive power. All three main lines crossing the Border carried growing quantities of freight, largely heavy industrial materials for, and

229 A down Royal Scot at Greenholme with EE class 40 1Co-Co1 No 236 at the head. *D Cross*

230 Stanier class 5 4-6-0 No 45135 lifts a goods train southwards past Thrimby Grange signalbox on the climb to Shap in March 1967. *B Stephenson*

229

products of, Scottish industry. The 0-6-0 goods engine was in general use, although by 1914, 0-8-0s were being developed by the LNWR and other railways for mineral traffic. The four-wheel wagon with traditional loose link coupling was ubiquitous and goods train speeds were low. On both East and West Coast routes, parcels trains, fish (from Scottish ports to markets in the South) and other perishable-traffic trains were being worked by mixed-traffic (largely 4-6-0) engines characteristic of 1900-14.

War brought decelerations. Among Anglo-Scottish passenger workings were many troop trains. There is the terrible memory of the collision on the Caledonian Glasgow-Carlisle main line at Quintinshill. Creation of the naval base at Scapa Flow in the Orkneys, combined with the increasing dangers of the sea route, caused immense flows of naval personnel and stores traffic between the South and Thurso (for Scapa Flow) in Caithness. Large quantities of coal for the fleet were moved by rail from South Wales collieries to Thurso, and coal trains and returning empties were an operating problem not only on the single-line Highland Railway but also on the main lines already carrying heavy traffic.

From the Armistice of 1918 to grouping was a period of rehabilitation, and for some time after 1923 the four new

companies, because of the run-down condition of their systems, were not in a position to start on improving Anglo-Scottish passenger services. The London & North Eastern absorbed the three East Coast companies and the London Midland & Scottish swallowed the LNWR, CR and GSWR. The Waverley route became the LNER's, so that St Pancras to Edinburgh expresses were LMSR to Carlisle and LNER beyond. No steps were taken for some years to rationalise it or other through workings that dated from the great age of competition.

The beginning of a revolution in British locomotive design was the appearance in 1922 of the first successful Pacific design by Sir Nigel Gresley for, and built at Doncaster by, the GNR. It was the forerunner of subsequent LNER Pacific classes that performed all heavy East Coast work until dieselisation. Even so, advantage was not taken of their great power to accelerate Anglo-Scottish East Coast trains, though some loads were increased.

Not until 1927 did rivalry between the LNER and LMSR show itself in improvements. They were still bound by the pre-1914 agreement on London to Edinburgh and Glasgow timings and so began to vie with each other in the length of non-stop runs. In the summer of that year the LMSR restricted the Royal Scot to Glasgow and Edinburgh passengers but with stops at Carnforth for changing engines for the climb over Shap and at Carstairs to divide or join the Glasgow and Edinburgh portions. The LNER in the following year started the Flying Scotman's 393-mile non-stop run between Kings Cross and Waverley. It resulted in the corridor tenders which could be joined by vestibule gangway to the leading vehicle — a costly gimmick while the schedule was still 8¼ hours. Meanwhile the LMSR was introducing its Royal Scot 4-6-0s. Both companies provided new stock for their trains. The LNER's 1928 sets for the Flying Scotsman included such novelties as a coach with cocktail bar, hairdressing room and women's retiring room.

By 1932, 8¼ hours between London and Scotland's two big cities was so patently ridiculous that timings were being cut (in fact, all over the country) and accelerations began on the East and West Coast lines. In May 1932, the Flying Scotsman's overall times were cut (for the first time for 32 years) to seven hours 50 minutes. Further accelerations followed by stages and by the outbreak of war in 1939, the Kings Cross to Waverley summer non-stop timing was seven hours exactly, and Aberdeen was only 10¼ hours from Kings Cross. In the 1938-39 winter schedule, with stops at Grantham, York and Newcastle, it was seven hours 20 minutes. Composed of yet newer train-sets, the total weight exceeded 500 tons and was often 600 tons at peak traffic periods. In 1933, the LMS Stanier Pacifics started to enter service and West Coast transits also were progressively shortened. The Royal Scot's Euston to Glasgow timing was down to seven hours by 1939.

In 1935, King George V's Silver Jubilee year, the LNER introduced its first highspeed streamlined train, the Silver Jubilee, between Kings Cross and Newcastle; it was highly successful. In 1937, the year in which King George VI was crowned, it inaugurated the Coronation between Kings Cross and Waverley, with a six-hour schedule including stops at York and, later, Newcastle. The nine-vehicle sets were air-conditioned and the last vehicles were the so-called beavertail observation cars. The Pacific locomotives also were streamlined. Much retiming of other trains was needed to provide paths for the streamliners and on some sections of line an additional block had to be kept clear. The rival LMSR train was the Euston-Glasgow Coronation Scot, which consisted of nine vehicles of standard stock specially adapted and, including the streamlined Pacific engine, painted in a bright blue-and-

white livery.

Meanwhile there had been steady accelerations on the Midland route, although no attempt was made to effect spectacular timings. Midland-route passenger traffic with Scotland continued to originate and end in the Midlands and North West. The St Pancras to Glasgow St Enoch timings of the Thames-Clyde Express was cut to eight hours 38 minutes with the aid of 5XP-class and other 4-6-0s. The LNER worked the St Pancras to Edinburgh Waverley Thames-Forth Express with Pacifics over the Waverley route north of Carlisle.

Development of eight-coupled goods engines before 1939 allowed many freight trains to be as long as track layout and signalling allowed. The number of goods trains with continuous brakes (fitted freights) running at higher speeds was increased, as were fast parcels trains on Anglo-Scottish routes.

The 1939-45 war again caused decelerations, in circumstances generally more difficult than in the previous war. Attempts to continue refreshment car services had to be given up. Thanks to good motive power, which was maintained under enormous difficulties, trains, notably on the East Coast route, became very heavy. Accelerations began again in October 1945, but the Anglo-Scottish steam services never again reached pre-war levels — but not because of motive power. Whatever the reason, the failure ensured that the great age of steam traction in Britain remained the later 1930s when Gresley and Stanier Pacifics headed the fastest Anglo-Scottish trains.

Dieselisation, which started in earnest on British Railways in the 1950s, unquestionably brought Scotland nearer. The unique Deltic Co-Co diesel-electric locomotives then reduced the Kings Cross to Waverley time by the Flying Scotsman to just under 5¾ hours and it came down to 5½ hours exactly in June 1973. The Deltics will continue to maintain the service until the first high-speed diesel train (HST) multiple units take over when there will doubtless be further accelerations, with the promise of still shorter transits, perhaps down to 4½ hours for the nearly 400 miles, in the more-distant future if the advanced passenger train (APT) project is successful.

The West Coast route is now electrified throughout providing the fastest ever timings from London, the Midlands and the North West to Glasgow and Edinburgh.

BR Britannia Pacific No 70032 'Tennyson' heading a parcels train in the Lune gorge, south of Tebay, in March 1967. *B Stephenson*

231

232

233

231 English electric class 40 diesel-electric No D373 heading a
freight train on inhospitable Ais Gill in December 1967. *R Bastin*

232 Thomson A2 No 60520 *Owen Tudor* leaving Grantham for
the north with a Gresley A3 in the background. *M Tye*

233 Deltic No 9010 *The King's Own Scottish Borderer* enters York
with a northbound express in October 1972. *V Bamford*

234

235 A double-headed Mallaig-London train in the Monessie gorge, in April 1968. *D Cross*

The West Highland Railway

CRAIGENDORAN JUNCTION! What a sonorous name for a once lovely place. What an apt name, moreover, for the start of Scotland's most romantic railway into the wilds of Lochaber and the lonely lost North West. The first syllable, Craig, was southern Scots; the middle could have been anything or anywhere; but the last long-drawn-out doran could only have been of the west Highlands, and after all, that is what the West Highland Railway was all about.

The line was intended to link the empty north-west of Scotland with the more populated industrial lowlands, thereby profiting both. As in the case of so many railways built in the last century, the anticipated profit did not materialise, but the WHR was a superb line otherwise. It was also a line very nearly unique in Britain and had more than a passing affinity with some of the lines built in New Zealand and other parts of our then far-flung Empire for it was built, not as the great English lines were built to link established centres of population, but to open up a countryside thought at the time to be of rich potential. Fort William was simply a fortunate excuse, as there was an established settlement there.

To be blunt, the West Highland was built to put the population back in the high windy places of Lochaber that the Highland Clearances considered better suited for sheep. In retrospect, the sheep have proved the better bet; the displaced population realised it and failed to respond to the invitation to return, so the West Highland was left to link Glasgow with Fort William and little else besides. There is Celtic irony in the fact, as originally Fort William and Lochaber had nothing to do with the WH project, which was to be the Glasgow & North Western Railway pioneering a new route to Inverness, intended to circumvent the evil Caledonian and inept Highland companies. Fort William might with luck have been graced by a branch, so long as some private company put up the money, just as Fort Augustus was to be later. The ideas failed, making a great deal of money for the lawyers but leaving the Loch Ness monster in peace — no doubt both profited.

The genesis of the present West Highland line goes back to 1882 with the presentation of the Glasgow & North Western's Bill to parliament, with Inverness as its goal. That was the heyday of romantic Scotland, with Landseer, the reticent Victoria, and rumbustious John Brown summering at Balmoral in the ascendant. Far-away places were in vogue. Also, on the national conscience was the plight of the fishermen and crofters of the far north-west, a plight which could only be alleviated in those days by building a railway: just as at the present time a provincial town cannot become an 'area centre' unless a motorway is built through it and destroys at least half of it. Rather surprisingly, the GNWR's Bill was thrown out, mainly due to dogged opposition from the Highland Railway. Parliamentary sound and fury died away, the lawyers laughed all the way to the banks, Lochaber slumbered.

Still, the Lairds of Lochaber were stubborn men to whom next day's weather was of more importance than the vapourings of politicians; they wanted a railway, so a railway they would have. Now, where there were no railways men had to have horses, and thus the term 'horse trading' came to our language, and that sort of excellent balance between compromise and outright bribery was used in 1889 for the West Highland Railway to get parliamentary powers to build a railway from Craigendoran Junction, on the North British Railway, to Fort William; so long as the name of Inverness was not mentioned, the Highland did not object. The builders' ultimate intentions had nothing to do with it.

The contract for the West Highland line as subsequently built was let to the Glasgow firm of Formans & McCall, with Charles Forman as engineer and he was to prove a sound choice. He was also a lucky man, as he and sundry directors, while surveying the line, set out to walk across wild Rannoch moor towards the end of January in the bad year of 1889; they made it, but only just. Charles Forman was a man of many parts. He first made his name building underground railways in Glasgow and, both from the structure of them and his gaunt yet functional work on the West Highland, proved himself, if not a great engineer to be a very practical one. He shared with Joseph Locke a flair for using the countryside, and the West Highland brief needed every trick he knew in avoiding heavy earthworks and expense.

Locke did the same on the Lancaster & Carlisle from choice; Forman did it on the West Highland through sheer financial necessity, for even with backing from the North British, at first tacit then more active, the West Highland was built on a shoe-string. Part of Forman's genius was to realise that, given such ferocious terrain and so limited a budget, he could never build a fast main line on the scale of the neighbouring Highland, built by Joseph Mitchell through equally difficult terrain. The West Highland was a colonial-type railway built as cheaply as possible to link as many centres of trade or population as possible — and no matter how long a time or many miles it took to get to Fort William, it would be far quicker and easier than anything that had gone before.

Of the line itself, the overriding impression is one of water. It is seldom out of sight of lochs or rivers — first the great sea lochs at the head of the Firth of Clyde, then Loch Tulla and the many smaller ones on Rannoch moor, finally Loch Treig and that great arm of the sea, Loch Linnhe.

236 View from a locomotive cab towards Ben Doran, approaching Bridge of Orchy, in September 1972. *D Cross*

236

There are also Loch Lomond, the rivers Falloch, Fillan and Orchy, flowing to the south, east and west coasts respectively, and then the Spean flowing, at last, to the sea at Fort William. Alas the line was no water-level idyll, for there were mountains in between and, dominating all, the great cold bleak moor of Rannoch.

There might be more lonely places in Scotland; there can be few as bleak and treacherous, for Rannoch is a vast upland bog, the dumping ground for all the debris from the last age. A horrible sterile mixture of peat, boulders and water; a place of ghosts and marshlights, of legends and superstition, where the West Highland line literally floats across the moss for miles, buoyed up on sheepskins and brushwood, and tons and tons of debris and stone poured in on top of that make-shift raft. It was the most difficult and dominating feature of the line when it was built; it still is today. It always will be, for it is unique in Britain. Not for nothing was the first very early morning goods train from Fort William known as The Ghost — anything could happen out on that great upland waste.

Why build a railway across so terrible a place, where only a few sheep and fewer shepherds lived? Why indeed? The answer was the same as bedevilled nearly all British railway building: a rival company was making nasty noises on or near the logical route, in this case the Caledonian down by the sea at Ballachulish! If the moor of Rannoch dwarfs everything else on the West Highland, it is relative — the big man dwarfed by a giant. From the moment it leaves the North British suburban line to Helensburgh at Craigendoran, the West Highland is one of the more remarkable feats of man against nature; the Settle & Carlisle was another, but it was built with the financial

resources of the Midland behind it. The West Highland had the goodwill of the North British Railway, but for a long time no more, and goodwill does not build viaducts or lay rails across the moor of Rannoch.

The line was built by the determination of a few powerful local men, the pittances of their tenants and the thrifty genius of their engineer. The passengers who use it today look, and marvel at the scenery displayed with near-wanton abandon outside the carriage windows. They see the country, they might even spare a shred of sympathy for the motorist on that ghastly road up Loch Lomonside, but they do not see the line as the engineers and builders must have seen it. That can only be seen from the cab of the locomotive and in the autumn of 1972 the Scottish Region of British Rail very kindly gave me the chance to do just that. It was a shattering experience.

The start of the West Highland's own metals at Craigendoran Junction sets the scene. It is a line of contrasts throughout; behind is the grimy overpopulated 'conurbation' (a horrible word for a no less horrible place) of Glasgow, to the west a coastline rapidly becoming another victim of 'commutermania' and ahead a signalbox. The obviously more prosperous line, now electrified, hugs the coast to Craigendoran pier and that stately bastion of civilisation known as Helensburgh. But the other line, which keeps straight on up the hill and through the rhododendrons, looks even in diesel days to be a line of character; and it is a line of character, for it is the start of the West Highland.

For the first 19½ miles to Arrochar and Tarbet, the line twists and turns along the Western slopes of the hills, with one or other of the great sea lochs in view to the west. The

length also boasts the first of the three summits, at Glen Douglas of 564ft, a poor thing compared with what is to come, and approached by gradients which are short though steep. The most impressive facet of this section is the curvature; time and again from the cab it looks as if the line is going to run straight into a wall of rock and only at the last instant does it snake around the base. Another feature of the area is the woods which tumble down the hillsides to the water's edge. The trees are mostly deciduous, with only the odd conifer among them. Past Arrochar, the woods continue to the head of Loch Lomond and then are gone, yet another of the West Highland's many contrasts.

At Arrochar the line crosses a small saddle between the salt waters of Loch Long and the fresh of Loch Lomond. Just below the station, there is a most unusual building, once a church, now converted to a garage. (In view of the dangers of the road up Loch Lomonside, it might have been better had those two functions been combined!) Apart from Helensburgh (Upper) and Garelochhead, all the stations on the first section are now closed — they were built for residential traffic which never came. Surprisingly, all the other original stations remain open, apart from Gorton which was never much more than a halt and passing loop. The next eight miles to Ardlui are a repeat of what has gone before, with the curvature if anything more severe and Loch Lomond to the east of the line.

Beyond Ardlui, the nature of the line changes dramatically as it climbs up Glen Falloch. The curves are still there but less demanding, though that mercy is tempered by steadily increasing grades. The trees are left behind and at the head of the glen the first isolated remnants of the old Caledonian forest stand forlorn near the track; thence to Crianlarich, the crossroads of the West Highlands. A pleasant spot, Crianlarich, down there in Strath Fillan, with an importance thrust upon it by geography that it did not really want. First, it was the meeting place of several 'drove roads'; then, when the West Highland Railway came, that line crossed the Callander & Oban line of the Caledonian there; and, finally, it became an important road junction in the motoring era.

Remarkably, and after a lot of pressure, a spur was built between the W H and the C&O lines, but it was little used until British Railways days. It is still in use for timber traffic from the old Caledonian yard to the paper mill at Corpach, and for trains from Glasgow to Oban since the eastern part of the Callander & Oban was long since closed and lifted.

Beyond Crianlarich, the hard work begins with a six-mile climb, mostly at 1 in 60, past Tyndrum station to the County March summit of 1,024ft. The countryside has become bleak and treeless, but dead ahead from this summit there is one of the most remarkable views on any railway — the conical peak of Ben Doran. It is a fitting prelude to the famous Horseshoe bend, where the line uses the flanks of three mountains to lose height round a perfect horseshoe curve, completed by two of Forman's typical truss-girder viaducts on stone piers. The next station, at Bridge of Orchy, is another typical island-platformed structure, with a steeply pitched roof to shed

the snow so prevalent in those upland parts. From there, the line climbs again for another six miles through country getting ever bleaker until, just short of the site of Gorton loop, it cuts through the middle of the famous Black Wood of Rannoch, yet another remnant of the great forest that was burnt from Aviemore to the Orchy valley.

For fifteen miles, trees are left behind and the line turns northwards to tackle the dreaded Rannoch moor on short sharp grades and incessant curves around peaty lochs and bottomless bogs. Rannoch station at least has a road eastwards to civilisation, a hotel, and a few houses nearby. The station to the north, at Corrour, has nothing but a cluster of cottages, a shooting lodge and a road built by the Forestry Commission leading from nowhere to beyond. Between Rannoch and Corrour, there is the only snow shed in Britain, near the Rock of Cruach, where the line cuts through a vast nose of granite sticking up among the bogs. This was the playground of the snow demons, as the West Highland Company soon found to its cost: conventional snow fences had little effect so the snow shed was built.

The summit of the line, at 1,347ft, comes a few yards north of Corrour station; an unspectacular place merely a mound of glacial debris slightly higher than hundreds of others. Then, a mile farther on, the line sweeps to the right and literally falls off the moor down a six-mile-long inclined plane, starting far above Loch Treig and ending up at water level at its northern end. The line was diverted there when the water level of the loch was raised by the British Aluminium Company in connection with its new smelting works; it now runs through a short tunnel near the new dam. And so to Tulloch and the Spean valley, to be followed all the way to Fort William. The remaining three stations of Tulloch, Roy Bridge and Spean Bridge are two-platform affairs, the first since Craigendoran and somehow out of place on the West Highland.

Just before Roy Bridge, there is one of the amazing changes of scenery so much a feature of this fascinating railway. The valley narrows and road, railway and river writhe and wriggle through the Monessie gorge; with its strange twisted rock walls and cataracts, this mile is one of the highlights of the whole journey, just as what follows is the great anticlimax. From Spean Bridge to Fort William, the line drops gradually along the northern flank of Ben Nevis, once described rudely but with justification as 'That muckle great flat-topped hill'. The eastern approaches to Fort William are dull and untidy, all scattered about with factories and motels. The Mallaig line trails in from the north, and then, quite suddenly, the West Highland fires the last shot in its scenic locker; it bursts out from the houses on to the shore, with beautiful views across Loch Linnhe, and runs over a level crossing and into its charming but far too small terminus.

The Mallaig Extension line, opened in 1901, is another 41 miles of loch and mountains every bit as beautiful, even

237 K4 Mogul 2-6-0 No 61998 *Macleod of Macleod* on a Mallaig-Glasgow train in July 1954. *A J S Paterson*

238 Corrour station on the WHL, from the cab of a diesel locomotive in September 1972. *D Cross*

239 Fort William-London train at lonely County March summit in October 1971. *D Cross*

240 Class 27 D5356 crossing the River Lochy with a Fort William-Mallaig train in 1971. *D Cross*

241 An early morning Mallaig-Glasgow train headed by an NBL class 29 diesel skirts Loch Enil, in typical Mallaig extension scenery. *D Cross*

more curvaceous, and although its gradients are far shorter than those on the 'main' line, they are also steeper since, while the West Highland was built on a shoe-string, the Mallaig line was built on government charity, which was worse. Its more interesting feature is the use of reinforced concrete for many of its bridges, including the graceful curved viaduct at Glenfinnan, for a long time the biggest concrete structure in the world. There was once another branch from Spean Bridge to Fort Augustus, built mainly on the proceeds of Burton beer. Alas! That soon went flat and Fort Augustus was left to its monks and its monster. For a few years the Highland Railway got its hands on this branch — probably the last example of the great axiom of Scottish railway companies: 'We don't want it, but we have to have it to keep the other chap out!'

Although technically an independent company from its opening in 1894 until it was formally absorbed by the North British in 1908, the West Highland never owned its own locomotives or rolling stock, and was worked by the North British from the outset. The train services were to a great extent governed by the sailings of the Outer Isles boats from Mallaig, once the extension there was completed in April 1901. Basically, there were two trains each way throughout the year from Mallaig to Glasgow, with extras in the summer. From the summer of 1901 the down train in the morning and up train in the evening conveyed through coaches and sleeping cars to London Kings Cross. Freight traffic was mainly fish and agricultural produce until the British Aluminium Company started operations at Fort William in 1936. Even then, apart from fish traffic at certain times of year, the goods service was never very intensive until about ten years ago, when the great new paper mill opened at Corpach, three miles from Fort William on the Mallaig line. The paper mill has saved the West Highland and now, after seventy years, the goods traffic is its most important feature.

Speeds on the line, never high, were governed more by curvature than the gradients, though the latter are hardly easy. Trains in the winter tended to be light, but for all that, the present-day schedules leave very little in hand. To keep time over the line even with modern diesel power requires a standard and skill of driving without peer anywhere.

When the West Highland line opened and the North British Railway agreed to work it (presumably in case the rival Highland company should be, as it never was, a gold mine!), the NB was in no way niggardly and provided both new locomotives and rolling stock. The latter, by NB standards, was good, and the locomotives were a superb series of inside-cylinder 4-4-0s designed by Matthew Holmes and built at Cowlairs (Glasgow). They were simple, strong and rugged machines and came to be known as the West Highland Bogies. Their great success led to their becoming the basis of all the engines on the line until Gresley and the LNER epoch. The ultimate development of the Bogies was the famous Glen class designed by Reid and also built at Cowlairs; one of them, *Glen Douglas*, is preserved in the City of Glasgow's transport museum.

When the London & North Eastern Railway swallowed the North British in 1923, things remained as before until the early 1930s, when some of Gresley's standard K2 class Moguls (2-6-0s) were slightly modified for use on the West Highland and named after prominent lochs on the line. They were strong engines but very rough, and so not very popular with the crews. Then, in 1937 there emerged from Darlington the first locomotive since its inception that was specially designed for the West Highland, the K4 class Mogul. They were splendid engines but there were only six of them, although in the dying years of the LNER they were augmented by Edward Thomson's two-cylinder variant, the K1s, which also were deservedly popular.

With the advent of British Rail in 1948, various trials were made with the Thomson B1 and standard Class 5 4-6-0s. Both classes did well, but were not much improvement on the Gresley Moguls that had preceded them. In NB & LNER days, the freight traffic was in the hands of the strong but sluggish classes of NB 0-6-0, plus a scattering of Gresley J39s for the fast fish trains.

It was not until the last few years of steam working that the West Highland got its greatest engine of them all, the Stanier Class 5. What remarkable engines they were; everywhere they went they conquered, even on the fiercely individualistic West Highland. To quote a diesel driver: 'Oh, they Black Fives were grand injuins apart from their damned injectors . . . they may have been Caley injuins but they were far better than oor ain.' There could be no higher praise.

THE STORY OF THE RAILWAY CARRIAGE

242

Development of the Railway Carriage

THE RAILWAY PIONEERS of the early nineteenth century in planning to carry passengers were soon faced with the problem of what type of vehicle to use, since never before had there been any such thing as a railway carriage. Indeed, of the four essential features which went to make up early all-purpose railways — track, steam locomotives, goods wagons, and passenger carriages — only the last item was unknown in rail transport. Track of a sort had been developed over two centuries, culminating in the use of the iron rail by the end of the eighteenth century. Steam locomotives had gradually evolved from the static engines of the mid-1700s, through the experiments by Trevithick and Watt in the late 1700s and the primitive machines of Murray and other engineers, to the improvements evolved by George Stephenson, in developing what became the universal pattern for the railway locomotive.

Wagons running on tracks for the transport of coal, stone and so on had been used for nearly 300 years, but passenger carriages, specifically for railway use, had not been seen before. Thus it was inevitable that the engineers of the first passenger railways, the Swansea & Mumbles in 1807 and the Stockton & Darlington in 1825, should have turned to existing road vehicles for inspiration and the first railway coaches were little more than road coaches on railway wheels. Indeed, with horse traction employed on the first lines there was hardly any difference between road

and rail carriages. With the adoption of steam locomotives which could haul far greater loads, several carriages could be coupled together to form a train. It was soon realised that it was not necessary to provide individual wheels to each single carriage body and two or three bodies were mounted together on one underframe to form a longer carriage with separate compartments. Thus was born, at the dawn of railways, the traditional British compartment carriage which is only now disappearing from the railway scene.

The British class system, with its divisions into the wealthy, the middle class and the poor, immediately made its mark on the railways. Until the coming of the steam railway the horse had been the fastest means of transport, travelling at speeds of 20mph or more singly with a solo rider, between 10 and 15mph in pairs or fours hauling road coaches, and at little more than walking pace hauling the great lumbering goods wagons which usually carried a fair proportion of poorer travellers. In practice, it was largely only the wealthy who travelled around the country, for the average working man was tied to his place of work on the farm or the developing factories of the industrial revolution. The wealthiest had their own private carriages

242 Engraving of a 'summer saloon' coach produced at Saltley works, Birmingham, for the Viceroy of Egypt. From the *Illustrated London News* of 29 May 1858.

243 A mixed-class coach of the Bodmin & Wadebridge Railway (originally all first class) showing direct descent from road coaches typical of earliest railway carriage practice.

244 Mixed-class coach of the LNWR of 1862, still retaining traces of road vehicle styling. *Science Museum, London*

247 Artist's impression of a first-class railway carriage based on road coach practice, as used on the London & Birmingham Railway in the early 1840s, from the Wills' cigarette card series.

248 and 249 Passenger coaches of the Liverpool & Manchester Railway, formally opened in 1830: an open-top third-class and a first-class vehicle. Both are replicas at the Birmingham Railway Museum.

and horses, while merchants and others who needed to travel frequently took the express stage or mail coaches. Many road carriages had two classes of travel — inside or outside. Inside was the most luxurious with well-padded seats for four or six passengers, but outside passengers were subject to the vagaries of the English climate. Apart from the main passenger compartment, the coach usually had a boot at the back for the carriage of mailbags or valuables, while luggage was carried on the roof between or behind the outside passenger seats.

It was this sort of vehicle that was adapted for railway use, even to the boot, and racks on the roof for luggage. The road coach body was followed almost to the last detail, with the curved panelling and decorative mouldings of the body-sides. However, for obvious reasons passengers did not ride on the roofs of railway coaches; second-class passengers were given separate coaches, more austere in design than the best, sometimes consisting of little more than a wooden box on wheels with seats inside, and a door with a space instead of a glazed window. The equivalent of the slow road wagon used by the poorest travellers was the open carriage, in effect nothing more than a goods wagon fitted with seats, with holes in the bottom to let out the water when it rained; such was the miserable beginning of the third class. Some railways did not even take third-class passengers; if they did the carriages were often attached to goods trains, or ran only at night. Flat wagons were also run on some railways to carry private road carriages for those who preferred to travel in their own vehicle — virtually a forerunner of today's Motorail trains.

These primitive railway carriages were very small by today's standards; nearly all were four-wheelers with a length of about 20ft, a width of about 6ft and a body height of 6-7ft. There was little improvement when the first of what became trunk railways — the Liverpool & Manchester (1830), London & Birmingham (1837), and the London & Southampton (1840) — were opened. Only the Great Western, which opened its first section in 1838, brought any marked improvement, largely because the company adopted the broad gauge of 7ft 0¼in compared with the standard Stephenson gauge of 4ft 8½in. From the start, Great Western first and second-class coaches were carried on six wheels and the bodies were much wider (9-10ft) and longer, (30ft or more). The Great Western also built some saloons of much the same size but with a central entrance and seats arranged around the sides of the coach, facing inwards. These coaches were also distinguished with clerestory roofs, that is, a roof in which a centre section is raised along its length above the side sections with windows in the sides of the top deck. This form of construction was often used in buildings, churches for example, and it was to be seen in railway use on and off

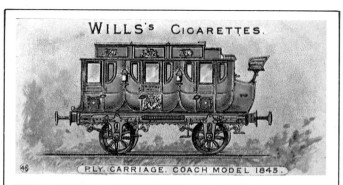

247

248

249

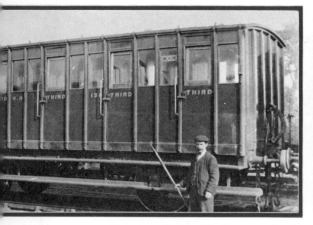 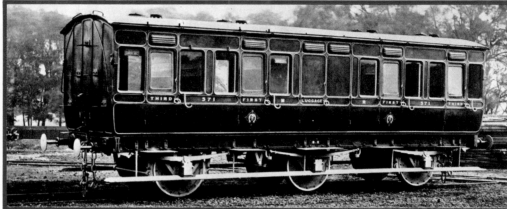

245 Third-class Highland Railway coach of the 1860s; end smoking compartments are enclosed, others are open above the seatbacks.

246 Standard Midland Railway six-wheel mixed-class coach of the 1870s. *British Rail*

for nearly a century. Other than that carriage roofs at that period were almost flat, with only a slight trace of curvature.

It was not possible to stop a train travelling at speeds higher than 20mph very quickly using the locomotive brakes, certainly not as rapidly as a horse-drawn road carriage, so hand brakes were fitted to railway carriages and were operated by guards or brakesmen riding on the roof of selected coaches of each train. They took their cue from the engine driver or front guard who signalled to apply the brakes. Because of the smoke and cinders from the engine, which might have injured the brakesmen, special brake carriages were fitted with enclosed observation look-out positions above roof level to allow the brakesmen to see over the top of the carriages ahead. This form of vantage point was given the name of a lantern or birdcage roof and could be found on certain brake vans in Britain until recent times. Other railways provided guards with a side observation window known as a ducket.

Gradually passengers were provided with lights at night, but they consisted of nothing more than an oil lamp which was sometimes shared between two compartments. Lamps were dropped in through the roof by a lampman who walked along the train at a convenient station.

During the 1840s and 50s passenger amenities improved slightly; after the passing of Gladstone's Regulation of Railways Act in 1844 — which among other things provided that railways must run at least one train a day conveying third-class passengers in covered carriages, at an average speed of not less than 12mph, for a fare of not more than one penny a mile — the lot of the third-class passenger was better than it had been. Carriages themselves had also improved: they were longer — between 30 and 35ft, wider — between 7 and 8ft (except on the Great Western), and there was usually one light to each compartment. First-class coaches were luxuriously upholstered with padded seats and backs, arm and head rests and carpets. Second-class coaches usually had some form of padding in seats but were more austere, while third-class coaches had wooden seats and plain wooden partitions, if indeed they had partitions at all. Some third-class coaches were arranged in the form of one open saloon with benches across the middle and only one or two external doors. Sometimes there were no windows other than in the doors. If the third-class coaches seemed very poor and spartan to our eyes today it must be remembered that the habits and manners of some travellers were not exactly hygienic and many did not know how to behave in public. Clothing, too, was often dirty.

From the middle of the 19th century private saloon carriages began to make their appearance on railways. They were vehicles equipped for carrying families with servants, and were attached as required to ordinary trains; some even contained a bed for carrying invalids. It is in the private carriages, and the royal saloons of the period built for Queen Victoria, that we see the first signs of real improvement in passenger comfort. Many features now taken for granted as a normal part of rail travel — toilet facilities, heating, refreshments and sleeping berths — first saw the light of day in a primitive form in mid-Victorian saloon carriages. The first sleeping facilities, for example, were in what were known as bed carriages, in which a form of stretcher bridged the gap between facing seats in a compartment to allow the passenger to lie down. This can be seen today in the surviving bed carriage preserved in the collection at Clapham Museum. It was originally used by Queen Adelaide on the London & Birmingham Railway from 1842, but because the compartment provided no more than 5ft between partitions the bed extended into the boot at the end of the coach.

Toilets were provided in some saloons, consisting of simple hoppers opening out on to the track beneath the floor, a primitive and extremely unhygienic system, but one which survives in modified form today. Queen Victoria's pair of six-wheel saloons built in 1869, respectively for day and night travel, had inter-coach gangways to allow the royal passengers to pass from one to the other through the coach ends, and a pantry in which hot drinks could be prepared.

By the 1870s sleeping saloons with proper beds had also been introduced. They were not always arranged in compartments and some beds were in large saloons, respectively for men and women. Nevertheless, the sleeping saloon did not come into wide use for another 20 years or so. During the 1870s railway carriages again increased in size, particularly in length, a development permitted by the introduction of bogies, that is pivoted trucks carrying the wheels, placed at each end of the coach underframe. Bogies gave a much smoother ride than rigid four- or six-wheel types, or indeed the fixed eight-wheel arrangement which had been tried by some companies. Bogies were able to take curves more easily and could ride up and down track imperfections without transmitting the inequalities to the coach body. They were adopted first in Britain from the early 1870s but had been used in America, particularly, for some years before that.

Indeed, in North America the four- and six-wheel rigid-wheelbase coach was virtually unknown. So, too, were compartments, for American carriages were usually massive clerestory-roofed saloons entered through open balconies at the ends, with the seats arranged on each side of a central passageway. This was the traditional American carriage (or car as it was known) from the start of railways in North America. In Europe many railways followed

250

251

252

253

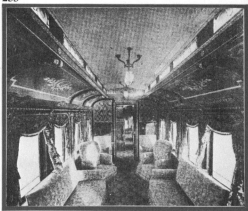

254

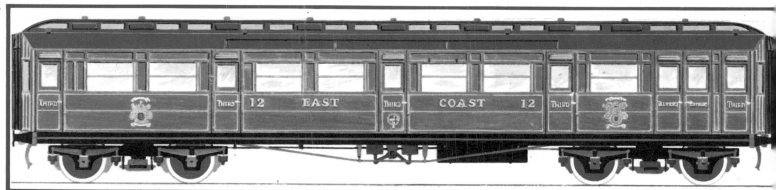

250 Magnificent interior of the sitting room of Queen Victoria's saloon on the LNWR, built in 1869. *British Transport Museum*

251 GWR carriage for Queen Victoria, as restored and preserved by the Dart Valley Railway. *G R Hounsell*

252 and 253 Two views of the luxurious first-class accommodation in a South Eastern Railway vestibule train, from the *Graphic* of 9 November 1897. *Illustrated London News*

254 Preserved corridor-third carriage of East Coast Joint stock, built in 1898 by the North Eastern to Great Northern design, as restored for the Kings Cross station centenary.

British practice, inevitably perhaps, since numerous lines were built or designed by British engineers. Thus the compartment coach was normally used in Europe, although some railways preferred the American-pattern end-balcony type.

The 1870s marked the end of what might be termed first-generation railway carriages, for gradually from that time onwards carriages took on the shape more familiar to our own eyes and looked less like the road coaches of the previous century. The introduction of bogies, while allowing longer coaches to be built, brought a problem. On some lines carriage length was restricted by the need to avoid bridging fouling bars at facing points in the track. Fouling bars consisted of a length of steel angle connected to a bolt which locked point switches one way or the other, depending on which route the train was to take. The bars were made longer than the distance between any two pairs of wheels on a passing train and were located alongside the rail in such a way that the wheels of a train passing over prevented the bar from being lifted and the points unbolted. This was a safety device evolved to prevent points being moved under a train. On some lines before longer coaches could be built all facing point lock fouling bars had to be lengthened.

Nearly all coaches in ordinary service, whether for main or local lines, were of the non-corridor compartment type and it was not until the 1870s that toilets began to be provided on a few coaches used on long-distance trains. Even then they were at first connected to only one or two compartments and only for first-class passengers. It was not until 1882 that the first side-corridor coach appeared, a six-wheeled vehicle on the Great Northern Railway in which passengers in the compartments could reach toilets at the ends of the coach.

The Midland Railway created a stir in railway circles in the mid-1870s by abolishing second class and conveying first- and third-class coaches by all trains. Moreover, it provided third-class passengers with padded seats. Not content with such a revolutionary move it introduced Pullman cars to Britain. They were massive American-built cars with end balconies and domed clerestory roofs. There were several types of car, including day saloons with open interiors and armchair seats, and convertible saloons for night use. They were equipped with pairs of facing seats, on each side of a central passageway, which could be extended towards each other to form a bed, while a second upper berth, folded away against the roof during the day, could be lowered at night to allow passengers to sleep one above the other. Curtains on each side of the passageway provided privacy between each section.

Despite the Midland's enterprise, Pullmans were not an outstanding success, although the cars survived for many years and spread at times to other railways. A noteworthy user was the London-Brighton line, where daytime Pullman saloons were a feature of Brighton services for the next 90 years, culminating in the Southern Railway electric Pullmans, including the Brighton Belle, which survived until 1972.

In 1879 the Great Northern Railway introduced the first dining car to Britain, a Pullman vehicle, and during the following decade railway-owned dining cars appeared on a number of long-distance routes, particularly those between London and the North. Apart from Pullman cars there was still no means for passengers to move from one coach to another while the train was running and passengers had to join and leave dining cars at an intermediate station or travel all the way in the diner. It was not until 1892 that the first true corridor train with inter-coach gangways was introduced, on the Great Western Railway. The ordinary coaches were still of the compartment type but with a side corridor extending from one end to the other; dining cars

255 GWR corridor brake-third of 1892, one of the first side-corridor coaches for full-length corridor trains. *British Rail*

naturally were of the open pattern with a centre passageway and seats on each side.

Other improvements to passenger comfort were taking place with better lighting and heating. Old oil lamps gradually gave way to compressed oil gas, and experiments were being conducted with electricity. Unfortunately electrical equipment of the time was very heavy and cumbersome and gas was the principal means of illumination on trains for some years to come. It was also highly imflammable, which the railways found to their cost in the number of accidents when crashed carriages caught fire. Primitive forms of heating were being tried by using steam from the locomotive passed through a pipe down the train to heat radiators in the coaches. But many companies still provided no heat at all and passengers had to rely on warm clothing and footwarmers, metal containers filled with hot water and sodium acetate which could be hired by passengers.

By the last decade of the century all trains had to be equipped with continuous power brakes, which had been made compulsory by the Regulation of Railways Act in 1889. They were operated by differences in air pressure in either a compressed-air or vacuum system in such a way that if the train became uncoupled or if a passenger operated the alarm signal the brakes were applied automatically, apart of course from normal brake applications by the driver.

This was a period of considerable contrast in railway carriage design; there were still thousands of four- and six-wheel coaches on local and main-line stopping services and they appeared quite diminutive alongside the newest bogie vehicles. By then the latest of them were massive 12-wheel types on two six-wheel bogies, more than 60ft long and 9ft wide, mostly with clerestory roofs. Indeed, the clerestory roof reached its zenith towards the turn of the century and was used by many railways in an attempt to provide better daytime lighting and ventilation. On the debit side was the higher cost than the otherwise low-arc roof and the fact that it was not always weatherproof, so that rain sometimes seeped through joints in the clerestory deck.

Gradually other companies, particularly those in the north, followed the Midland's example by abolishing second-class accommodation; sleeping cars had become general on overnight services between London, the North of England, Scotland and the West Country, but were still only for first-class passengers. The standard form of sleeping car was a side corridor compartment coach with single berths or beds in each compartment.

The turn of the century marked the start of a period of great opulence in railway carriage design and passenger comfort. The period had also brought a vast increase in train weights, which meant that locomotives had to be larger and more powerful.

The decade between the end of Queen Victoria's reign and the outbreak of the First World War saw the peak of British carriage development; until that time coaches had gradually been getting longer, higher and wider, to reach

the maximum dimensions permitted by the British loading gauge. This allowed a width of about 9ft and a height from rail of nearly 13ft, with lengths varying between 50ft and 65ft. On the Great Western, however, the broad gauge had left its mark, for the generous clearances provided by Brunel's 7ft gauge, finally abolished in 1892, meant that even after standard gauge had been adopted throughout the GWR the principal former broad-gauge lines could take coaches and locomotives wider and longer than on other railways. In 1905 the Great Western produced some of the widest and longest coaches seen on a British railway until that time, or indeed since. Nicknamed Dreadnoughts, they were no less than 70ft long and 9ft 7in wide, with high elliptical roofs.

The same period saw the beginning of the decline of the clerestory roof on all railways that had used it, except the Midland, which continued to build clerestory stock until the end of the 1914-18 war, and on London Underground stock, where it was employed more for ventilation purposes than added daylight, until the mid-1930s. A few clerestory-roofed examples survive today on one or two lines of London Transport and on former underground coaches currently in use on the Isle of Wight. The true clerestory as used on main line stock, however, was employed to improve natural lighting with windows in the roof-deck side. A disadvantage was that after dark, lighting a clerestory coach was a problem; if only one light was provided in each compartment it tended to be suspended high in the clerestory, causing shadows; alternatively two lights (and greater cost) were needed. At that period gas lighting was generally employed and the incandescent burners, reflectors and massive glass globes took up a considerable space below the roof.

There were other disadvantages. The construction of the clerestory roof was complex since the roof itself was in three parts, respectively the two lower side decks and the raised top deck, all of which needed separate framing. Although a wooden-bodied coach did not stand up very well in a serious accident in any case, the clerestory roof weakened the whole coach by virtually breaking the back of the coach down the middle. Until the coming of the clerestory, the normal shape of roof was in the form of a low arc but the new century saw the development of non-clerestory stock with higher roofs, first the semi-ellipse with the sides curving sharply down to meet the body side, and then the high elliptical roof, familiar today. Modern construction in fact gives a much lighter and more spacious effect, despite the loss of natural light through roof glazing.

Although gas continued to be the normal lighting

256

257

258

259

260

medium for several years to come, and did not disappear finally in Britain until the early 1960s, electricity was gradually adopted for carriage lighting for its greater effectiveness and better safety in an accident. The first experiments in electric lighting had taken place in the 1880s but some railways were slow to adopt it because the method of generation, which had become standardised, by belts from coach axles driving dynamos to charge batteries, added to the friction and rolling resistance of the train, so that more-powerful engines were needed. It was all part of the general trend towards heavier trains brought about by the introduction of corridor stock, which increased the train weight per passenger and was considered a retrograde step by some companies. It took a number of accidents just before the 1914-18 war, culminating in the worst disaster ever on a British railway at Quintinshill in 1915, in which train wreckage caught fire from escaping gas, to convince the pro-gas faction of its dangers.

Edwardian main-line railway carriages also reached a peak in sumptuous appointment, particularly in first-class coaches, with deep well-padded and sprung seats, velvet upholstery, carpets, padded body sides, ornate decoration, including panelled ceilings, curtains and, on electrically-lit stock, ornamental lighting. Second class, although still

well in evidence, was dying and becoming merged with third class (except in the South of England where second class survived until the 1920s). Third-class compartments had become comfortably appointed, if at times somewhat spartan. From the Midland Railway's revolution of the 1870s by providing the third-class passenger with padded upholstered seats, all railways provided reasonably comfortable third-class accommodation, far superior to anything found on the European mainland.

The movement of commuters by rail (to use the comparatively recent and convenient American description) by the turn of the century was beginning to reach large proportions, although journeys were generally short and the suburbs around London at least were only five to ten miles out from the city centre. The underground system had hardly begun, the motorbus and private car had yet to be developed, and electric tramways were in their infancy. Thus the railways had a monopoly in taking people to and from work and the new habit of living at a distance from one's workplace was encouraged by a policy of frequent trains and cheap workmen's fares. The trains themselves were almost invariably formed of long rakes of four-wheelers with narrow compartments. The third-class coaches had low seat backs and no partitions, just like their predecessors 60 years earlier.

256 Midland and Glasgow & South Western joint stock 12-wheeled dining car with clerestory roof, built in 1914 and now preserved. *British Rail*

257 SECR non-corridor composite formed into three-coach sets and used extensively in Kent. *G M Kichenside*

258 Standard GWR third-class corridor coach of the late 1920s. *British Rail*

259 Saloon and buffet of a GWR twin diesel railcar set of the late 1930s. *British Rail*

260 LMS semi-open first of the early 1930s, featuring corner seating at the near end for every passenger. *British Rail*

261 Stanier corridor third *circa* 1935, the standard LMS type for the decades before and after the Second World War. *G M Kichenside*

262 Southern Railway Maunsell 1st/3rd corridor coach of the 1930s, found all over the system on the SR steam services. *G M Kichenside*

263 Great Western Dreadnought 1st/3rd composite coach dating from 1905. *G M Kichenside*

264 British Rail MkII open second in general use on most Inter-City trains today. The latest version is air-conditioned. *G M Kichenside*

261
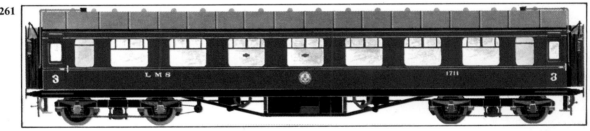

262

263
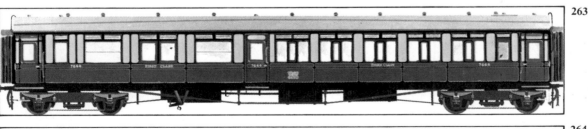

264

The problem was to get as many people on to a train as possible, in the 8ft width of what had become the basic standard suburban carriage, which permitted only five passengers to sit side by side. The Great Eastern Railway, realising that its loading gauge allowed coaches to be another foot wider, and not wishing to scrap its existing stock, carried out a surgical operation by cutting the 8ft-wide coaches down the middle lengthways, splicing in new frames and panelling which increased the width to 9ft, thus allowing 12 passengers to be seated in each third-class compartment instead of the previous ten. Moreover, some of the four-wheel coach bodies were placed in pairs on new bogie underframes, which improved the riding. In fact, bogie coaches were generally built from then on for suburban use, although four and six-wheelers continued to be built by some companies up to the 1914-18 war, and by the Caledonian as late as 1923 (by which time it had become part of the LMS).

The 1914-18 war marked the end of an era, for it changed the way of life, not only for everyone in Great Britain but throughout Western Europe. It hastened the development of the internal-combustion engine which brought the expansion of private motoring and a resurgence of public road transport which challenged the railways for traffic. The electric tram had eaten into city suburban rail services, many of which closed down, and

although another 40 years were to pass before major rail closures began to take effect, life on the railways was never quite the same after the war. In all aspects economy became the watchword and although the railways regained some of their vitality during the 1920s and '30s it was not in the same form as in Victorian and Edwardian days.

After 1918 the railways, which had become run down by wartime activities, recovered only slowly and it was clear that the 100 or so companies in existence needed a massive reorganisation. Under a 1921 Act of Parliament, four major companies were set up to take over practically all the companies in existence until that time. The grouping opened the way to standardisation of equipment, including locomotives and coaches, to bring considerable economy in construction and maintenance.

Although nobody realised it at the time, it was also the start of the decline of the steam locomotive. Pioneer electric railways appeared in the 1880s and the first conversions of main lines to electric traction took place in the Edwardian years with the introduction of electric working in the Newcastle, Liverpool and London areas in 1903-5. All three of those early electric systems employed similar types of coach which were new to passengers used to the traditional compartment carriage. They were based on American designs, and internally were laid out in open saloons with seats each side of a central passageway and

265 Standard third-class non-smoking compartment of LMS corridor stock from the mid 1930s, featuring armrests, a new addition to LMS long-distance third-class stock. *British Rail*

266 BR Mk IIC open first coach employed on Inter-City services. *British Rail*

267 Great Eastern Railway turn-of-the-century device for widening suburban coaches. *British Rail*

268 Typical BR diesel multiple-unit of the 1950s; this one was built by Wickham of Ware and is seen at Kings Lynn, Norfolk. *G M Kichenside*

269 Great Western railcar No 4 at Didcot. *C M Whitehouse*

entry through end doors or open end balconies. In London, the saloon coach had already been used by the first deep-level tube railways of the 1890s, in which side swing doors were precluded by limited tunnel clearances; it was now adopted on the sub-surface Metropolitan and District railways also. In Liverpool, the Mersey Railway used saloon coaches, as did the Lancashire & Yorkshire on its Liverpool-Southport line. The Liverpool-Southport coaches were distinguished by being the widest in the country, with a body width of 10ft.

During the 1914-18 war, further London suburban lines were converted to electric operation, accelerated by the need to release steam engines for war traffic. The London & North Western adopted saloon coaches with end doors but the London & South Western employed traditional compartment coaches; indeed, its electric trains were rebuilt from steam-hauled vehicles. Conversion was also used extensively on the newly formed Southern Railway after the grouping for its suburban electrifications of the 1920s and 1930s. Often the rebuilding was quite elaborate, with parts from two or even three older carriages being mounted on new bogie underframes. Although the Southern carried heavy commuter traffic, the 8ft-wide coach body surprisingly persisted and there was nothing like the Great Eastern's splicing operation.

For main-line service, new designs soon appeared on the four group companies, some bearing a considerable likeness to previous pre-grouping types. On the LMS, for example, it was the Midland carriage superintendent, R. W. Reid, who took over the similar post of the newly formed company and it was not surprising that Midland practices became the new standard. Timber bodies on steel underframes were standardised and Derby Works was reorganised to produce wooden bodied coaches on mass-production lines. Although coaches could be built much more quickly by new methods the demands of the LMS re-equipment out-paced the capacity of the various LMS carriage works and over 200 all-steel coaches were built for the LMS by outside contractors. All were open vehicles

with seats on each side of a central passageway and end doors; open coaches had been used for dining purposes from the 1890s, but they were a complete break from the traditional side-corridor compartment coach for ordinary travel.

Yet the time of the all-steel coach had not really arrived and timber construction was still cheaper than steel. On the LNER, Gresley, who had come from the Great Northern Railway, continued to use the teak-bodied coach, unpainted on the outside and simply varnished over the natural wood. The Great Western had begun to use steel body panelling over timber framing, which obviated the need for decorative wooden mouldings covering body panel joints which had characterised railway carriages for nearly a century. On the LMS steel coaches, mentioned above, it was felt that the plain steel sides needed decoration, so an ornate panel lining was painted on to look like wooden mouldings!

On the Southern Railway, Maunsell, the chief mechanical engineer, introduced new designs; until then, apart from a few corridor trains on the London & South Western and for Continental boat train use on the South Eastern & Chatham, corridor trains were a rarity in Southern England. Distances were, of course, fairly short and most runs were under 100 miles in length. The Southern inherited from all three of its principal constituents large quantities of non-gangway lavatory stock, that is compartment coaches with toilet facilities serving only one or two compartments, or with only a short internal corridor linking three compartments. From the outside it was not always possible to determine exactly which compartments had toilet access.

The LMS and LNER also built quantities of this type of stock for longer-distance stopping services.

In contrast, the Southern did not build any locomotive-hauled non-corridor stock throughout its 25-year existence; with its vast electrification programme it did not need to. In 1933 came the first of the various Southern main-line electric conversions for which Maunsell designed

270 Metro-Cammell Pullman built for East Coast services in the 1960s. *R Bastin*

corridor electric stock similar to his steam stock for other lines. The newly electrified lines serving Brighton, Hastings, Worthing and other places on the South Coast were served by Pullman cars in the new electric units, and a speciality was the all-electric complete Pullman train for the Brighton Belle, certainly a luxury on a 55-mile outer suburban run. It lasted until mid-1972 when the train was given an honourable retirement; most of the Pullman cars have been sold for continued use as restaurants, mostly far from their native haunts and in some cases far from a railway line.

The other three companies also produced their special trains for particular services; some were no more than special sets of coaches hardly differing in their appointments from ordinary stock but for exclusive use on a named train. The LNER specialised in luxury coaches for several of its named expresses; the coaches for the streamlined Coronation and West Riding expresses were formed entirely of open saloon vehicles but the first-class coaches had the seats partitioned off in groups of four or six, with a central passageway.

By the end of the 1930s steel was being used to a far greater extent in coach body construction, usually for side and roof panels, with the timber framing retained. Once again designers turned their attention to all-metal coaches and the LMS built some lightweight electric vehicles using steel and aluminium components for Liverpool area lines. However, the outbreak of war in 1939 interrupted further development. Quite soon after the war ended, the four group companies were again producing new coaches, including all-steel types on the LMS, but individual development was again halted in 1948, this time by nationalisation of the four companies to form British Railways.

One important development did take place during the 1939-45 war, when Bulleid, who had taken over as chief mechanical engineer of the Southern Railway, introduced a new type of suburban electric train for the Southern with 9ft-wide bodies of welded steel construction. Inside, the seats were taken almost up to the outer body skin and the early coaches were very austere and cramped, not surprisingly as Bulleid had succeeded in fitting 11 compartments, each seating 12 people, into a coach 62ft long. At the time of nationalisation Bulleid was also experimenting with double-deck trains and eventually produced an eight-car electric train with interlaced compartments on upper and lower levels. Only one train was built and the Southern standardised on a traditional side-swing-door coach, open throughout, with a central passageway and two-plus-three seating. A similar arrangement was adopted for nearly all subsequent BR suburban electric stock, although Glasgow suburban trains had sliding doors. Now the pendulum is swinging the other way for BR is likely to standardise sliding door coaches for future commuter trains.

From the start, the new British Railways main-line corridor coaches were entirely of steel, but internally they differed little from previous designs, with wood-grain decor and rather dull moquettes for seating. There was little change in design for more than a decade, despite the production of numerous prototypes and the Mark I fleet, as it became known, spread to all main lines throughout the country. From the mid-1960s, big double-glazed windows, better heating, ventilation and soundproofing, wide doors and modern decor, have gradually been introduced, to provide a Mark II standard, and the latest version, which has reverted to small windows, is fully air conditioned. At the other end of the scale, from the mid-1950s BR introduced a large fleet of coaches formed into diesel multiple units. They were built for local and suburban use and some had bus-type seats.

Latest BR development having entered service in a new high-speed train is the Mark III coach, a longer vehicle than has been seen before on British Railways. It has a body length of about 75ft and a width of 9ft, is designed for speeds up to 125mph and is fully air conditioned. A feature is the abolition of individual compartments and all seats for both first- and second-class passengers will be in open saloons. In some proposed layouts for the second-class saloons, some of the seats will not coincide with windows and some passengers will sit alongside solid panels between windows, a retrograde step reminiscent of some of the worst features of 60 years ago.

The other important development for the 1970s is the Advanced Passenger Train, designed for speeds up to 155mph on existing track, and possibly much higher speed on specially prepared tracks. To allow a train to take existing curves at a higher speed than at present the coach bodies will tilt. To keep them within the loading gauge the body sides are inclined inwards so that from the waist upwards coach interiors will be narrower than at present. Although they will have very advanced running gear, the general design of the air-conditioned passenger accommodation of the APT saloons will be little different from the standard Mark III coaches.

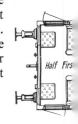

Half First

London and North Western Radial

ALTHOUGH THE London & North Western claimed for itself the title of the Premier Line, its progress in coaching stock improvements lagged behind that of the neighbouring Midland Railway. During mid-Victorian years the standard British main-line coach was a six-wheeler with a length of about 30ft, but in 1876 the Midland introduced bogie coaches 54ft long, carrying more passengers than a six-wheeler and in greater comfort since the pivoted bogie trucks at each end of the coach gave a smoother ride than the rigid wheelbase of older vehicles.

The London & North Western Railway, or at least two of its chief officers — Francis Webb, locomotive superintendent, and Richard Bore, carriage superintendent — could see no advantage in bogies, nor in such long coaches as those of the Midland. In any case, the length of LNW coaches for many years had been restricted to 33ft or less by a traverser at Euston station used for transferring coaches from one line to another.

During the early 1880s the restriction on LNW carriage length was lifted after the removal of the traverser, but even then Wolverton works designed new stock no longer than 42ft. This was too long for a six-wheeled underframe, so eight wheels were adopted, but not in independently suspended bogie frames. The two centre axles were rigidly attached to the coach underframe by axle guards bolted to the solebars in the normal way, but the outer axles were carried in separate frames sliding in curved guide blocks which allowed a few inches movement towards each side. Thus as the coach entered a curve the rail forces pushed end wheels sideways and with the thrust of the curved guide blocks turned the truck frame radially so that the end wheels took up a position more in alignment with the curve.

271 A tricomposite 42ft North Western Radial, providing for first, second and third classes, with a lavatory for first class and a luggage compartment. Second class was not finally ended on the LNWR until about the turn of the century.
Clifford and Wendy Meadway

It was rather a hit-and-miss arrangement since the radial frames could move only in a fixed radius according to the amount of side-play, which only aligned the wheels truly to one particular size of curve. On curves of any other radius, larger or smaller, the wheels were not truly tangential to the rail because of the restricting influence of the two rigid centre axles. The radial coaches were almost as rough riding as six-wheelers and certainly not as steady as bogie coaches.

Large numbers of radial eight-wheelers were built during the 1880s, both for internal LNW services south of Carlisle and the West Coast Joint Stock, an independent fleet of coaches owned jointly by the London & North Western and Caledonian railways for Anglo-Scottish services. It was during this period that improvements in passenger amenities began to be seen with the provision of toilets and many 42ft radial coaches had between-compartment toilets for long-distance journeys. Toilets had made their appearance during the previous decade for first-class passengers but their use had gradually been extended for second and third-class travellers. There were no corridors in these coaches and each compartment usually had its own toilet facilities, although not all were so served. Some coaches had small luggage compartments so that the cases and trunks travelled in the same vehicle as their owner; because of the internal layout variations some of the end compartments were half-compartments or coupés.

C. A. Park, who succeeded Richard Bore as LNW carriage superintendent in the mid-1880s, soon realised the defects in the radial arrangement and started a programme for rebuilding them on conventional four-wheel bogies. Even so, some of the radials lasted for many years in their original condition.

The standard long-distance LNW and Anglo-Scottish expresses of the period were usually made up of a mixture of six-wheel and radial vehicles, even on overnight services, which included some of the pioneer first-class sleeping cars. It was not until the 1890s that longer bogie vehicles, at first 45ft, then later 50ft and 57ft in length, came into general use on LNW services, 20 years or so after their introduction on the Midland.

One radial eight-wheeler survives today, a West Coast Joint Stock travelling Post Office coach, preserved at the National Railway Museum, York.

272 Layout of the LNWR Radial coach. *Ian Allan Library*

Great Northern Six Wheelers

UNTIL THE 1870s coaches on the main line from Kings Cross to the North, in common with most railways in the country, were little more than box-like four-wheelers, but that decade saw the introduction of more-spacious coaches of between 30ft and 35ft in length and 7ft 9in or 8ft wide, mounted on six-wheeled underframes. On the Great Northern Railway, coach bodies were of varnished teak; the use of natural varnished wood finish lasted for a century on this route, since it was adopted early on by the infant Great Northern in the 1850s and remained standard for Great Northern, East Coast Joint Stock and London & North Eastern Railway coaches until nationalisation in 1948.

The Great Northern six-wheelers of the 1870s were built to a body shape that remained well in evidence for 80 years; they had low, almost flat, roofs curving sharply down at the edges to meet the body sides, a form used by few other railways. Great Northern bodyside panelling was also distinctive for it did not have the round-cornered waist, window, and top panels enclosed by the mouldings favoured by other railways, but instead had half-round beading below the waist dividing the lower body side into two horizontal panels, broken only by doors. Above the waist the panels were recessed slightly from those below the waist so that the whole body side was on three levels, so to speak.

During the next 30 years large numbers of six-wheelers were built to this basic pattern for both the Great Northern and the East Coast Joint Stock, provided by the Great Northern. The East Coast Joint Stock was a special pool of coaches built for through services between Kings Cross, York, Newcastle and Edinburgh and beyond, jointly owned by the three railways which made up the route.

At first the normal GN main line six-wheeler was a compartment coach with no special facilities but gradually toilets between certain compartments were introduced, for first-class passengers only at first, and later for the other two classes of travellers. Provision of toilets was a long overdue requirement, but even then it was not altogether satisfactory since only one or two compartments in each coach were served by toilets, and unless passengers took a

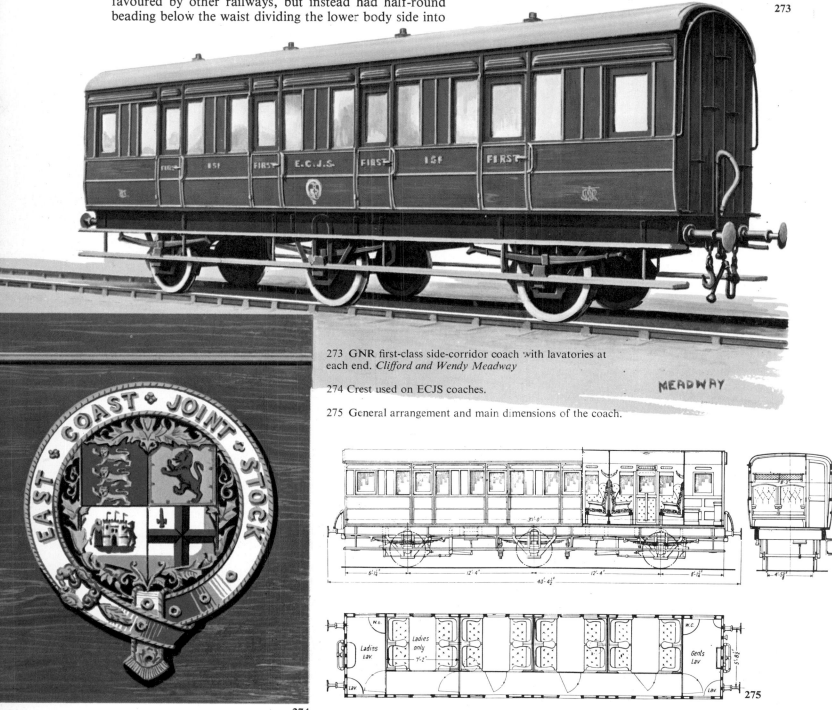

273 GNR first-class side-corridor coach with lavatories at each end. *Clifford and Wendy Meadway*

274 Crest used on ECJS coaches.

275 General arrangement and main dimensions of the coach.

118

good look into a compartment before joining the train it was a matter of luck whether long-distance passengers found a compartment with toilet access. In 1882, to remedy this deficiency, the Great Northern introduced a six-wheeled coach with side corridor linking four first-class compartments to two toilets, one at each end respectively for ladies and gentlemen. Thus was born what became the traditional side-corridor coach, although at that stage it was still not possible to pass from one coach to the next. Apart from Pullmans, that was a development of the 1890s.

The Great Northern and East Coast six-wheelers were many and varied in design. Indeed there were so many that when trains with through corridors between coaches were introduced in the 1890s it was not possible to provide trains of completely new stock and many six-wheelers with internal corridors were rebuilt with flexible gangway connections.

The six-wheeled underframe gave a very hard ride but the Great Northern, like the rival LNWR, did not take kindly to bogies, at least in mid-Victorian times. The GN even built some rigid eight-wheelers which were just as hard riding and with a less flexible wheelbase than the

London & North Western radial eight-wheelers of which they were contemporaries. It was not until almost the end of the last century that the Great Northern really adopted bogie vehicles, but when it did the designs were a complete contrast to what had gone before. The new coaches were massive vehicles with clerestory roofs mounted on two six-wheel bogies. They were designed by Howlden, the Great Northern's carriage superintendent from the 1870s until 1905, and with those of Gresley, who succeeded Howlden, they gradually ousted the six-wheelers from front-line service.

Even so, the six-wheelers remained on local cross-country and branch-line duties until the Second World War. Indeed, it was fairly easy to find a train of six-wheelers in 1938 to run on special trips with one of the celebrated Stirling 4-2-2s (No 1) which was brought out of York Museum for celebrations to mark the introduction of a new Flying Scotsman train. The last of the Great Northern six-wheelers survived until the 1950s and it was a great pity that none of the restored 1938 special train coaches were preserved, like the locomotive. Nevertheless, one or two have survived on preserved railways, but not in original condition.

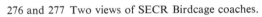

276 and 277 Two views of SECR Birdcage coaches.

South Eastern Birdcages

ON THE PIONEER TRAINS of the 1830s and 1840s, the only brakes on a train were hand-brakes on the locomotive and on selected coaches through the train. The carriage brakes were applied by brakesmen who had to be positioned to see lineside signals and to see and hear hand or whistle signals given by the engine crew if they wanted to stop a train in an emergency.

The best view along the train was obtained at roof level and the brakesmen were consequently seated outside the coach end in such a way that they could look over the top of the carriage roofs. The exposed position was, in fact, a relic of road coach days when the guard sat high up at the back of the vehicle where he could keep an eye open for highwaymen. While railway guards and brakesmen did not have to contend with armed hold-ups, the guard's position persisted. In contrast, another danger appeared on the railway, for guards and brakesmen had to be careful not to sit too high when passing under bridges. Moreover, they bore the full effect of smoke, steam and cinders from the engine.

To afford protection, some coaches were provided with enclosed observatories above general roof level, with windows all round to give the guard a good view. The observation projections were known as lanterns or birdcages and were gradually adopted by a number of railways in mid and late Victorian times.

The requirement from 1889 for railways to use

automatic brakes applied by variations in air pressure, with the brakes on the whole train controlled from the locomotive, meant that there was no longer any need for the guard to assist in braking, except in an emergency, but he was still required to keep a good look-out just in case the driver missed a danger signal. Other railways provided side look-outs, called duckets, but the view from them was limited because the ducket could protrude no more than about six inches at the most from the coach side.

As coaches began to be built with higher roofs, soon after the turn of the century, there was less room for the birdcage, since it depended for good visibility on a low roof profile right through the train. One company that made extensive use of the birdcage roofs for its guards was the South Eastern & Chatham, which covered the whole of Kent and parts of East Sussex. A number of routes operated by the SECR included tunnels and other structures which limited the width of SECR coaches to eight feet, a restriction which still applies today on the line from Tunbridge Wells to Hastings. For that reason the SECR could not use side ducket look-outs and stuck to the birdcage for almost its entire existence, with coaches having low semi-elliptical roofs.

Since large quantities of South Eastern & Chatham stock survived until the Kent Coast main-line electrification schemes of 1959-62, the birdcage look-out remained in evidence until recent times. Because of the

short distance between London and the Kent coast the SECR made little use of corridor stock. However, toilet facilities were required and to cater for medium and long-distance passengers, the SECR built large quantities of non-corridor stock equipped with between-compartment toilets or with short internal side corridors serving two or three compartments.

The SECR also maintained three classes of travel to the end of its existence and another of its quirks was its love of saloons. The company built large numbers of three-coach sets containing three-class accommodation, toilets, a first-class saloon and end coaches equipped with birdcage look-outs. The SECR also provided coaches for through services to other parts of the country; they were unusual for the SECR in that they had through gangways and side corridors. One is the subject of our illustration below. It was built in 1907 and had two first-class, two second-class and two third-class compartments, and a guard/luggage compartment with the inevitable birdcage.

Although the SECR was the most extensive user of the birdcage, it has a descendant today in the periscope look-out which was widely used by the Southern Railway and in more recent times by British Railways. By means of two suitably arranged mirrors, the guard sitting at his desk at normal level was given a view along the coach roof. A problem with the device is the difficulty of keeping the upper mirror clean.

Now even the periscope is being abandoned, as in today's locomotive controls and signalling systems automatic safeguards reduce the need for the guard to act as the driver's second pair of eyes.

278 The lookout end of a South Eastern Birdcage. *Clifford and Wendy Meadway*

279 Also by the Meadways, from a BR LMR photograph, this is the interior of a large first-class compartment, with sofas.

London and North Western Twelve Wheelers

THE LONDON & North Western Railway did not adopt bogie coaches until late in life, indeed not until after C. A. Park had become carriage superintendent in the late 1880s. Even then the coaches were generally short, no more than 45ft or at the most 50ft in length, such as the first corridor coaches built for West Coast route Anglo-Scottish services in 1893. There was nothing like the large Midland clerestory 12-wheelers of the mid-1870s.

But before the century was out, Park thoroughly revolutionised LNW carriage design, particularly in respect of dining and sleeping cars. While ordinary LNW and West Coast stock after the turn of the century was standardised at 57ft, carried on two four-wheel bogies, Park's designs for sleeping and dining vehicles were massive 12-wheelers, 65ft long with clerestory roofs, sloped at the ends. Bodies were built to the full width permitted by the loading gauge, which meant that they were inclined slightly outwards from roof level to waist, with a turn-under towards the underframe. They were handsome coaches, distinguished by ornate panelling and mouldings on the bodyside, with finely applied gilt lining contrasting with the deep purple brown and white of the main bodyside livery.

In 1907-8 Park produced what many authorities consider to be the most sumptuous coaches ever built for

ordinary service on a British railway. They were special sets built for the London-Liverpool American boat trains and the London-Glasgow afternoon service respectively. In general appearance the coaches were very similar to the sleepers and diners of the previous decade, but they were given high semi-elliptical roofs instead of the clerestory type, which was beginning to go out of fashion. Unlike corridor coaches for other LNW services, which until then, and, indeed, for the next 20 years, had side doors to each compartment, the coaches of the American boat trains and the afternoon Anglo-Scottish services had only end doors and vestibules, and access to all compartments was by the side corridor. This feature was not new in itself since it had already been seen on earlier dining and Pullman cars, and on the Great Western Dreadnought coaches of 1905. But the British public were not yet ready for this amenity, which obviated interruptions at stations when passengers joining the train sometimes had to step their way across the already crowded compartment to reach the corridor, if it was on the far side.

The three trains built for the American boat traffic were formed of eight coaches each, a 50ft luggage van at each end, a 50ft kitchen car in the middle, two first-class side-corridor coaches, a first-class diner, a second- and third-class corridor coach and a second- and third-class diner. Each of the two first-class corridor coaches had one large compartment laid out rather as a drawing room with sofas and armchairs, while most of the normal-size compartments included armchairs; the furniture in the compartments also included small tables. The object was to recreate the private rooms found on American trains at that time. Second- and third-class passengers had normal compartments with fixed seating, but decor and appointments were superior to contemporary coaches on other services. The trains were electrically lit throughout, with the exception of the kitchen car which had in any case to carry gas for cooking, and was also gas lit. The American boat trains were remarkable so far as the LNW was concerned, since they presented a uniform appearance throughout. If any other LNW or West Coast train consisted entirely of coaches of the same width and roof profile it was purely by chance!

Even the new trains built for the afternoon Anglo-Scottish service were not uniform since new dining cars were not provided and earlier clerestory-roofed cars were included in the formation and one or two older coaches were included to form through portions detached en route. These trains, which left Glasgow and Euston simultaneously at two o'clock in the afternoon, were still known by their unofficial nickname, The Corridor, since

280 LNWR 12-wheel second/third class corridor boat-train coach. *Clifford and Wendy Meadway*

281 Interior of a second-class compartment of the American boat-train stock. *British Rail*

281

they were the first on the route to be given coaches with through coach to coach corridors in 1893. The new 12-wheel stock was more conventional in having fixed seating for both first and third-class passengers (second class had been abolished on Anglo-Scottish services some years earlier) but in other respects the coaches were almost as grand as those for the Liverpool boat trains.

As railway carriages of that period go, the vehicles were not all that long-lived. They remained on the 14.00 service until the mid-1920s when they were replaced by standard LMS vehicles, but their weight, size, and non-standard seating layout made them unsuitable for other main line services; although individual coaches of this stock could be seen from time to time on secondary duties, most had been withdrawn by the 1939-45 war. Nothing quite like them was ever built again, for, after the 1914-18 war, commercial restraints brought more functional and austere designs, even though standards of comfort have improved over the years.

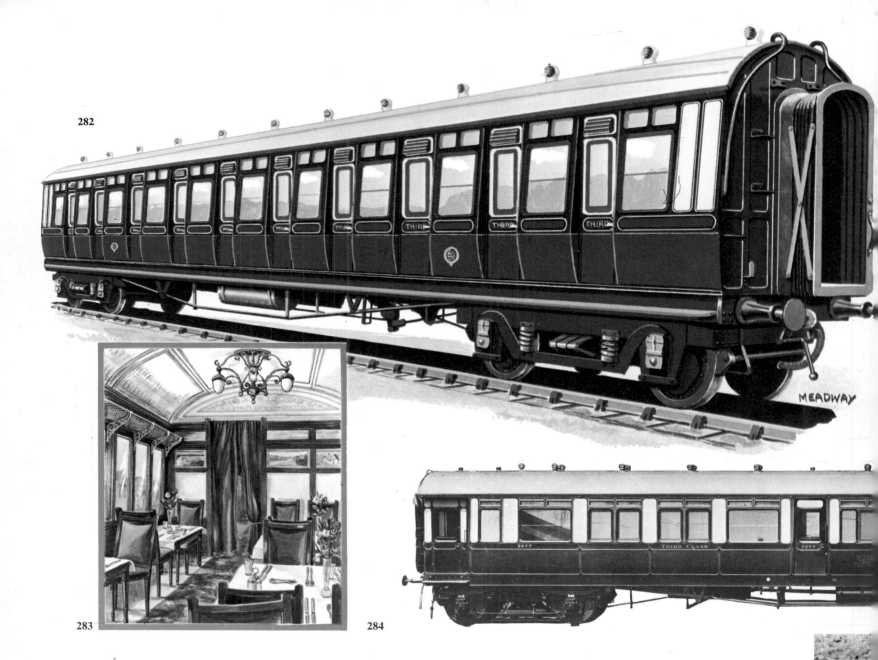

282

283   284

MEADWAY

Great Western 70 Footers

BRUNEL'S 7ft 0¼ in broad gauge, which at its maximum extent stretched between London and Penzance, South Wales, and Wolverhampton, even after its final abolition in 1892, left the Great Western Railway with probably the most spacious principal main lines of any railway in the country. Lineside structures and particularly over-bridges had been designed to allow for engine and coach widths of 10ft and while some realignment had taken place to bring track centres to the correct distance from platform faces when the broad gauge was abolished, generally speaking there was ample clearance on each side of the main standard-gauge tracks to allow the continued use of wide stock. The Great Western did not immediately make full use of the facility after the final demise of the broad gauge and the first standard-guage coaches built for ex-broad-gauge lines were no more than 9ft wide, which was the general limit on most standard-gauge railways.

The end of the broad gauge coincided with a number of new developments in passenger coach comfort; for example, the introduction of restaurant cars and corridor trains. When Churchward succeeded William Dean as the Great Western's chief mechanical engineer, about a decade after the end of the broad gauge, his engineering flair provided the basis of a sound motive power policy that was to last the Great Western until the end of its existence in 1948. Moreover, he introduced new coaching stock designs, some quite unlike anything that had gone before; others brought in new features in advance of their time to which the Victorian and early Edwardian public did not take kindly.

In 1905, after the building of one or two prototypes, the

Great Western built some of the largest coaches that have ever run on a British railway before or since; they had a body length of about 70ft and a width of 9ft 6in and, judged by British standards, were massive vehicles, with high elliptical roofs and recessed end and middle doors. They were fitted with separate compartments and corridors that changed from one side to the other at a centre vestibule. The compartments did not have external doors and it was this feature which seemed to be disliked by a travelling public brought up on doors to every compartment.

Because of their size, the coaches were nicknamed Dreadnoughts after the contemporary battleships. They were not built in large numbers and soon afterwards a new GWR design reverted to individual side doors to each compartment. The new coaches were also 70ft or thereabouts in length but the width was the more normal 9ft; again the doors were recessed and for that reason the coaches received the rather apt nickname of Concertinas.

Two or three years later another type of coach became known as the Toplight, from the fact that it had small windows of frosted glass above the main windows. The Toplights became the standard Great Western coaches for the next decade. Although they were produced in shorter lengths for routes where normal size restrictions applied, some were built to 70ft length. Their successors, the steel-panelled coaches of the early 1920s, also included 70ft vehicles, particularly for use in some special sets for Paddington-South Wales trains.

By that time, however, since the long — and in the case of the Dreadnoughts, extra wide — coaches were restricted

to former broad-gauge lines, it was becoming a problem with so many variations of size to prevent coaches being misdirected on to more restricted routes. So the GW did not build any more 70-footers, although in the following 20 years it occasionally indulged in odd flights of fancy with small batches of shorter but extra-wide coaches. It was, perhaps, a step backwards and one wonders whether any real assessment was made of lineside structures to see whether normal standard-gauge routes could be made to accept long coaches with comparatively minor adjustments.

In recent years BR has adopted a standard body length of 64ft 6in for passenger coaches. Now, the closure of many intermediate stations and the ripping up of sidings has brought the removal of many structures that have restricted loading-gauge dimensions. The assessment of principal main lines all over Britain has shown that there are now few places that cannot accept coaches 75ft in length, provided the body width is limited to 9ft; consequently, 75ft will be the size of BR's next generation of coaches, making the first real increase in length since those first Great Western 70ft Dreadnoughts nearly 70 years ago.

282 GWR 70ft third-class 'Concertina' coach of 1906/7. *Clifford and Wendy Meadway*

283 Interior of GWR 1904 'Dreadnought' restaurant car. *Clifford and Wendy Meadway*

284 Third-class 70-footer of 1905/6. *British Rail*

285 Preserved Pullman car *Topaz* pictured at Brighton. A 31-seater built in 1914 by the Birmingham RCW Co, it continued in service until 1960. *British Transport Museum*

286 Ornate interior of *Topaz*. *British Transport Museum*

286

285

Pullman Cars

TO THE BRITISH travelling public of mid-Victorian years, used to enduring long journeys in hard-riding four- or six-wheel coaches with all accommodation in self-contained compartments, without heating and toilet facilities, and only the miserable flickering flame of an oil lamp for lighting, the spacious bogie Pullman cars, introduced on the Midland Railway in 1874, must have come as something of a shock.

For those days, they were massive carriages, with clerestory roofs, open balconies at each end and seats dispersed for the most part on each side of a central passageway; they were heated in winter by a hot water stove at one end of the car, and were equipped with toilets.

Some of the early Midland Pullmans were fitted out for sleeping on night journeys, with berths formed either from two facing seats with extensions which pulled towards each other to form a bed, or by an upper berth hinged to the body side and folded up against the roof by day and lowered by night, supported by chains, over the top of the lower berth. Cars used for daytime services only were equipped with single armchairs, pivoted so that they could face in any direction.

Introduction of the Pullman vehicles on the Midland Railway followed a visit in 1872 by the Midland's general manager James Allport to the United States, where he met George Mortimer Pullman, who had previously introduced luxury Pullman cars on North-American railways. Pullman built the cars for these early Midland experiments in America and shipped over what amounted to kits of parts for assembly at the Midland carriage works at Derby. The cars remained the property of Pullman and operated under contract with the railway, and passengers paid a supplementary fare for using them.

The Midland placed in service trains composed entirely of Pullman cars, which were all first class, and additional coaches of similar appearance but with ordinary seats of the then three classes for passengers not wishing to pay the supplement. The advantage was the through corridor access from all coaches to the lavatories, a feature unknown in ordinary British trains at that time.

With hindsight, it seems difficult to understand why the luxury trains were not received with wide acclaim, but the fact is that the British public did not take to the American-style centre-gangway cars, nor did they like paying a

287 Major exterior Pullman features: the clerestory roof, end balcony and highly decorative finish. *Clifford and Wendy Meadway*

288 Mock-up of a Pullman interior of about 1890, in the old British Transport Museum, Clapham. *J Benton-Harris*

289 Clerestory-roof Pullman car *Prince* built at the LBSCR Brighton works from US Pullman Co parts in 1888 and scrapped in 1929. *British Transport Museum*

290 Interior of an earlier Golden Arrow Pullman, with the *Trianon* bar in the background. *British Rail*

291 Interior of Pullman kitchen car *Malaga* after modernisation for Golden Arrow Service in 1949. *Malaga* is preserved by the Ian Allan Group at Shepperton and used as the group's boardroom. *British Rail*

292 The last down run of the Brighton Belle electric Pullman unit on 9 May 1972, crossing the Ouse viaduct north of Haywards Heath. *J C Morgan*

288

289

290

supplement for their use. As a result the first all-Pullman trains on the Midland were soon abandoned, although individual cars, and in particular sleepers, survived and prospered on new services.

Five years later, in 1879, a Pullman car running on the Great Northern Railway from Kings Cross to Leeds and Bradford became the first regular dining car on a British railway in which food was prepared and cooked on the train. Meanwhile, Pullman cars had been introduced to other lines, including the unlikely short London-Brighton run which created a Pullman link to that popular South-coast town which lasted for over 90 years. By 1881 an all-Pullman train was running between London and Brighton and was remarkable for the fact that it was electrically lit, the first train in the world to be so fitted. By that time, refreshments were being served in a number of Pullman cars, either main meals on the longer journeys or buffet snacks and drinks on short runs.

Although Pullman cars, all of which had by then come into ownership of a British-based Pullman company, ran on a number of lines, their success varied from railway to railway and cars were often transferred from one line to another. Gradually, moreover, Pullman services in Britain became confined to daytime journeys, and sleeping-car services were taken over by the railways themselves. Pullmans were found widely on services between London and the South Coast and came and went on other lines. Eventually they disappeared from the Midland route and, after the railway grouping in 1923, were to be found only on the Southern and LNER lines, apart from a short appearance on the Great Western between London and Torquay. LNER services were all-Pullman formations, while the Southern's operations included both all-Pullman trains and isolated Pullmans in ordinary service.

The normal Pullman parlour car consisted of an open vehicle with seats on each side of a central passageway, forming the main saloon, and single compartments known as coupés served by short side corridors at the car ends. A kitchen car would have about half its accommodation laid out similarly for passengers and the other half devoted to kitchen and pantry facilities.

The hallmark of Pullman operation was personal service by attendants, and meals or refreshments at every seat. Indeed as standards of comfort on ordinary coaches rose during the 1920s and 1930s, it was the extra service found on Pullman cars that made them such a success in the 1930s and after the Second World War. The Southern Railway even found it worthwhile to include Pullman cars in its new electric trains for the various South Coast electrification schemes of the mid-1930s, including the all-Pullman Brighton Belle, the only Pullman electric multiple-unit in the world — and on a mere 55-mile outer-suburban journey! It was the unique feature of the service, with its high staff costs, that made it uneconomic in today's conditions; sadly, the Brighton Belle came to an end early in 1972, just 40 years after it was placed in service.

In more recent years Pullmans in Britain have bought even greater advances in standards of comfort, with air conditioning and sound insulation, first seen on the diesel Pullmans on the London Midland and Western regions, which brought Pullmans back to the Midland route from St Pancras, on which they first appeared in England, for a short period.

Today, however, improvements in general rolling stock design have brought comparable luxur to ordinary trains.

Moeover, higher speeds on many routes mean that it is no longer possible to serve more than one sitting for main meals and it becomes necessary or desirable for passengers to be served in their own seats. Tomorrow's coaches now entering service on BR in experimental form bring the highest standards to ordinary trains and there is no longer any need for Pullman cars. But it has taken almost a century since the introduction of the first Pullmans to Britain to achieve this.

291

APART FROM early pioneering railways, such as the Stockton & Darlington and Liverpool & Manchester, most of the British railway system was built during the reign of Queen Victoria. Indeed, the young Princess Victoria inherited the throne in 1837, the year in which the first section of the London & Birmingham Railway was opened, and within a few years members of the Royal Family began to appreciate the advantages of rail travel.

By 1842 the London & Birmingham Railway had provided a carriage for use by the Dowager Queen Adelaide, widow of King William IV. It was very similar to that company's standard first-class mail carriages, with two-and-a-half compartments and a boot at one end. In normal circumstances the boot contained the mail, a relic from road coach practice, but in Queen Adelaide's carriage the boot formed an extension from the adjacent compartment which could be fitted out for sleeping. Stretcher bars placed across the gap between the facing seats supported an intermediate cushion so that a bed could be made up across the compartment.

The small size of early coaches, with between-partition widths of little more than 5ft, would have made it impossible for a passenger to lie full length, and a flap in the coach end allowed the bed to extend into the boot. The London & Birmingham bed carriage was thus one of the first sleeping coaches. In fact, almost throughout railway history, royal or other private saloons have pioneered improvements in standards of comfort which did not come until later years in ordinary stock.

Queen Victoria and Prince Albert made a number of journeys by train, travelling in small saloons similar in size to ordinary coaches of the period, but much more ornately decorated and furnished. The Great Western Railway, with its royal connections at Windsor, built two or three saloons for use by the Queen in the 1840s and '50s, one of which at least was an eight-wheeler, although not with bogies, since the axleboxes were rigidly attached to the coach underframe. An oddity on one of these saloons was the roof-mounted signal by which instructions could be passed from the senior railway officer accompanying the train to the crew on the running of the train. Those were the days before continuous brakes and it would not have been possible to stop the train in an emergency merely by hand brakes on the saloon itself. It was always said that the Queen disliked travelling fast and would not permit a speed of more than 40mph.

Undoubtedly the most important of the Victorian royal saloons was the pair of six-wheelers built by the London & North Western for the long Anglo-Scottish journeys between Windsor and Balmoral in 1869. One coach was laid out as a daytime lounge and the other with a bedroom for night accommodation. They were the first British coaches to have flexible gangways to allow free passage between them while the train was moving, although it was not possible to pass into coaches on each side. The saloons included toilet accommodation and a small pantry in one of the attendant's compartments which allowed the preparation of light refreshments. Full meal facilities were not required, as the Queen normally took meals at an extended station stop, usually Perth. The saloons were sumptuously appointed internally with sides and roof quilted with silk or damask. The two six-wheel coaches were rebuilt in 1895 on a single underframe carried on two six-wheel bogies; the rebuilt coach is preserved as part of the national collection, now to be seen at the new York railway museum.

This saloon lasted in use until the early years of the present century, but the new King, Edward VII, ordered a new royal train. It made its first appearance in 1903 and consisted of two royal saloons on six-wheel bogies, less fussy internally than the Victorian coaches, and generally similar to the standard LNW and West Coast Joint Stock sleeping and dining cars of the period. with clerestory roofs and ornate panelled body sides.

294 The King's day saloon of the 1903 train, built by the LNWR for long royal journeys, and now preserved.
Clifford and Wendy Meadway

293 and 295-300 Exterior view and interior details of Queen Victoria's LNWR saloon, now preserved in the National Railway Museum, York. *British Transport Museum*

301 and 302 Interior of the smoking room and a general view of King Edward VII's LNWR saloon of 1903.
British Transport Museum

Each coach combined day and night facilities respectively for the King and Queen, and there were a number of detailed differences between the two coaches: the King's saloon, for example, included a small smoking compartment. Entry was by double doors into a large end vestibule. The complete royal train was made up of a number of matching semi-royal saloons (which when not in use for royal journeys could be hired by the wealthy as family saloons) for the personal attendants, and a dining car, as well as coaches for other royal staff and railway officers. In later years a bathroom was provided in one of the royal saloons. This calvacade lasted for nearly 40 years, and indeed one or two vehicles of the train survive today for royal use.

In 1908 the Great Northern and North Eastern Railways built a pair of royal saloons more modern in appearance since they had high elliptical roofs which had then recently been adopted by Nigel Gresley, carriage superintendent of the GNR. One of this pair also survives today for use by Queen Elizabeth II on short daytime journeys. For night travel, however, and particularly where a large number of royal staff accompany the Queen, today the LMR royal train is used. It includes not only one or two coaches from the 1903 LNW train and various semi-official saloons of LMS origin, but also the two principal royal saloons built for King George VI and Queen Elizabeth in 1941, today used by the Queen and Prince Philip. At the time they were built they had some unique features, including double-glazed windows and full air conditioning, again pioneering facilities, which only some 30 years later, are coming into general use on ordinary coaches.

Travelling Post Offices

IN THE eighteenth century the British Post Office was bitterly opposed to Palmer's suggestion of the use of stage coaches to speed the mails, but half a century later its controllers were more broadminded and within two months of the opening of the Liverpool & Manchester Railway on September 15, 1830, letters were being carried by the trains. This was even before freight traffic began. By the time the Grand Junction Railway opened between Birmingham & Newton on July 4, 1837, the Post Office was able to offer a 16½-hour transit from London by stage coach to Birmingham and thence by rail to either Liverpool or Manchester. A sorting carriage (a converted horse-box) ran from Birmingham to Liverpool from January 6, 1838, on the suggestion of Frederick Karstadt.

It was decided to provide a specially built vehicle for the service and John Ramsey (appointed Inspector General of the Post Office for his idea) devised the apparatus for exchanging bags of mail at stations without stopping the train. The apparatus was incorporated in the new vehicle and used in conjunction with lineside catching nets and standards on which the bags to be collected could be hung.

Sir Rowland Hill, instigator of Post Office reform (including the penny post) was a member of the board of directors of the London, Brighton & South Coast Railway on its formation in 1846 and throughout his service with the Post Office (1846-1864) powerfully advocated maximum use of railway facilities for mail services. As a result travelling post offices became used to a larger extent on railways in Britain than anywhere else in the world. Not only is time saved by being able to sort letters in transit, but 'late fee' letters can be posted actually on the trains.

The parcels post was inaugurated in 1883 and two years later special Post Office parcels sorting vans were in service on the railways. At one time the requirements of HM Postmaster-General were said to dominate the compilation of the railway timetable, with meticulously observed exchange points, such as Tamworth, between the West Coast route and the Midland's South-West to North-East links. Although the Great Western, with the rather pompous phrase about 'compliance with directions received from Her Majesty's PMG', was first with exclusive night mail trains in 1840, the most famous night

303 Jubilee No 5659 heads the down West Coast Postal at the Harrow pick-up point in June 1947. *Ian Allan Library*

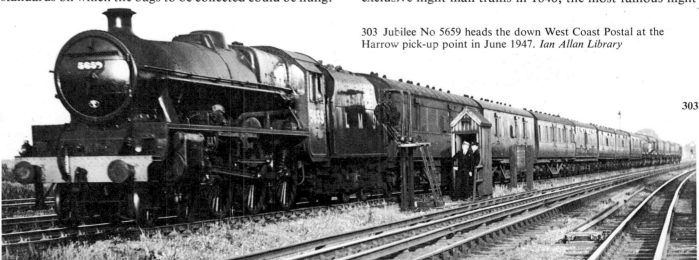

304

305

307

306

309

308

mail was the West Coast Postal Limited, which became all-mail in 1885, had some very high-speed running between stops, and was the subject of the famous documentary film which had the theme poem:

'This is the Night Mail crossing the Border
'Bringing the cheque and the postal order.'

At the maximum there were nearly 200 TPO services and 132 apparatus stations on railways in Britain. The special services have been much reduced, owing to the development of the Inter-City regular-headway passenger network, road connections and air services. During 1971 the apparatus stations, which had been eliminated of recent years on many routes, vanished entirely, their ingenious techniques having outlived their usefulness.

304 Preserved 1838 postal coach of the Grand Junction Railway. *British Transport Museum/B Sharpe*

305 Late-fee posting box on an 1885 postal sorting van of West Coast Joint Stock. *British Transport Museum/B Sharpe*

306 Catching net rigged on the side of a postal sorting van. *John Topham Ltd*

307 Vanside rig ready to drop a bag into the trackside net and snatch one into its own net. *Ian Allan Library*

308 Sorting mail inside the travelling post office. *John Topham Ltd*

309 Trackside rig for mailbag exchange, manned by post office staff, with bag ready for pick-up. *Ian Allan Library*

FREIGHT

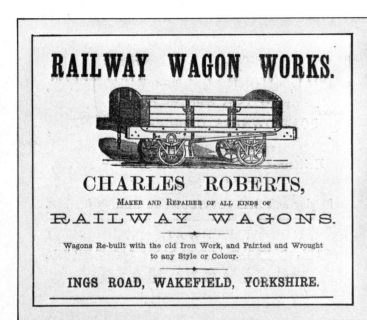

310 Wagon builder's advertisement of 1866.
Charles Roberts & Co Ltd

311 One of the early pieces of railway goods yard mechanisation, the loco crane. *A Wood collection*

310

311

Development of Freight Services to 1900

ALTHOUGH THE railway originated with the mineral business, the commercial railways which spread so quickly after the Liverpool & Manchester success of 1830 were not very eager for freight business; several, such as the London & Birmingham, put it in the hands of an agent, former stage-coach proprietor Horne. However, it was soon seen to be a highly remunerative branch of business and by the end of the nineteenth century there was a complex series of sundries services throughout the country, with 'road vans' doing station-to-station business, numerous direct services on the heavy traffic flows and tranship depots for making fast transits over less popular routes.

With the coming of the Great Northern Railway to London, there was a determined effort to sell coal by rail and the GNR did its own marketing. Coal had hitherto come to the Metropolis by sea and the North London Railway was used by the Northumberland & Durham Coal Company, which had its own engines and wagons, to deliver coal from West India Docks into London suburbs, until it bought out the cuckoo in its nest in 1859. In the eighteen-seventies the Midland became so enthusiastic for the coal business that it helped the District Railway to build a connection from Hammersmith to Ravenscourt Park to get depots on the District at West Kensington and High Street. In 1882 it went further and built a coal depot at Maidstone, 40 miles from its system, on the London, Chatham & Dover line.

Towards the end of the century, with horse-and-cart delivery from stations, small towns vied to be within five miles of the railway and places over 10 miles from the line were thought to be in the wilds; but they were rare — around Hartland Point in Devon and west of the Cheviots in Northumberland in England.

As steam shipping made the import of iron ore cheap the railways had a freight bonanza, with coal for shipment going down to the South Wales ports and ore going back up to the steelworks of Ebbw Vale and Dowlais. Consett began to rely on Swedish ore imported through the Tyne; from the west coast of Cumberland haematite ore went over Stainmore to Durham steelworks and Durham coke passed it on the 1,300ft climb going to the furnaces of Workington.

Despite many unbraked and dumb-buffered wagons in mineral service, the hand-braked 6-ton and 10-ton wagons in Britain offered speedy services, compared with the 10mph or so of the Continent, in the latter part of the 19th century. Trains of 200 tons or so ran at 30mph from London to Exeter on the GWR and the LNWR had some runs nearly as good between London Camden and Stockport. Midland Railway London to Manchester services and Great Eastern Doncaster to London Spitalfields timings came out at 23mph and the Great Northern got the goods from Kings Cross to Liverpool between nine o'clock at night and half-past seven next morning, with 28mph running on the main line to Retford, including stops. For many years the fish and cattle came from Aberdeen to London faster than the passengers!

With British business largely in the brown-paper-parcel category, there were not the opportunities that existed in America for the big bogie wagon and 1,000-ton or more loads, hauled over long distances; such services depended on bigger locomotives, developed with a more generous loading gauge and the universal use of the air brake, where British railways made a grudging application of the vacuum brake to a few thousand of their 1,200,000 wagons used on express freight trains. The British burden of 600,000 private owners wagons had much to do with this.

312 (facing page) An Ivatt class 4 2-6-0 heading a coal train over Ashington viaduct in Northumberland in September 1966.
M J Esau

31.

Twentieth Century Freight Services

BY THE BEGINNING of the twentieth century the depots for handling goods had grown from the 'wharf' of the early railways to a multiplicity of small goods yards set up at frequent intervals over the entire railway system, very often with domestic coal in mind as the principal traffic and with their spacing largely governed by the convenient delivery radius within the compass of a horse and cart. There was a leaven of larger depots between which regular services of sundries traffic were provided, sometimes with the aid of transhipment sheds en route.

Various degrees of sophistication were discernible, coal yards ranged from those without any mechanical aids, beyond a sack-weighing scales to comply with coal delivery regulations, to those where traffic had to be conveyed in hopper-bottom wagons to be dropped into the appropriate merchants' bins. The Midland Railway had a number where the wagons were positioned by electric traversers taking power from overhead wires, an improvement over rope and capstan methods and a considerable step from movement by pinch bar and muscle. Horses were used to move wagons in many depots and to save space in layouts. Turntables were made use of to a considerable degree; as they were usually designed round the dimensions of a 10-ton four-wheeled wagon, they helped to limit wagon sizes and explain the lack of interest in bogie freight stock.

There was discernible about 1920 a period of over-mechanisation, when too many cranes were installed in some depots; the work accomplished did not match the capital expenditure. On the other hand, hand-barrowing, wasteful of manpower and time, was still the rule in many. Scientific investigation of needs, and equipment to provide logically for those needs, was initiated by the LMS in the 1930s. Wagons were placed in depots by wagon-hauling mules and power capstans instead of shunting engines; they were loaded for outward journeys by the collection vehicle circulating in the depot; inwards consignments came on to a narrow platform and were conveyed away to the delivery round vehicles by slat conveyors. Derby St Mary's and Birmingham Lawley Street were made showpieces and many others were used for various experiments, but they were brought to an end by the war of 1939. Classic depots of the period were those rebuilt by the Great Western at such points as Bristol Temple Meads, Wolverhampton and Paddington.

While wagon-load traffic and the return of empty private owners' coal wagons remained a supreme traffic consideration, marshalling yards for wagon sorting,

315

316

317

usually mechanised for operation of points leading to the balloons of sorting sidings and with primary and secondary retarders to reduce the speed of wagons running by gravity off the hump, were vital to operation. The block train concept and the development of the container into the Freightliner has reduced the use of marshalling yards and many built by British Railways in the first flush of modernisation after 1955 have already been abandoned. Slat conveyors or adaptations from moving walkways and gantry cranes for shifting containers sideways to ships and road vehicles seem to be essentials of the late twentieth-century goods depot. One can be sure also that the depots themselves, more productive through mechanisation, will be spaced very much more widely to take advantage of the mobility of motor delivery vehicles.

313 Goods station at Hereford served entirely by horse transport shortly after the turn of the century. *A Wood collection*

314 Modern metamorphosis of the railway yard at Sotteville on the SNCF, now being equipped with automatic control by the French Westinghouse company. *WABCO/Europe*

315 Typical scene at a Freightliner depot with two cranes busy on road-rail container transfer, although rubber-tyred cranes have how largely been replaced in BR service by high-capacity rail-mounted machines. *British Rail*

316 Scene at British Rail's Parkeston Quay, Harwich, land-sea container terminal. *British Transport Films*

317 Half-height containers of china clay being transferred by ordinary mobile crane from road to BR Freightliner wagons for the trunk haul by rail from Par in Cornwall to the London area. *T E Corin*

318 (overleaf top) Shunting a Freightliner train at Heysham in connection with Irish Sea container traffic in 1968. *D Cross*

319 (overleaf bottom) At the British Railways Willesden Freightliner depot 30-ton travelling cranes have lifting heads (spreaders) that are instantaneously adjustable to handle any container of the principal international standard sizes. *I Krause*

318

319

Coal by Rail the Modern Way

COAL IS THE traffic round which the earliest railways were built; they were the most practical way of moving heavy loads in the mines and the track spread the load instead of sinking into the ground as the wheels of common carts did when loaded. But long-distance conveyance of coal from colliery to market took some time to become commonplace — for some years it was a short downhill transit from mine to staith and then shipment by coaster the traditional way to reach London; Midlands works received their coal supplies largely by water also, but in that case by canal barge or narrow boat.

The London & North Western Railway had a snobbish inhibition against carrying coal, ranking it with manure as something to be kept out of the sight of first-class passengers — hence the screens between platforms and goods lines at their typical large stations. A decade passed after the railway reached London before a modest coal depot was built at Camden. The Great Northern on the other hand, when it reached Kings Cross, brash and out to do business wherever it could, opened a depot for the sale of Yorkshire coal in 1851. The general manager's brother, moreover, was the monopolist merchant.

Competition soon brought an end to that and the Midland began to bring Leicestershire coal to London at prices competitive not only with seaborne coal but with the Great Northern's commodity brought from half as far again. With the growth of steam shipping and appreciation all over the world of the virtues of coal as a heating agent, for gas production or the basis of steam power, enormous quantities of coal were moving from mine to factory, to every home and to ports for shipment by the end of the century. It was so cheap and labour so plentiful that no great sophistication developed in its transport. Coal was moved in 6-ton, 8-ton and 10-ton wagons which were mainly supplied by collieries and coal merchants; there were about 600,000 private owners' wagons on railways in

Britain, mainly in the coal trade, and they roughly equalled the numbers supplied by the railway companies. These small units had to be marshalled to return empty to the right collieries and outward to the correct consignees and despite several attempts to suppress the private wagons, traders clung to their rights, established from the pre-steam railway days when the railway was looked upon as a special sort of toll road.

Wagons were cheap to build and their use as warehouses either by coal merchants or by exporters was tolerated undeterred by theories about demurrage charges. Nearly every great port was distinguished by miles of sidings filled with coal wagons awaiting shipment and the railways accepted this as a penalty for handling such vast tonnages; for many years the total carried came to more than 200 million tons, although this figure counts a good deal of tonnage twice as it exchanged from one company to another — crossing London by the widened lines of the Metropolitan and Blackfriars Bridge, en route from the northern companies to the London, Chatham & Dover company's depots, for example. In South Wales alone nearly 60 million tons of coal were raised in the peak years; in 1913, 37 million tons were exported and 11 million tons went through the loading plants at Barry Docks — a record figure for Great Britain — for export.

The horse-and-cart era of delivery from goods and mineral stations set a pattern of small lots, no more than two tons at a time, to domestic and industrial premises and brought about a proliferation of railway depots at frequent intervals along the routes, since the ideal horse haulage radius was thought to be about three miles, with a resultant inefficiency in goods train working. There were 74 goods depots in the London area alone and each of the

320 BR class 37 diesel No D6894 with empty coal hoppers at Sunderland in August 1967. *B Stephenson*

322

northern companies, with the exception of the late-arriving Great Central, secured coal depots south of the river to which they sent their own trains by means of complicated running powers. One Midland establishment was at Maidstone, to which its trains toiled, for a short period, over 42 miles of alien tracks from St Pancras by way of the Metropolitan and London, Chatham & Dover Railways.

The coal wagon gradually increased in size until the 10-ton wagon was commonplace and some owners went nap on 12-tonners. High-sided wagons came into operation in the coke trade, but the biggest types could not get under the colliery screens and coal owners seemed unwilling to invest in improved railway loading arrangements. So although early in the twentieth century several railways were experimenting with 30-ton wagons for general goods, mineral wagons remained of modest size. When after 1920 the Great Western Railway tried to improve coal shipment traffic in South Wales by building 20-ton wagons it became apparent that what they had succeeded in most was arousing the enmity of their customers. Although between 1919 and 1939 much lip-service was paid to the virtues of all wagons in the coal trade being owned by the railway companies, it was not until the 1947 Transport Act that anything positive was done about it, although during both wars steps had been taken by pooling their use to ensure that unnecessary sorting of wagons was curtailed.

Under the 1947 Act the railway companies were nationalised and 585,000 po wagons, mostly for coal, were taken over; as a result the stock issued in compensation was dubbed 'wagon stock' at the Stock Exchange. In the meantime Mr Duncan Bailey of Charles Roberts & Co Ltd, a well-known railway wagon builder, had designed a 16-ton all-steel wagon which would fit into any colliery loading bay and British Railways set about improving on it with 21-ton and 24½-ton wagons, designed to suit more liberally designed colliery screens. A 32-ton hopper was also designed, but as it stood nearly 12 feet above rail level a cut-down version of lower height and only 26 tons capacity was quickly made available, to suit the National Coal Board.

It was in that period that it became increasingly realised that the most satisfactory and economical operation of a railway was obtained by running block trains from colliery sidings to one destination only, without going through a marshalling yard. As far as possible, consistent with the qualities of coal required by the consumer, that is now the pattern of BR coal transport. House coal concentration involves co-operation between National Coal Board, British Railways Board and local coal merchants to provide mechanised plant for dealing with many thousands of tons of fuel a year.

There have been many difficulties. Among them are the

321 Horse-drawn wagons at Blaenavon colliery in South Wales. *D Huntriss*

322 NCB-owned 0-6-0T *Sir John* at Mountain Ash colliery in South Wales in April 1969. *D Huntriss*

323 A BR J27 0-6-0 leaving Sunderland with coal wagons in July 1967. *D Huntriss*

324 BR merry-go-round wagons discharging in the hopper house at Ferrybridge power station. *British Rail*

independence of small coal merchants; the cost of the necessary plant; the shortness of the haul, which allows little in the way of the charge for the traffic to be allocated to paying for the investment; and in some areas, the small demand for coal, which by the nineteen-fifties was meeting active competition from oil fuel and the threatened competition of North Sea gas. Nevertheless it was in 1957 that a start was made by a Sheffield firm, Burnett & Hallamshire Fuel, which made a decision to concentrate all its solid fuel business in the city on a pioneer mechanised handling plant in the Eastern Region Nunnery depot. It was a private venture, as was one the next year put in by Charringtons at Palace Gates in North London as a pilot scheme, which was closely watched by the trade.

Further action was slow to come, but things began moving in 1962, when the Eastern Region persuaded merchants from a large number of stations to take their coal from plant it erected at Enfield Chase. Bulk tipping lorries were provided for delivery to the merchants' own premises, which are run for the railway today by National Carriers Ltd, the company that took over railway collection and delivery fleets under the 1968 Transport Act. This arrangement enabled small wayside coal depots on the main line, such as New Southgate, to be closed, and what is more important, from its benefit in shutting down a costly freight train operation, the night service to be given to the yards on the High Barnet branch, where the passenger service is provided by London Transport electric tube trains. Enfield line depots between Wood Green and Bayford were also closed, with consequent saving in freight train mileage.

Another event in 1962 was the coming together, after much negotiation, of the National Coal Board, the British Railways Board, and the Coal Merchants Federation of Great Britain, in a tripartite agreement which, based on the experience so far obtained, settled the general lines of concentration for the future, but left local details to be cleared up by regional and local committees. As a result coal movement has been rationalised almost everywhere, although not all of it moves in lengthy block trains and not so many mechanised depots have been erected as was at one time hoped.

Mechanical plant is very costly and consequently it requires a reasonably long haul from the coalfield to keep the traffic profitable to British Railways and at the same time to permit some contribution towards the interest on the expenditure, so a big annual throughput is also essential. A typical plant was one of the first to open under the tripartite agreement at West Drayton on the Western Region, where it was bounded by the Frays River and the curve of the West Drayton to Staines branch. It was designed for an annual distribution of 200,000 tons of fuel

325 An 8F 2-8-0 with a long coal train at Peak Forest for Buxton in November 1967. *D Huntriss*

and the 40,000-ton stock provides 23 varieties. The designed daily peak movement is 1,200 tons, or on a weekly basis 6,500 tons. Trains come from the South Wales or the East Midlands coalfields and are composed of 21-ton hopper wagons. The siding layout is simple; the train engine backs the train in to discharge its load into a chamber below the track and the train of empty wagons then proceeds towards London to turn back at a convenient point. A conveyor takes the fuel at 120 tons an hour from the receiving hopper to the selected one of 12 60-ton delivery hoppers or 10 10-ton hoppers. The hoppers feed 46 bagging points where lorries are loaded for the western suburbs of London. A transfer point on the conveyor feeds an automatic boom stacker which takes fuel to the desired part of the 40,000-ton stacking ground. As required the stacker can retrieve the fuel and dispatch it to the delivery hoppers.

At Taunton in 1964 the Western Region opened an interesting combined freight and coal concentration depot, designed to serve by road destinations in the 30-mile radius. The local coal merchants joined in the £300,000 combined investment through Taunton Coal Concentration Ltd. It was intended, on the solid fuel side, to handle up to 500 tons a day, but in the seasonal nature of the coal trade this means about 80,000 tons a year.

To avoid heavy investment in conveyor belts and large hopper structures, some non-mechanised concentration depots have been set up. They are necessary in the green fields areas where block trains are unjustified but the haul from the nearest mechanised depot would be too costly by road. The equipment varies from portable conveyors and digger shovels to plain old-fashioned shovel and muscle power. But there are also manually operated concentration depots in highly urbanised areas where the run from the coalfields brings only small remuneration to the railway and it has been agreed with the coal merchants that while block trains are desirable, heavy investment in plant is not. In the West Midlands it was intended to concentrate the

work of 168 depots in the then Birmingham Division into eight new establishments, but apart from the investment aspect there were environmental reasons for not adopting a size of depot that would have involved annual throughputs of 350,000 tons a year in the heart of the conurbation, with the concomitant congestion of coal delivery lorries in central area streets. A plan was therefore hammered out for use of two dozen smaller depots, designed to pass 40,000 or 50,000 tons of fuel a year as a minimum, or at least two trainloads a week.

Three depots in Birmingham, at Aston, Monument Lane and Lawley Street, opened on November 4, 1963, and Stratford-on-Avon and Leamington Spa followed a week later. The first block coal train to a non-mechanised depot ran on December 2 to Aston, and the entire programme was on its way to completion in about a year. The distance from the pithead to many of these depots is only 15 or 20 miles, making for a low rate out of which to recoup extra investment costs. The depots are under mixed management, but there are also some private depots, such as the one on the Pensnett Industrial Estate (connected with the ancient Pensnett private railway which served the Earl of Dudley's steelworks and collieries) where conveyors take the fuel from undertrack drops to overhead bins from which the lorries are fed. The Pensnett depot also has a railhead for pig-iron to serve Black Country industry from the steelworks at the Ford Motor Company's Dagenham plant.

Coal concentration has enabled wagons to go into intensive circuit working and the regular runs have improved locomotive utilisation. This is exemplified still better in the principal industrial use of coal — in the generating stations of the Central Electricity Generating Board, where despite the rivalry of oil fuel and nuclear power, aided in a small way by paraffin-powered gas turbine plant, the demand for electrical energy is so great that use of coal increased from 34 million tons in 1962 to 66 million tons in 1971, thus compensating to a large

degree for the reduction in domestic demand. A 2,000-megawatt power station, of which six were completed during the last part of the 1960s, will absorb 20,000 tons of coal a day and some are able to accept the output of several collieries. A little of it is waterborne, but a considerable proportion of the coal required comes by rail.

Where possible coal is handled by modern 'no hands' methods, the train running over the generating station hoppers at slow speed and the bottom doors of the hopper wagons being opened automatically by mechanical tripping gear. The unloading equipment is provided by the Generating Board under an agreement signed with British Railways in a glare of publicity at the beginning of 1964. The counterpart of automatic loading into a moving train at the colliery end has been implemented much more slowly by the National Coal Board, which has no doubt taken note of the CEGB endeavours (so far frustrated by teething troubles) to rely to an increasing extent on the commercialisation of nuclear fission. However, the ideal merry-go-round system, with the train not stopping at either end for loading or unloading, is quite practicable, and ensures that maximum utilisation of the wagons is obtained.

The first English merry-go-round at a power station to get off the ground was West Burton, in Nottinghamshire, then the largest coal-fired power station in Europe, with a consumption of about five million tons a year. Trains of up to 50 permanently coupled 46-ton-gross (32 tons of coal) wagons are chute loaded at 14 pits, including for a start the super-modern Bevercotes, and hauled by diesel-electric locomotives to West Burton where, controlled by the signalman in a modern power box, the train enters the merry-go-round loop and the six whole-width bottom doors are automatically opened while the train moves at a steady half-a-mile an hour, despite the diminishing load, under the control of a very precise locomotive speed control. Discharge takes place at a rate of 2,500 tons an hour; although the hopper capacity below the track is only 1,200 tons, the conveyor belts discharge coal into the power station at 3,000 tons an hour. In all, about 50 collieries are involved in 15 merry-go-round schemes, which beside power stations include working to the vast Northfleet cement works in Kent and the Immingham jetty for export coal.

In Scotland the South of Scotland Electricity Board station at Cockenzie was the first to have circuit working, from Monktonhall colliery over part of the Tranent-Cockenzie wagonway, which is so old as to have figured in the official account of the Battle of Prestonpans. There 84 wagons, running in 28-wagon trains, do the work that by the old rule-of-thumb methods would have needed more than 1,500 wagons and at Monktonhall four acres of sidings replace the 250 acres that would have been needed formerly. The wagons on this circuit generate three million ton-miles a year instead of the 22,000 ton-miles of the conventional coal wagon in old-time wagon-load working.

Another interesting railway task is to take import coal of certain specialised grades from port to steelworks; for the block trains to carry it wagons of 50 tons gross weight have been designed, with 25-ton axle-loads — about the maximum that can be sustained in Britain. A new form of friction-damped pedestal suspension has been developed for working the new wagons at 60mph or more. So although the tonnage of coal moved by British Railways was only 107,318,000 in 1971, the prospects of profitability, owing to rationalisation, are bright. There are several factors that help: closing of wayside depots to the tune of over 200 in Greater London alone in 15 years to 1970; consequent movement of block trains to the remaining larger depots; circuit working and merry-go-rounds from colliery to consumer; and maximisation of wagon size with aids to quick discharge. Far from declining, railways show in their handling of coal traffic technological advance and managerial and marketing skills.

326 Modern BR merry-go-round coal train of 32-ton capacity wagons. *I Krause*

327 An ex-BR pannier tank at work at Merthyr Vale colliery in January 1969. *D Huntriss*

328 BR Type 47 diesel-electric locomotive with a block coal train passing Nottingham in March 1972. *I Krause*

327

328

326

SHIPS, ROAD AND AIR

Railways and Dock Ownership

FEAR OF MONOPOLY inhibited Parliament from freely giving powers to railway companies to own port and harbour undertakings, just as it was hesitant to let them become proprietors of steamer services. The logic of a railway and its interface with shipping services being in the same ownership, was most obvious in the case of mineral exports, but the first commercial railway to get into the port business seems to have been the South Eastern in 1843. It probably did it by the side door, as the chairman bought Folkestone Harbour for £18,000 from a speculator-contractor who acquired the silted-up port for £10,000 a few weeks previously. Nevertheless, purchase was sanctioned by an Act of June 27, 1843.

The little St Helens Railway, a coal-exporting line which resulted from an amalgamation of 1845, obtained powers to build Garston Dock in 1846 and was in business there in 1852; the mighty London & North Western first leased the Garston branch and then in 1864 took over the entire undertaking, thus becoming a dock owner. The North Eastern Railway opened Tyne Dock at Jarrow in 1859 for coal shipment; through amalgamation, it took over docks at Hartlepool and it purchased the Hull Dock Company in 1893. Later work at Hull was joint with the Hull & Barnsley Railway (originally the Hull, Barnsley & West Riding Junction Railway and Dock Company when incorporated in 1879 with the eager support of Hull Corporation).

The Great Western contributed money to Millbay Docks at Plymouth in 1846; the Plymouth Dock business was absorbed under the South Devon Act of 1874. The GWR's greatest creation was the new port of Fishguard for the Irish — and in the early days for transatlantic — traffic, opened in 1906. In the latter part of the nineteenth century the Furness Railway opened Devonshire Dock at Barrow in 1867, the Alexandra (Newport & South Wales) Docks & Railway began business in 1875, the Lancashire & Yorkshire opened Wyre Dock, Fleetwood, in 1880, the Great Eastern graduated from Harwich to Parkeston Quay in 1882, the Barry Railway initiated an entirely new port for coal shipment in 1889 and the London & South Western bought Southampton Docks in 1892. But Newhaven, which the London, Brighton & South Coast had power in 1878 to assist financially, did not become Southern property until 1925.

This is by no means all the story; the North British, for example, developed a string of coal-shipping ports round the Fife coast and along the Forth. The Great Central persuaded King George V to open its wonderful new dock at Immingham in 1912 and he dubbed the general manager, Sam Fay, a knight on the quayside in a spontaneous gesture.

Between them the grouped railways owned a great variety of ports and had done wonders in developing many others not in their ownership. Nationalisation allocated them to an Executive of the British Transport Commission and, since 1962, to a separate body, the British Transport Docks Board.

329

329 Harwich Parkeston Quay in the 1960s; the harbour was
founded by the Great Eastern in 1882. *B Coaley*

330 A 1929 picture of the Southern Railway's port of
Southampton, originally bought for railway use by the London &
South Western in 1892. *British Rail*

331 The GWR's Fishguard harbour in 1922, with the company's
hotel on the hill above. *British Rail*

330

331

Railway Ships

PARLIAMENT at one time considered that railway companies should operate railway services and should not own steamers. The matter was considered in depth in 1848 when four railways sought permission to become shipowners, having previously relied on contractors or loosely related concerns. However, at the 1848 hearing powers were granted to the Chester & Holyhead Railway on the grounds that the service to Ireland was the sole reason for a railway to Holyhead and for a steamer connection to be operated by the Furness. The Brighton and the South Western companies were the other applicants; the Brighton proposal was turned down, and afterwards the company was reprimanded for attempting the task through a subsidiary; the LSWR was granted permission for 14 years but did not exercise its rights.

The Chester & Holyhead powers were exercised by the London & North Western Railway. The next successful applicant was the South Eastern in 1853. In the eighteen-sixties there was a spate of grants, namely London Chatham & Dover and the London Brighton & South Coast in 1862; the Great Eastern in 1863; the Manchester Sheffield & Lincolnshire to specified ports across the North Sea in 1864.

The Great Western powers were obtained in 1871 and operation started the next year. Having been granted powers, the Lancashire & Yorkshire purchased the fleet of the North Lancashire Steam Navigation company jointly with the LNWR in 1873, and soon built up a big fleet on the North Sea. The Lancashire & Yorkshire eventually had the largest fleet of the pre-grouping companies, with 28 ships wholly owned and seven joint with the LNWR. Last-comer to the field of railway ship operators was the Midland Railway, which became interested after the purchase of the Belfast & Northern Counties Railway in 1903 and the opening of Heysham habour the following year. To meet the requirements of the French postal service, some London Chatham & Dover ships sailed for a time under the French flag.

The railway ships have maintained high standards of comfort, especially on overnight services such as Parkeston Quay to Hook of Holland; the LC&D made several experiments with double-hulled ships to mitigate the effects of rolling in the Channel and it was the Southern Railway which first applied the Denny-Brown stabiliser commercially, having built 29 new ships in the first ten years of its existence. Previously, the South Eastern & Chatham had been among the first to order turbine-driven vessels, back in 1902. In 1938 the Southern Railway introduced a vessel with Voith-Schneider propellers on the Lymington-Yarmouth service which traverses a sinuous river estuary and precise directional control at low speed is essential.

When the main-line railway companies were vested in the British Transport Commission in 1948, the fleet transferred included 122 ships totalling over 60,000 tons net. The business has been developed as the Shipping and International Services Division of British Railways Board, trading as Sealink. Today, the Sealink fleet includes not only train ferries (developed by the Great Eastern Railway in 1922 for freight and the SR in 1936 for through sleeping car trains from London to Paris and Brussels since the war) but roll-on/roll-off car and lorry ferries, container ships, and passenger/vehicle hovercraft operated by an associate with which tickets are interavailable.

332 The SS *Picard* leaving Tilbury for Dunkerque, from a painting by Norman Wilkinson for the LMS. *British Transport Museum/B Sharpe*

333 London, Chatham & Dover train and ships at Admiralty pier, Dover. *A Wood collection*

334 London & North Western steamer *Cambria* on the Holyhead-Dublin service started by the Chester & Holyhead Railway. *A Wood collection*

335 Midland Railway steamer *Londonderry* for Irish services to and from Heysham. *A Wood collection*

336 Engraving from the *Illustrated London News*, 16 February 1850, of the train ferry operated on the Forth between Granton and Burntisland by the Edinburgh, Perth & Dundee Railway.

337 London & North Western Railway ferry *Hibernia* leaving Dublin North Wall for Holyhead. *A Wood collection*

338 Heysham harbour of the Midland Railway as pictured in a Chown-series postcard in 1913. *A Wood collection*

333

334

335

336

337

338
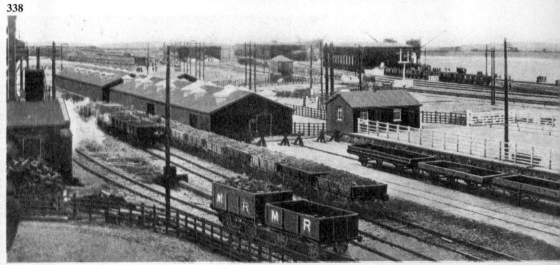

Railways and Road Transport

FROM THEIR beginnings, railways have needed to work co-operatively with road transport, and often to develop specialised means of working efficiently with the universal means of transport and access to premises — the road. On the road, long before the railway era, transport had been organised by stage-coach or mail-coach operators and before that by stage-wagon proprietors; and despite the much-publicised 'foul state of English roads' in the eighteenth century, road transport had also worked to timetable, even if it was one of weeks rather than minutes.

The first commercial railway, the Liverpool & Manchester, gathered passengers to its stations by advertising connecting bus services. When the Great Western terminus opened at Paddington, buses connected the green-fields station with the Bank, and when the GWR suggested a lower bus fare was needed, the railway subsidised the bus service.

After 1835 stage-coach proprietors saw the red light and supported Cort's Anti-Railroad Society, but leading coaching men, such as Chaplin & Horne, soon sold out and invested in railway shares; Chaplin became chairman of the London & South Western and Benjamin Horne became parcels agent of the London & North Western. Despite the ownership of very large collection and delivery fleets and thousands of horses, the railways continued to use numerous independent cartage agents, especially in the autumn peak of sundries traffic.

Freight haulage on the roads was represented by the country carrier, including businesses such as Pickfords, founded 1646, and new town parcels carriers such as Carter Paterson, upstarts of 1860. Pickfords eventually took over Chaplins, by then Southern Railway agents, in 1936.

Railway ownership of motor vehicles began with Great Western's purchase of lorries in 1902; on August 17, 1903 the GWR began a bus service from Helston to The Lizard, where a light railway had been demanded. It had no Parliamentary powers to operate motor buses, but acquired two Milnes-Daimlers which had been operated by the little Lynton & Barnstaple Railway for a few weeks until harried by police; they had dared to go faster than 8mph!

The four grouped railways at last obtained a clear title to operate buses and to engage in freight operation on the road away from the rails in 1928. Instead of competing with existing bus operators they quickly decided to invest (usually not more than 49 per cent) with the established road operators, including four municipal undertakings. In haulage they similarly invested in such firms as Carter Paterson, Pickfords or Wordies, but more usually making outright purchases.

Railway investment in buses was transferred to the British Transport Commission under nationalisation in 1947, but haulage became a responsibility of the Road Haulage Executive; under the 1968 Act the buses operate under the aegis of the National Bus Company, with some railwaymen directors to ensure co-ordination, but even the railway collection and delivery services have gone to the National Freight Corporation with the railway sundries business.

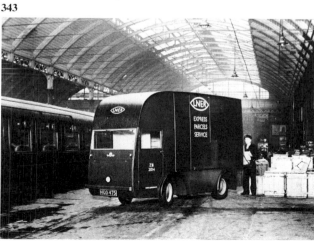

Road Railers

SINCE THE EIGHTEENTH century there has been considerable thought given to devices by which all the virtues of the railway — its ground-load-spreading ability, its smooth riding and low horsepower per ton — could be made available to the handy independent road vehicle in suitable circumstances and a galaxy of inventors and patents can be marshalled to trace a story of both success and failure, but with indifference the most abiding end-product.

The railway had become well established as a necessary adjunct to collieries, lime works and iron works, or wherever heavy haulage was needed, when John Curr began to develop a scheme for common carts to make use of the rails. His enterprise arose from the disgust, leading to riots, with which the people of Sheffield viewed the Duke of Norfolk's attempt to bring coal into the town by rail. It was thought to be an attempt to frustrate users from collecting the coal in their own vehicles from the pithead. The railway, which the duke had commissioned in 1774, was burned. It might well be that John Curr, the duke's manager, wanted to retain both the virtues of a railway and the ability to accommodate customers' own carts. He therefore transferred the flange from the railway wheel to the side of the rail — and so the cast-iron plateway was born in 1776. Curr's designs included run-off rail sections where carts could transfer from rail to road and vice-versa. He also devised switch-plates that made railway junctions possible.

Charles E Lee, in *Evolution of Railways*, has pointed out that the plateway was intended to provide a highway for flat-tyred vehicles that were required to make part of their journey by ordinary road. There seems to be little evidence that plateways were, in fact, used in tthat way by common carts; so many of them had narrow gauges, especially in the Midlands and Wales (down to 1ft 6in), that such use would have been quite impracticable. More than that, regulations framed by the world's first public railway, the Surrey Iron Railway of 1801, and by others, seemed to prevent ordinary carts from using the plateways, although Parliament made toll regulations in the spirit that railways and plateways were merely a particular form of toll road.

Plateways with flanged rails enjoyed a vogue lasting only about a quarter of a century and although locomotives were used on some, the fragile nature of cast-iron tram plates caused many to be discarded or to be relaid with edge rails for flanged wheels. The pattern had been set by Trevithick's engine of 1804, which scored a notable triumph for steam traction and a sad day for tram plates on its notable journey from Penydarren Ironworks to the canal wharf at Abercynon.

It is therefore of distinct interest that in 1885 the whole question was raised afresh by the promoters of the

339 A Southern Railway 5-ton lorry being loaded from rail wagons in 1929. *British Rail*

340 Complete train of BR Roadrailer vans on trial on the Cambridge-Newmarket line. *British Rail*

341 Early railway mechanical transport – a steam wagon of the LNWR in North Wales. *A Wood collection*

342 British Rail's Scammell 'mechanical horse' and trailer for local deliveries.

343 A 1-ton battery-electric van produced by Crompton Parkinson for the LNER in 1947. *British Rail*

Bessbrook & Newry Railway in Northern Ireland. The line was 3ft gauge, taking electric current from a third rail, except at level crossings, where short lengths of overhead conductor intervened. The rails were of great interest, however, as bracketed alongside them were flat plates on which ran four-wheeled carts hauled by the electric rail-cars. The reason was that the line was primarily an industrial railway to serve a linen mill at Bessbrook and freight had to be collected by road from several points in Newry and then delivered to the factory and vice versa. On the run between town and plant the carts were coupled to the electric cars and the plain wheels of the carts were guided by the electric railway rails standing ⅞in proud of the flat plates on which the carts ran. The scheme was designed by Henry Barcroft of Bessbrook Spinning Company.

There were a number of other attempts to combine rail and road tracks, but most of the later inventiveness in this field has been devoted to making permanent adaptations of road vehicles to run on rails and to making road and rail wheels quickly interchangeable so that a road vehicle can take advantage of the low rolling resistance of the rail for a fast journey over the trunk portion of a route.

There have been several schemes in which vehicles ran upon either a single-rail or double-rail track (for low rolling resistance) but were driven by road wheels (for the better tractive adhesion). The driving wheels were steel-tyred in the nineteenth century and rubber-tyred in more recent years. The Larmanjat system using a single rail to carry the vehicles and road wheels for balance and traction, originated in France and a most elaborate system was intended for Lisbon. The Manchester company Sharp, Stewart built a locomotive running on double-flanged wheels on leading and trailing bogies and steel road wheels for driving. It was tried on a line set out in the fringes of Epping Forest and seems to have disappeared into limbo.

A system designed for South Africa was first recorded as using a Dennis-engined tractor in 1912, when introduced by Colonel F Dutton, motor transport superintendent of the South African Railways; it blossomed 12 years later at Wembley Exhibition, after General Stronach had developed the system as the Stronach-Dutton through Roadrail Loco-Tractors Ltd. The system was based on a 2ft gauge rail track flanked by parallel strips of road surface for pneumatic-tyred driving wheels. The Wembley installation demonstrated two Sentinel steam tractors or locomotives and four petrol-engined tractors. Converts to the necessary belief in the economy of this form of

road/rail co-operation were few — the cost of laying a road plus a railway was not considered justified by the potential advantages when viewed in the light of the flexibility of ordinary road transport and the growing efficiency of the 2ft-gauge railways with which South Africa was already liberally provided.

Sixty years ago there began a cult of adapting road vehicles to run on railways by the simple expedient of changing the road wheels for flanged railway wheels. The Caledonian Railway was a leader in the practice; having purchased an Arrol-Johnston with an archaic charabanc body, which did not prosper as a road vehicle, the company transferred it in 1911 to the Connel Ferry railway bridge on the Ballachulish branch and operated it on a shuttle service from Connel Ferry to North Connel, giving it a new lease of life on flanged wheels. In that guise it saved pedestrians a boat trip across the mouth of Loch Etive by the reversible falls, which change direction with the ebb and flow of the tide; by attaching a light trailer to carry motor cars, it saved motorists the 96-mile run from one side of Loch Etive to the other via Glencoe. The service became so popular that when the Arrol-Johnston wore out a road was made alongside the rails on the Connel Ferry bridge. Cars had to be signalled in between the occasional trains because of the tight clearances.

It is difficult today to realise that the Act for a Trans-Canada Highway was passed only in 1949, that the route was not completed until 1964, and that as recently as 1951 the road passage of the Rocky Mountains over miles of washboard gravel was considered an adventure, shrouded in dust in dry weather and daunting through mud in wet spells. In those circumstances it is not surprising that determined motorists with something near the standard 4ft 8½in track on their cars should have taken to flanged wheels and with the approval of the railways, motored into British Columbia over the Canadian Pacific and Canadian Northern tracks. Elsewhere many uses for converted motor cars were found; South African Railways bought Austin Sevens in the 1920s for conversion to 3ft 6in-gauge inspection cars by Wickham of Ware, for example.

At home the North Eastern Railway, a pioneer of motor bus operation on the roads, had a yen for the use of road vehicles on rails. It resulted eventually, under LNER auspices, in a 26-seat Leyland bus on flanged wheels which plied between York and Strensall for some years from 1924. Steps were provided to allow passengers at low-

344

platform halts to mount or alight. The idea was copied across the Irish Sea, but there the Great Northern of Ireland used AEC single-deck buses (the first had 24 seats and the second 31) with Gardner diesel engines, and Howden-Meredith wheels which permitted use of existing road wheels on rail track simply by enclosing the pneumatic tyre in a flanged wheel rim. Among other advantages it added to comfort. One was placed in service on the Scarva-Banbridge connecting link, enabling a line closed in 1933 to be re-opened the following year. Similar vehicles were converted at Dundalk for use on the Sligo, Leitrim & Northern Counties Railway and on the Dundalk, Newry & Greenore (LMS-owned) line. The County Donegal Joint lines (3ft gauge), owned by the Great Northern and the LMS (Northern Counties Committee), saw the use of several steel-tyred bus-type vehicles converted to run on rails, starting off with one converted from standard gauge which had inaugurated the Ford back-to-back railcar period on the Derwent Valley Light Railway in Yorkshire.

The back-to-back railcars began life in the 1923 period as the brainchild of Colonel H F Stephens, who horrified his commercial assistants by using adaptations of Ford Model T one-ton trucks and building austerity coachwork at an East Anglian bodybuilders. They were supplied to the Kent & East Sussex, Selsey, and Shropshire & Montgomeryshire lines and seem to have succeeded in frightening off the remaining passenger traffic. The author's memory of a journey in 1927 from Llanymynych to Shrewsbury serves as an awful warning how not to popularise rail travel — the harsh attack of the wheels on every railjoint, the groaning transmission in the front car (the second unit ran dead when going backwards), the rolling on the Ford transverse front spring, and the agonies of a wooden seat endured for nearly 20 miles of violent pitching and rolling must have tested many a Salopian heart. It is not surprising that the competition of a local busman had run the S & M passenger service to a standstill by 1933.

From the early vehicle conversions, and especially those that combined pneumatic tyre and flanged wheel, it is not a far cry to the vehicle that would be equally at home on rail and road. Much thought has been devoted to such a concept in Britain, the United States and Germany, but the opportunities for application appear to have been much more restricted than were at one time thought likely. Karrier Motors Ltd, then at Huddersfield, was encouraged by John Shearman, road motor engineer of the London Midland & Scottish Railway, to build a road/rail vehicle. The almost conventional bus bodywork of the day, to seat 26, was by Cravens Railway Carriage and Wagon Co Ltd, of Sheffield; the flanged wheels were by Lang Wheel Company and the road wheels by Goodyear. Two bars across the radiator carried railway-type buffers and a towing hook before railway operators were satisfied that the Ro-railer, as it was named, would not be an obstructive nuisance if it suffered a failure. They made a bizarre contrast to the road licence plate, UR 7924. The vehicle was registered in Hertfordshire as the first public demonstration of its versatility was given at Redbourn in that county.

The nub of the Ro-railer design was the eccentric gear which could take the road wheels from their normal position for road use at the ends of the axles into a retracted position, thus permitting the railway wheels to be guided by the rails and flanges. A prepared stretch of road raised to the level of the rail heads was necessary so as to put the railway wheels in contact with and lined up with the rails. The changeover either way could be carried out in less than 2½ minutes. The prototype vehicle had doors on each side amidships so as to serve railway platforms, but steps were provided for road use. Measuring 26ft by 7ft 5½in, it was pointed out that a three-axle double-deck bus or a 10-ton goods vehicle could equally well be adapted to the system. The overall gear ratio was 7 to 1 for road use, with a 60mph top speed and consumption of eight miles per gallon of petrol, and 4.2 to 1 for rail operation giving 75mph top speed and 16 miles to the gallon. The wheel arrangement made the Ro-railer about 3½in higher as a road vehicle than when on the track.

Little imagination or enterprise appear to have been shown in putting the prototype to work and its operation did not arouse much enthusiasm with the LMS hierarchy; so far as is known the Ro-railer was not tried on any of the

344 Lowering the road wheels of a BR Roadrailer by hydraulic power. *British Rail*

345 BR Roadrailer adapter bogie to couple the first vehicle in the train to the locomotive. *British Rail*

346 The prototype 1930 Karrier Ro-Railer for the LMS had eccentric gear for switching between road and rail wheel use. *Chrysler Corporation*

347 Mobile hydraulic power was used to change running modes between road and rail on the BR Roadrailer. *British Rail*

348 Modern adaptation of a standard bus to rail operation – the Sadler railcar. *F L Pugh*

many possibilities foreseen by Shearman — projection of country branch services right into the villages they were intended to benefit, weekend reliefs and excursions with road cruises between seaside resorts or across picturesque country, and many others. Eventually it mouldered in the Commer-Karrier company's yard at Luton. The vast LMS was unable to organise its use in the light of the licences required by the Road Traffic Act 1930, and the attitude of its new partners, the bus companies.

It has to be confessed that none of the other users of Ro-railer devices made much of them; the most notable was the projection of some suburban tram or light railway facilities around Rotterdam beyond the end of the track. The London & North Eastern Railway took delivery of a Karrier Ro-railer freight vehicle which was used to transport permanent-way material by road to parts of the West Highland line and so avoid track occupancy on long single-track sections. The distances between road access points made the ability to run on rails most useful.

There have been both American and German variations on the Ro-railer theme. In the USA and Canada the Evans Auto-railer surrounded the bus wheels with a four-wheeled railway bogie and had some popularity in the nineteen-thirties. Unhappily the Arlington & Fairfax Railroad experience was all too common. This inter-urban electric line on the fringes of Washington, DC, embraced the petrol-engined Auto-railer, took down its overhead wires and sold off its ageing electric railcars. The line, in the fashion of inter-urbans in the horse-and-buggy days, sailed past most of the villages it was intended to serve at some distance. The hybrid replacements of the electric cars ran to a grade crossing, became road buses, served a village and came back to the railroad tracks for the run to the next place that the tracks did not serve. A year or two seems to have passed before the owning company realised that with a straightforward road bus there would be no track-maintenance costs, no time wasted changing from railcar to road bus, and a much more direct run out from Washington. The universality of the purely road vehicle argues strongly in its favour.

In the 1930s the prospects of providing a door-to-door freight facility with the Ro-railer were neglected, but they were taken up afresh by the Pressed Steel Company comparatively recently. Rather regrettably, it was not a revival of interest in the Karrier patent, but was engendered by a British Railways visit to see the Chesapeake & Ohio company's Railvan device in the fifties. As developed here, the Roadrailer equipment of British Road Services (later operated by British Roadrailer

Services Ltd) had compressed-air operation of the retracting equipment and each single-axle vehicle was designed to run on the road as a conventional semi-trailer; on the railway they were coupled Talgo-fashion to an adapter wagon which followed the locomotive.

By the time the 51 vehicles built had had the bugs ironed out of them on the East Coast main line, where they were intended to work London to Edinburgh, injudicious handling of the trade union situation resulted in them being banned by the National Union of Railwaymen, along with the nascent Freightliner express container train. It was sad that when the ban was lifted, authority left the Roadrailer vehicles to langsish in a shed at Peterborough without commercial trial, on the ground that the net payload was less efficient than Freightliner and container operation. Had further development been carried out the situation might have been reversed as a number of firms had promised their support with consignments. The costly crane facilities of Freightliner depots would, of course, be unnecessary with Roadrailers.

The striking fact of the present situation on transporting road vehicles by rail is that the greatest use is made in America of piggyback and similar methods by which road vehicles are carried on railway flat trucks. In the USA numerous tunnels have had the invert lowered so as to afford greater headroom for the lorry trailers and this has presumably been a paying investment. The slightly tighter European loading gauge has resulted in the use of pockets in the wagon floors to accept the rear wheels of road semi-trailers at the lowest possible height and such 'kangaroo' services operate on established traffic flows. Here again, a movement which began in Britain has seen little recent development. The trailer-building firm of R A Dyson, of Liverpool, provided large numbers of drawbar trailers with milk tanks specially designed for placing on six-wheeled flat wagons on railways in Britain, clear of our very restricted loading gauge. The LMS method of carrying edible oils in insulated road-rail tanks put two semi-trailers on a six-wheeled railway underframe and practically anticipated the Continental kangaroo system.

Another road/rail device, developed in the 1950s and used fairly extensively in France in the 1950s is the UFR system. It uses specially prepared railway wagons provided with strong raves along the sides to make a continuous support which engages flanged wheel-like projections mounted outside the road wheels and the landing legs of normal semi-trailers; they provide a ready means of entraining the road vehicles and a safe anchorage for them in transit.

Besides the freight side of carrying road vehicles by rail, there is good business in the entraining of motor cars either for delivery for the motor trade or for private owners. Car-sleeper trains operate on most of the well-defined holiday car routes in Europe and in some cases all the year round (and by day without the complication of sleeping car facilities) on routes where businessmen welcome the relief from driving fatigue but want the benefit of their own motor vehicle at the far end. Special rail wagons of the double-deck type have been evolved to make an economical carrying unit and in America three-tier car carriers are in operation on a number of routes where the height of overhead structures is sufficient.

From time to time special railways have been mooted for carrying cars sideways-on over popular routes which would require vehicles 15ft or more wide. A 10ft gauge railway for the purpose has been proposed for a north-south route in Western Germany. In America the Westinghouse group a decade ago was advocating a novel method of drive for the big railway vehicles involved by such a proposal; fixed motored wheels in the middle of the track would start rotating on the approach of a vehicle and by friction give it a roll onward. The economics of the provision of such a number of driving wheels for an occasional passing vehicle are difficult to present in a favourable light. So far conventional 4ft 8½in railway vehicles seem to hold the advantage.

In France, Germany, Italy and Switzerland it is fairly common practice for industrial works to have railway sidings but no connection physically with the railway system. The railway wagons are delivered by road vehicle — a method not open to manufacturers in Britain because of our normal 32-ton weight limit on road vehicles. What the pollutionist lobby would say about 'juggernauts' if railway wagons on road trailers were a common sight in British streets can be imagined.

349 A LNWR motor bus on Watford-area services in 1906. *Topical Press Agency*

350 A LNWR horse bus on London services around the turn of the century. *British Rail*

349

350

Railways and Buses

THERE HAS ALWAYS been a tendency to think of the bus as a main rival of the railway but this is not wholly true. It has often been used by the railways themselves to supplement facilities, to test new territories or, in recent years, to replace lines that do not pay. It is often suggested also that the railways in their development ruined the stage-coach business, as well as canal traffic, both freight and passenger. That view overlooks the participation by a number of stage-coach owners in railway financing and how much of the railway traffic was due to the attraction of the facility and so was in fact of new generation.

In fact the siting of many stations at some distance from the centres of the towns they were intended to serve led to the development during the nineteenth century of many local horse-bus services. Some were instigated by the railways and aided by subsidy in one form or another and a few were provided by railway companies themselves directly or through contractors. With the advent of mechanical transport, however, many of the railways found that they had no legal powers to work such services and that, even if they sought them, they were not always easy to obtain. In a few cases the necessary steps were taken and in other cases it was decided to press ahead and operate services regardless of the lack of powers and to hope for the best.

As it happened the need had tended to diminish so far as local transport was concerned because of the development of street tramways. Although using horse or steam traction initially, electricity was more and more widely employed as the twentieth century progressed, both for the conversion of existing systems and for newly constructed ones. Railway companies in Britain mostly eschewed tramway operation on their own account, although there were the Burton & Ashby electric service of the Midland Railway, the Cruden Bay line — short but also electric — of the Great North of Scotland and the South Eastern's horse line between Hythe and Sandgate, to cite a few examples.

Roughly a score of railways had introduced motor buses in the British Isles by 1910, although, in truth, several had been so discouraged by the results that they had again abandoned their bus services before then. But a few had really taken up bus operation seriously. Most notably they were the Great Western Railway, the London & North Western Railway, the London & South Western Railway, the Great North of Scotland Railway and, in one respect uniquely, the Great Eastern Railway. The distinction of

351 A painting by C Hamilton Ellis of an LNWR bus in Watford High Street. *British Transport Museum/B Sharpe*

352 A Milnes-Daimler bus of the Lancashire & Yorkshire Railway. *British Rail*

353 Buses built and operated by the Great Eastern Railway at Lowestoft in July 1904. *British Transport Museum*

354 A Great Western 22-seat Milnes-Daimler bus on the Helston-Lizard service in August 1903. *British Rail*

355 A Guy bus of the GWR in 1929, used on the London inter-station service started that year. *Ian Allan Library*

the last-named was that it was the only railway to build its own complete buses. Not surprisingly several made use of their carriage works to provide bodies but only the GER went the whole hog, producing a dozen vehicles in all to a particularly robust design.

After starting a service in Cornwall between Helston and The Lizard on August 17, 1903, with two second-hand Milnes-Daimler wagonettes, the Great Western had about 300 buses on 168 services when its operations were at their peak at the beginning of 1929. The original motor vehicles emanated from a company which was a subsidiary of the narrow-gauge Lynton & Barnstaple Railway, which had used them to replace a horse-coach service between Ilfracombe and its station at Blackmoor the previous June, but had found local prejudice and police antipathy insuperable and therefore sold the vehicles. The GWR service was intended to sample the traffic possibilities of a light railway, for which there was strong local demand, and there is some significance in the fact that the railway never materialised. A similar reason lay behind several of the other services which were started and traffic was sometimes so sparse in the upshot that even bus operation, let alone a railway, could not be justified. A second service, from Penzance to Newlyn and Marazion was begun on October 31, 1903, and soon afterwards it was decided to develop the service and an order for 30 Milnes-Daimlers was placed in 1904.

Some of the routes begun in the early days remain today in original or extended form as testimonials to the perspicacity of their railway initiators. That from Wolverhampton to Bridgnorth was started in November 1904, and transferred to Wolverhampton Corporation on July 1, 1923. It passed in turn, with the rest of that undertaking's operations, to the West Midlands Passenger Transport Executive. The Penzance-Lands End and Penzance-St Just routes, which have been a Western National responsibility for more than 40 years, were both started by the GWR in 1904, a year which saw also the commencement of a Slough - Beaconsfield service.

In common with the other three mainline railway companies, the Great Western Railway obtained comprehensive road transport powers under its Act of 1928, which brought about a considerable change in its policy so far as passenger transport was concerned. It should, however, be stressed that it had previously taken a number of chances to reach agreement with major bus operators in various parts of its territory. In little over three years almost all the former GWR services had passed to operators in which the railway had a financial interest, although one of the last, that from Slough to Beaconsfield, was handed over to London General Country Services Ltd. Last of all to go was the Weymouth to Wyke Regis service, worked by the railway on its own behalf and that of the Southern Railway, which passed to the Southern National

356 A Thornycroft 36-seat bus of the LNER used in the Aberdeen area. *British Leyland Motor Corporation*

bus company on January 1, 1934.

It has already been mentioned that the London & North Western Railway was among the more ambitious operators of motor buses, which perhaps was only right since it had been a substantial operator of horse-bus services in the latter part of the nineteenth century. Its routes were, however, developed more slowly than those of the GWR and when what proved subsequently to have been the peak was reached in the summer of 1914 there were 40 vehicles at 6 depots. In fact 20 were at Watford, 9 at Llandudno Junction, 5 at Mold, 3 at Brownhills, 2 at Holyhead and 1 at Tring. In some cases buses were out-stationed, as for example those from Watford used on the Boxmoor Station-Hemel Hempstead service, which called normally for one bus and a standby. This service, extended in 1929 from Hemel Hempstead to Harpenden as a railway branch-line replacement, and that between Tring and Tring Station were to endure and to pass in due course to the London Passenger Transport Board.

What might be termed the true Watford workings had, in fact, begun to disappear before the 1914-18 war. The Watford - Harrow service, started in the summer of 1906, was given up eight years later when the London General Omnibus Co Ltd began a new route between South Harrow and Watford, although the services from Harrow to Harrow-on-the-Hill and to Pinner were maintained. They did not reappear after the war and it is only in quite

recent times that a bus service up the hill in Harrow has been revived. Most of the other LNWR services at Watford, such as that to Croxley Green, which had replaced a horse-bus service in 1906, and routes to Garston, Boxmoor and Hemel Hempstead, were covered by the LGOC in 1920 and from the following year were operated on its behalf by the National Omnibus & Transport Co Ltd.

As already indicated, these were by no means the only North Western services. Those in North Wales, which employed 16 vehicles in 1914, started in July 1905 with the Connahs Quay-Mold route, followed three months later by the service between Holywell town and its station which involved the then somewhat fearsome gradient of 1 in 9. The vehicles were later impressed for war service and the routes lapsed so far as their operation by the railway company was concerned.

The London Midland & Scottish Railway, as heir to the LNWR and to some degree the Midland Railway, was relatively passive in its earlier years but indulged in quite a flurry of bus-service expansion in 1928-29, through acquisition of a number of existing operators and the starting of various new services on its own account. At the same time it was, as were the other main line railways, negotiating the acquisition of interests in existing bus businesses and by 1931 most of its own services had passed to associated companies or corporations. The latter

151

constituted an aspect of interest which was followed also by the London & North Eastern Railway but not by the GWR nor the Southern Railway; it involved the establishment of joint committees. The LMSR was concerned on its own account with joint committees at Huddersfield and Todmorden and jointly with the LNER in those at Halifax and Sheffield. The two railways also bought jointly the Hebble bus business based in Halifax and a substantial interest in the Scottish Motor Traction Co Ltd.

Predecessors of the LNER were among the earliest railway operators of motor buses, with the North Eastern Railway starting a service between Beverley and Beeford as early as September 1903, the Great North of Scotland a 17-mile route from Ballater to Braemar — a lengthy service in those days — on May 2, 1904, and the Great Eastern a Lowestoft - Southwold operation in June of the same year. Nor were they the end of their ambitions and the GN of S had added a further 80 miles of bus routes within the next three years, which were to be maintained and expanded until they passed to an associate company in 1930. The original North Eastern route, which had been extended to Brandesburton, was abandoned in 1925, but other services that were opened in County Durham and developed steadily, had been augmented by the purchase of existing businesses, so that quite substantial operations passed to United Automobile Services and Northern General Transport at the beginning of 1930.

As was indicated earlier, the unusual feature of Great Eastern Railway bus operation was that it employed 12 vehicles of its own make. The routes were somewhat scattered, save for a group around Chelmsford begun on September 9, 1905, and transferred to the National Steam Car Co Ltd, as it then was, in July 1913. Earlier that year the original Lowestoft-Southwold service had passed to United Automobile Services, but the last routes to go survived into the nineteen-twenties and included one of the best known from Ipswich to Shotley, which was taken over by the original Eastern Counties company in April 1922.

The London & South Western Railway, which has already been mentioned, began a long service from Exeter to Chagford (19 miles) on June 1, 1904; it was suspended for the winter, but resumed the following summer,

thereafter to be maintained more or less uninterruptedly until it was sold in Southern Railway days in 1924. The railway's other main service from Farnham to Haslemere was worked for it for a year by contractors, John I. Thornycroft & Co Ltd, which built the bus. The results encouraged the railway to buy the vehicle and work the route itself from 1906. Seven years later it was handed over to the Aldershot & District Traction Co Ltd.

Reference should also be made to the Metropolitan Railway which, after being a sizeable horse-bus operator in London (though in later years at least mostly through contractors) appeared with motor buses in the Watford area on November 1, 1927, starting a service linking the High Street with the Watford (Met & GC) station which had been opened two years earlier. Because of inability to obtain road transport powers, operation was transferred to an associated company. Most of the other motor bus exercises by railways in Great Britain were on a fairly small scale and often, for one reason or another, of short duration. But there should be a mention of the Cambrian Railway, which inaugurated a Pwllheli-Nevin route in June 1906 with two Orion buses and maintained it, although with different vehicles, until its sale to the Nevin & District Omnibus Company early in 1913.

Railway bus operation in Ireland has, in general, been far more enduring than in Great Britain and attention has often been called to the fact that one of the few profit-making railway companies in the world — the Londonderry & Lough Swilly — achieves that result without working any trains. It was not, however, by any means the first of the Irish railways to take to the motor bus and the Belfast & Northern Counties actually instituted a steam-bus service between Whiteabbey and Greenisland in April 1902 and continued it until 1913; by then, for nearly nine years, it had been the Northern Counties Committee of the Midland Railway. An NCC-initiated service at Cushendall endured from 1905 to 1913 and in the south of Ireland the Great Southern & Western indulged in a certain amount of touring coach operation. The NCC, apart from one or two rather tentative efforts such as a Ballymena - Portglenone route in 1919, remained quiet until it obtained full road powers in 1927. From then on its development was rapid, so that it had no fewer than 130 buses when its services passed to the Northern Ireland Road Transport Board on October 1, 1935.

The Belfast & County Down had 14 buses which were taken over at the same time and its operations had originated with a service from Kilkeel to Newcastle (County Down) introduced on August 1, 1916. Crewing of the bus and its actual operation was by contract at the outset. The Great Northern Railway (Ireland) was in a different situation as it was working both sides of the border from the time its services started in 1929. All but certain cross-border services in Northern Ireland went to the NIRTB, with 50 or so buses, but the routes in what was then Eire were to remain the railway's responsibility for a further 23 years. About 180 vehicles passed to Coras Iompair Eireann, itself, of course, a railway undertaking as successor to the Great Southern Railways, when it absorbed its share of the Great Northern Railway Board on October 1, 1958. The GNR had, moreover, indulged in the construction of its own vehicles — fitting them with Gardner diesel engines — and about 70 of the buses passed to CIE. The Great Southern Railways based its development largely on its acquisition of the Irish Omnibus Company in 1933 after working in association with that company for six years. Partly by purchase, the IOC had built up an extensive network of services and there were comprehensive arrangements for ticket inter-availability between road and rail. Since then bus services have continued to grow and CIE, which is responsible also for Dublin city services, has over 2,000 buses.

357   358

359

357 A GWR Maudsley 'all-weather' coach in 1929, employed mainly on seaside tours. *Ian Allan Library*

358 A 1941 GNR-Gardner bus with a 1950 body at Letterkenny station on the Londonderry & Lough Swilly railway. *J F Parke*

359 AEC Regal coach of the Great Southern Railway (Ireland), used on tours. *British Leyland Motor Corporation*

Outside the British Isles the degree to which railways have taken part in bus operation, both horse and motor, has varied a good deal. In North America, particularly the United States, there have generally been legal obstacles to such participation and in Europe there are many variations in practice. In the Netherlands, operation in recent years has been through a series of subsidiary companies with which there is a great deal of co-operation; in Belgium the Belgian National Railways has used contractors and the SNCV (Vicinaux), which once had many and still has a few light railways, has a substantial bus fleet of its own which covers former tram routes as well as many others. It can be said that the railways are the largest bus operators in Austria, Denmark, Luxembourg (apart from the city undertaking), Norway and Sweden, and the German Federal Railway also has a very substantial fleet. French practice favours the use of contractors although there are various groups around the country which are based historically on light railway systems that operated in various departments.

The part played by railways in developing many overseas countries is well known and as the reliability of the motorbus improved it came more and more to share in that work. This has been the case particularly in New Zealand and South Africa where, although the railways do not have a monopoly, they are providers of very extensive road services and of tours. Smaller-scale operations by comparison, but nonetheless important, are those of the Mozambique Harbours, Railways and Transport undertaking, the Rhodesia Railways and the East African Railways and Harbours. In something of a contrast the Indian railways generally kept clear of bus operation, although in Hyderabad HEH the Nizam's State Railway began to develop bus services after it took control of the undertaking in 1930 and had built up quite a network of routes by the time that its operations passed to the appropriate regional undertaking.

Bus operation by railways themselves might have passed its zenith, but it has certainly had a substantial effect on services as they are today.

361

360

362

363

364

365

360 Town-service buses alongside the platform at Cullera station in Spain. *J R Batts*

361 SNCF bus on Paris inter-station service at Paris Austerlitz station. *J R Batts*

362 Albion country-service bus of East African Railways and Harbours. *East African Railways*

363 Crossley articulated bus in service with Netherlands Railways in Amsterdam in 1946. *J F Parke*

364 Modern Guy two-class bus operated by Rhodesia Railways. *British Leyland Motor Corporation*

365 Bedford bus of New Zealand Railways in service at Paihia in Northland. *J F Parke*

Railways Take to the Air

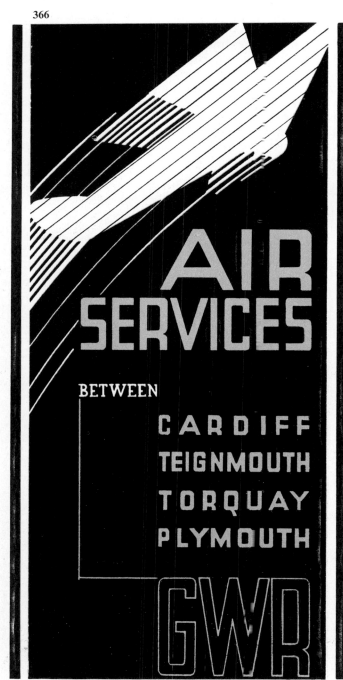

366 Cover of the Great Western Railway air service timetable of 1933. *J F Parke*

367 Several Junkers Ju52/3ms were used by BEA on ex-railway air services, but the one pictured, at Speke, was the only one to appear in RAS livery. *J F Parke*

ENTRY INTO air transport operation was managed more scientifically by the four main-line railway companies than the methods by which their predecessors had gained ownership of steamers and ports. The cloud no bigger than a man's hand, the first public air service from Hounslow to Paris, had appeared on the railway horizon in 1919; at first it was met with some of the same scepticism that American citizens displayed for some years after 1903 about whether the Wright Brothers had actually left the ground in a heavier-than-air machine.

However, it was soon plain that the new transport medium had high potential for making inroads into railway traffic, so, following the previous session's success in obtaining railway road powers, each of the four grouped companies promoted an Air Transport Bill in 1929; the Acts received the Royal Assent on May 10, 1929.

The Southern made an agreement with Imperial Airways for a shareholding interest but some time passed before much advantage was taken of the powers. Then on April 12, 1933, the Great Western Railway began a service from Plymouth to Torquay, Teignmouth and Cardiff, with aircraft hired from Imperial. On May 22 it was extended to Birmingham. In the meantime, on April 27, the Southern appointed a committee of directors to 'consider with the general manager the company's attitude towards aerial transport and to what extent, if at all, aeroplanes might be used in conjunction with railway services'. First action was to order a report from Norman, Muntz & Dawbarn, the consultants.

Early in 1934 the grouped railways joined Imperial Airways in forming Railway Air Services Ltd, with a capital of £50,000. In March, Sir Herbert Walker, general manager of the Southern, had arranged with Captain H Balfour, MP, chairman of Spartan Air Lines Ltd, to share receipts and expenses on a London-Isle of Wight service, on which the deficit for 1934 was estimated to be £2,880. This service was supervised by Railway Air Services and the GWR service was taken over and extended to run from Plymouth to Liverpool. Soon RAS was running from Croydon to Glasgow, but via the Isle of Man and Belfast. From August 20, 1934, it carried the mails.

In the days of 10-seat aircraft (Imperial operated 38-seaters on its London-Paris flights) RAS made a lot of progress through the drive and energy of K. W. C. Grand, afterwards to be general manager of the Western Region of BR and chairman of Coast Lines, and John (now Sir John) Elliot, later chairman of the Railway Executive and of London Transport. With Coast Lines (by coincidence) also a shareholder in RAS, that company provided much of the planning and know-how used after 1946 by British European Airways, by which Railway Air Services and its associates were eventually taken over. Its chairman was Sir Harold Hartley of the LMS Railway.

The SR consultants came up with many ideas that in a swiftly changing industry must seem old-fashioned, including strong support of Langstone Harbour as a flying-boat base, but they keenly advocated Gatwick as a rail-air interface. The Southern made another not-so-happy concession to an airport scheme, building a station at Lullingstone in 1939 for the great London air terminal that never arrived, because of the changes brought about by the 1939 war.

368 RAS (ex-Southern Air Services) and Spartan timetable of the mid-1930s. *J F Parke*

369 One of a fleet of 8-seat DH Dragons used by RAS, before the 1939-45 war, on Liverpool-Birmingham-Cardiff-Plymouth and Birmingham-Bristol-Isle of Wight services. *Richard Riding*

370 One of fourteen Avro 19s used by RAS on routes from Croydon to Dublin, Isle of Man and Belfast from 1945 until they were taken over by BEA in February 1949.

371 Great Western & Southern Air Lines DH89 Dragon Rapide in wartime camouflage paint, at Lands End on Scilly Isles service. *J F Parke*

372 Smart De Havilland DH86 Dragon in RAS livery, pictured at Croydon. *Hawker Siddeley Ltd*

373 One of Spartan Air Lines' three 8-passenger Spartan Cruiser IIIs, which in 1935 supplemented the same operator's earlier Cruiser IIs on the twice-daily return services between Croydon and Cowes. *Richard Riding*

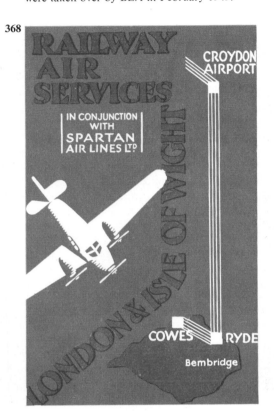

368

369

370

371

373

372

TRAIN OPERATION

Planning the Timetable

ONE OF THE MOST fascinating aspects of railway working is the complex task of preparing and publishing the timetable. In any large industrial undertaking production planning is an essential part of the business process and this is particularly so in the railway industry. Here the commodity produced— rail transport — is not normally a single standard unit, but a wide range of individual items embracing high-speed inter-city expresses, heavily loaded commuter trains and various types of freight working. The job of a train planning organisation is to co-ordinate the use of various resources — the track, signalling, stations, yards, locomotives, passenger stock, crews, wagons — so as to produce a passenger and freight timetable plan to meet the requirements of the railway's customers. They are also responsible for the production of both the public and internal railway working timetables and supporting publications, such as locomotive and coaching stock programmes, which are the means of communicating to the railway staff concerned the detailed information necessary to keep the trains on the move.

Since the business of a railway is to convey passengers and to move freight, the first stage of timetable planning is the basic commercial decision regarding the level of service to be provided. While the probable requirements of passengers can be fairly easily established, because of the nature of much of today's rail freight movement — bulk trains of cement, oil, steel, coal and high-speed Freightliner container services — finalisation of freight train schedules involves close consultation with the individual companies concerned.

Preliminary planning of passenger train services usually starts with analyses of ticket sales and train loadings, which are considered against estimates of the future level of business from certain passenger stations and on the trains in the service. From this data the commercial department defines the outline of the type of service to be offered. The outline would include: frequency of service on weekdays, Saturdays and Sundays; the time of first and last trains; selection of intermediate stops; average speed and journey time; train formation; proportion of first- and second-class accommodation; and type of catering. With the basic commercial requirements agreed, work can start in the train planning department on the first draft of the timetable.

There are many factors which affect the running of a train — the power of the locomotive and weight of the

374 and 375 Decorative covers of early timetables from the Great Western Railway and the London & South Western Railway. *Ian Allan Ltd*

376 Part of a BR Western Region timetable planning graph; it covers Saturday trains over a two-hour midday period for the Paddington-Reading section of the London Division. *British Rail*

374

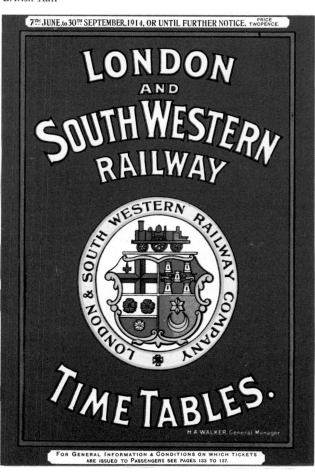

375

376

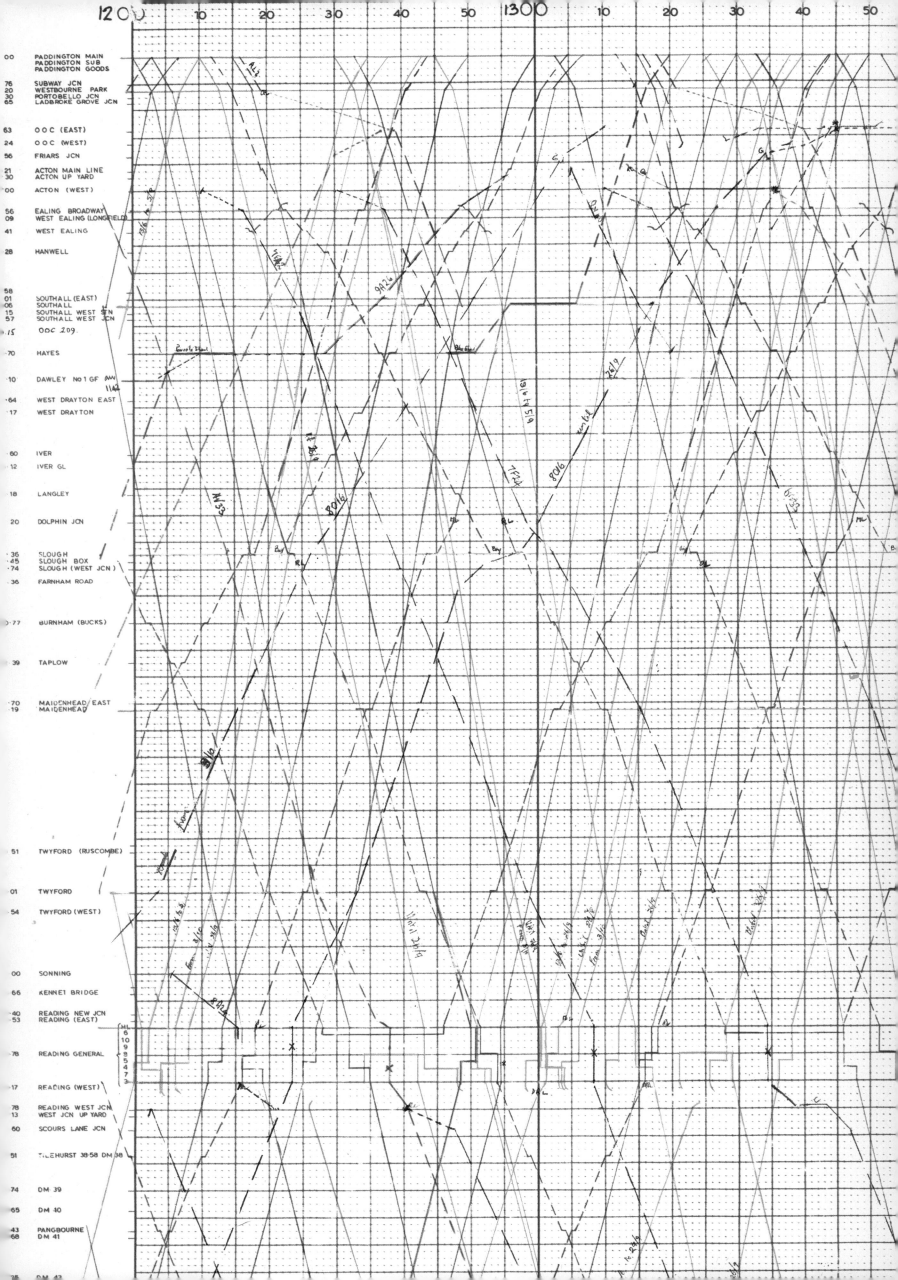

00	PADDINGTON MAIN
	PADDINGTON SUB
	PADDINGTON GOODS
76	SUBWAY JCN
20	WESTBOURNE PARK
30	PORTOBELLO JCN
65	LADBROKE GROVE JCN
63	O O C (EAST)
24	O O C (WEST)
56	FRIARS JCN
21	ACTON MAIN LINE
30	ACTON UP YARD
00	ACTON (WEST)
56	EALING BROADWAY
09	WEST EALING (LONGFIELD)
41	WEST EALING
28	HANWELL
58	
01	SOUTHALL (EAST)
05	SOUTHALL
15	SOUTHALL WEST STN
57	SOUTHALL WEST JCN
15	OOC 209.
70	HAYES
10	DAWLEY No 1 GF
64	WEST DRAYTON EAST
17	WEST DRAYTON
60	IVER
12	IVER GL
18	LANGLEY
20	DOLPHIN JCN
36	SLOUGH
45	SLOUGH BOX
74	SLOUGH (WEST JCN)
36	FARNHAM ROAD
77	BURNHAM (BUCKS)
39	TAPLOW
70	MAIDENHEAD EAST
19	MAIDENHEAD
51	TWYFORD (RUSCOMBE)
01	TWYFORD
54	TWYFORD (WEST)
00	SONNING
66	KENNET BRIDGE
40	READING NEW JCN
53	READING (EAST)
78	READING GENERAL
17	READING (WEST)
78	READING WEST JCN
13	WEST JCN UP YARD
60	SCOURS LANE JCN
51	TILEHURST 38-58 DM 38
74	DM 39
65	DM 40
43	PANGBOURNE
68	DM 41

377 Poster timetable of the South Eastern Railway for 1846.
British Transport Museum/B Sharpe

378 Poster timetable of a new service of the SER, issued in 1884.
British Transport Museum/B Sharpe

train, the maximum permitted speed on each section of route, the type of signalling governing the headways between successive trains and so on — so the train planning staff first settle the basic timetable data for each service. This would usually include: train timing based on power/weight ratio; additional recovery allowances to be added to schedules to offset the effect of temporary engineering work on the route; signalling; station allowances; focal point on which service is to be planned and principal connections. In addition the type of traction power, availability of crews and provision of rolling stock has also to be settled.

All the basic data required for train planning is of course established. The motive power department has on record point-to-point running times for each type of locomotive hauling varying train loads covering the entire system. Compared with steam power, where the performance of the locomotive depended on the quality of the coal and the physical efforts of the fireman, running times for electric or diesel locomotives can be calculated with much greater precision. The signalling characteristics of each route, which sets the headways necessary between trains, are also known to the planning staff. From the foregoing commercial and operating considerations train planning can then proceed.

Before describing the techniques of train planning and timetable production it would be helpful briefly to outline the scope and function of this part of a railway organisation. Past experience has shown that train planning activity is best organised on a centralised basis. The consultation necessary if the timing of trains is divided between different offices slows down the administrative process; also, as rolling stock is programmed to run not only throughout a railway region but, if circumstances dictate, anywhere in the country, centralised planning is an advantage. On British Railways today each of the five railway regions has its own centralised train planning organisation forming part of the chief movements manager's organisation. The largest of BR's five train planning offices is that for the London Midland Region located at Crewe. Over 200 people work on the planning and production of the London Midland Region timetable.

Broadly, the work covers the preparation of all train service details, programming of rolling stock and crews and the forward planning of new projects. Organisational arrangements vary on European railways, but most also seem to favour a centralised approach.

Despite the development of computer techniques and sundry trials and demonstrations, the traditional method of timing on a large graph is still used. A train graph consists of a time scale along the top from left to right and a distance scale, representing a specific section of line, along the side. In addition to the distance scale a plan of the track layouts, junctions, loops and stations is also set out on the left-hand side of the graph. Lines representing the position and progress of individual trains are plotted on the graph in accordance with the point-to-point running times. The lines drawn on the graph vary for different types of train, and different colours are sometimes used to identify trains running on fast or relief tracks.

Simple graphical presentation has many advantages. The capacity of any section of route can be seen at a glance and the situation at junctions or stations, where trains have to cross other tracks and possibly conflict with the passage of other movements, can be quickly assessed. The position at large passenger stations and freight yards is a particularly important part of the timetable plan, since no purpose would be achieved if a path for a train was established from say Crewe to Euston if no platform was available to receive the train at the proposed arrival time. The availability and occupation of platforms at large stations is sometimes worked out on a bar chart graph in association with the main train graph.

Although the feasibility of a proposed timetable plan is verified by plotting the paths for the trains on the graph, certain preparatory work is of course possible in advance. For example, the departure times of the principal inter-city services from large centres such as London, Manchester, Liverpool, Edinburgh, Bristol and so on can be settled at an early stage of the basic planning. As is the case on almost all main routes on BR, departure times from starting stations are standardised for particular destinations — on the hour from Euston to Manchester or Liverpool, 10 and 40 minutes past for Birmingham, five

minutes past for the North West and Scotland, for example — and as the paths for fastest trains have obviously to be allocated at first, the skeleton outline of the most important train times is decided prior to the graphing stage. The importance and value of the train graph occurs at the second stage, when track space has to be found for the many less important passenger and freight trains.

Preparation of a train graph thus starts with the plotting of the paths of the principal inter-city trains. Then follow stopping passenger trains, particularly those that have to be timed to connect with express services at certain stations. But although express services are usually given priority, it is not always the case; for example, city terminals often have to cope with the simultaneous requirements of homegoing commuters and the early evening inter-city trains for businessmen returning to the provinces.

A simple principle of timetabling is that a greater number of trains can be run over a section of line if they all travel at equal or near equal speed — a classic example is the London Transport underground where as many as 40 trains an hour can be worked at 1½-minute intervals on a given section, but only because they all stop at reasonably equally spaced stations and run at similar speed. Conversely, if the trains out of Kings Cross just mentioned were timed to depart in any order, without regard to the speed or sequence of stops, an absurd situation would ensue with fast trains forced to dawdle behind slow trains and wasting valuable line capacity. Hence, the grouping of trains in flights — railway operators call it the correct speed mix — is a widely used timetabling tactic.

As the timing and scheduling of each group of express trains is finalised, the train graphs for the sections of route are built up, showing the planner at a glance whether track capacity is being allocated efficiently and train timings are feasible.

With the important stage of planning of passenger trains completed, work will start on timing the slower — but no less vital — freight services. Compared with the situation 15 or even 10 years ago, the basic tempo of freight train operation on BR, and on many other railways, has drastically changed. Today a substantial volume of freight is moved in block trains running at speeds up to a maximum of 75mph. There is less of a problem running the fast freight services at night but slower freight trains continue to create timing problems at all times of day.

There is an interesting train timing situation on the West Coast main line between Crewe and Carlisle in the night hours. Between 23.30 and 04.30 no fewer than 18 trains — overnight sleeping car services; newspaper, postal and parcels trains; company freight trains and Freightliner services — have to be accommodated over the long two-track section of route on the climb up to Shap summit. Sleeper trains must not reach their destinations unduly early — passengers would not wish to be turned out of their berths at say 04.00 — and it is possible to run them on timings similar to the express freights. But the 45mph freight trains are difficult to work into the train graph paths. They are obviously allocated paths on relief lines wherever possible, but on two-track sections it is often necessary for slow freights to stand in loops or sidings and wait for a path to the next loop behind a group of faster trains.

Train timing is a continuing process and work on the next, or even the next but one, timetable is in progress before the current timetable year is brought into effect. To reduce the very high costs of timetable production BR opted several years back for an annual timetable to run from May each year, instead of separate books for the summer and winter periods. A year-round timetable only

became possible after a majority of inter-city routes were put on to fixed-interval timings and the one-time steep peak of July and August holiday train demand was blunted by the rise in air and road travel.

To ensure that the timetable is completed in time for implementation, the production of the timetable is itself strictly phased and controlled by a production schedule plan. Plans for the May 1973 timetable were already being considered before the May 1972 service had started. In fact, 1972-73 was an unusually complex year for BR timetable planning as the completion date for the extension of electrification over the West Coast route from Weaver Junction to Glasgow approaches. To avoid consequential extensive changes, the train services on the London Midland Region, and those on the inter-regional NE-SW route from Bristol and Cardiff through Birmingham to Lancashire, the West Riding and the North East, were already planned to fit in with the proposed 1974 Glasgow electric main-line service.

Timetable planning is not concerned only with use of the track. Among other equally important resources of the railway to be considered is, of course, the provision of rolling stock, locomotives and train crews. Simply stated, every train planned needs a set of carriages or wagons, a locomotive and a crew, and these requirements must be given due weight as part of the timetable production process. No separate part of the basic planning can be undertaken in isolation and the first ideas for even small changes to a service have to take account of the availability of passenger stock and locomotives. In practice the availability is established at the outset although not necessarily in finalised detailed form.

A simple case in point is the passenger stock situation of the LMR Euston-Manchester-Liverpool electrified service. On this route the utilisation of stock has reached a level of efficiency unheard of in steam days — many sets of stock run four single journeys each day and cover regular daily distances of nearly 800 miles. Other train sets only complete three or two trips. So when it was recently agreed to meet a public need for early-morning trains to get businessmen to their destination by 09.30, involving departures around 07.00, there was no stock problem as the additional early journeys could be programmed by bringing trains into service earlier than previously.

In contrast, an additional train in the middle of the day when all of the train sets are fully employed could mean the provision of an additional set of stock, which might or might not be economic. The situation is also true of

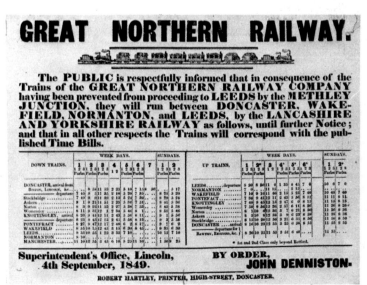

379 Great Northern Railway 1849 poster notifying changes to its published timetable, probably caused by an inter-company squabble. *British Transport Museum/B Sharpe*

locomotives. A planning factor for the 1970 Anglo-Scottish acceleration over the West Coast route, by double heading trains on fast timings with pairs of Class 50 diesel locomotives, was the availability of additional locomotives. As the peak employment period for Class 50s was at night, additional utilisation could be programmed during the daytime hours.

The magnitude of the programming side of train planning can be seen from the workload of the sections dealing with rolling stock allocation in the regional office at Crewe. There the detailed daily plan of work for around 1,000 diesel locomotives, 250 electric locomotives, and over 2,000 diesel and electrical multiple-unit vehicles and around 5,300 passenger coaches is produced. Systems for working out the daily programmes vary but are less formalised than the techniques of graphing train movements. In certain cases, where a fleet of special trains or locomotives is used exclusively for a special train service, it is often helpful to plan the use of the fleet on a bar chart graph, so that the actual hours in traffic of each separate unit can be seen at a glance and opportunities for further utilisation can be readily identified.

As an example, the programme of work for the 22 Deltic diesel locomotives working on the East Coast route is planned on that method; since the speed and performance of the Deltics are higher than the rest of the Eastern Region traction fleet, the programming of Deltics is settled at the outset when changes to the service are contemplated. There is a similar situation with the 10 Turbotrain sets on the Paris-Caen-Cherbourg route of French National Railways.

Locomotive programme and train crew work rosters are finalised and circulated to the various depots throughout the railway. Generally speaking — as can be seen from the accompanying illustrations — the detailed information is set out in tabular form. Various factors in preparing locomotive programmes have to be considered including suitability of the locomotive for the route, availability of crews authorised to drive that type of locomotive on that route, and the requirements for fuelling and maintenance.

Programming of locomotives and rolling stock is one of the most rewarding parts of the timetable production exercise and calls for a high degree of expertise. Staff involved in the work can see the results of their efforts where, by a judicious reshuffle of work programmes, they can provide for a number of additional trains by better use of the existing fleet. In order to make the best use of a fleet of locomotives or passenger train sets it is often necessary to arrange complicated cycles of work covering a wide geographical area for several consecutive days.

380 A London Midland Region timing clerk using graphs in timetable planning at Rail House, Crewe. *British Rail*

380

Slip Coaches

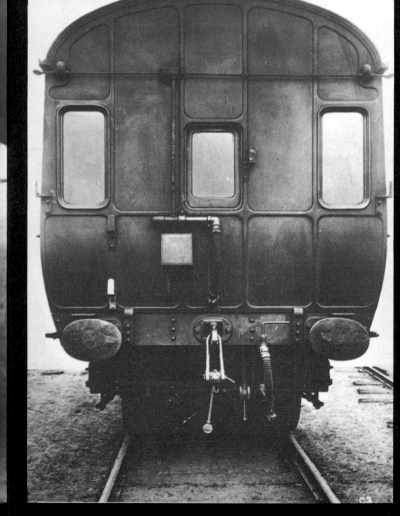

A RAILWAY OPERATING practice which had a considerable vogue up to World War I but gradually disappeared between the wars and is now almost forgotten was that of slipping coaches. In the 1850s it occurred to some fertile brains that non-stop runs might be extended and services thereby expedited if passengers could be set down at intermediate stations without stopping the main trains. To put this into practice it would be necessary to provide a specially equipped coach carrying a guard competent to uncouple it from the rear end of the main train at a short distance before the slipping station and bring it to rest at the station by the use of the coach brakes.

Obviously this could be a one-way service only; no-one ever succeeded in devising a method whereby a coach or coaches could be propelled out of a station on to the back of a passing express, but such a process would hardly commend itself from the safety point of view! In later years, as wages increased, it was realised that the use of a special guard to perform the slipping operation was an unjustifiable expense. For example, a train such as the Great Western Railway Cornish Riviera Express, with three separate slip portions for a number of years, needed four guards; but to this we will come in a moment.

The earliest slipping on record was performed between 1840 and 1849 on the London & Blackwall Railway; this line at first was worked by rope haulage, and coaches were detached from the moving rope at all stations between Mile End and Blackwall. But in 1849 steam locomotives superseded this unique method of working, and from then on the trains stopped at all stations.

The London Brighton & South Coast Railway appears to have been responsible for the first main-line slip-coach service. In its issue of December 11, 1858, *Herapath's Railway and Commercial Journal* contained the following item of news: 'A plan of dropping passenger carriages without pulling up the train or lessening its speed has been practised all the summer on the Brighton Railway. It is done by having a detent at one extremity of the draw-bolt chain, with a rope attached thereto, and passed to the guard at the head of the part of the train to be left. About half a mile or so before the train reaches the station at which the carriages are to be left, the guard pulls the rope, draws up the detent, and releases the carriages, which, by their impetus, run up to the station, and are there stopped by the brake.' Curiously enough, this quotation formed part of an article attacking the venturesome proposal of a certain Frenchman to attempt to attach coaches to trains in motion.

381 A slip in action; Ocean Mail coaches being slipped at 69mph at Bedminster. *British Rail*

382 Slip coupling and brake controls at guard's position at the front of slipped coach. *British Rail*

383 Outside detail of a GWR slip coach. *British Rail*

383

The LBSCR train concerned was the 16.00 from London Bridge to Brighton, which in order not to interrupt a non-stop run slipped a coach or coaches at Haywards Heath to be worked to Lewes. In the same year, 1858, the Great Western Railway, which was to become the principal British exponent of the art, from December in that year began slipping broad-gauge coaches at Slough and Banbury. By 1875 the number of slips detached daily in Great Britain had risen to 88, by 1890 to 122, by 1908 to 178 and by 1914, just before the outbreak of the war, to exactly 200. As just mentioned, the Great Western Railway took the lead, with 79 slips daily in 1908; in 1883 the Great Northern Railway temporarily assumed the lead, with 30 slips daily in that year as compared with the Great Western's 27; the Brighton total rose to 27 slips daily in 1914; and the Midland and Great Eastern Railways both attained totals of 25, the former in 1888 and the latter in 1904.

The most remarkable feature of slip coach working was that, although it was safeguarded in various ways — such as the substitution of a stop at the slipping station in the event of fog or falling snow — in actual fact it was in direct contravention of the rules of block signalling, for after the detachment of the slip two trains in effect were running at speed in the same block section. For that reason the slip guard was instructed to apply the hand-brake lightly immediately before uncoupling the coach(es) and then, when a fair-sized gap had opened up between the slip section and the main train, to release the brake until the point came at which to apply the air or vacuum brake to stop.

The only recorded case of a slip portion running into the main train after detachment occurred at Marks Tey, on the Great Eastern Railway; fog had descended unexpectedly, and when an adverse signal halted the main train at Marks Tey, the slip could not be stopped in time and ran into it.

In course of time slip coach equipment became more-or-less standardised. The coupling hook at the slipping end of the coach (at both ends, in some of the later Great Western and London & North Western double-ended slip coaches) was hinged; the coupling of the rear coach of the main train rested in it, the point of the hook being firmly held by a sliding bar which could be moved by a lever in the slip guard's compartment. Provision had to be made for sealing the compressed-air or the vacuum pipes of the continuous brakes at the moment of severance. With the Westinghouse brake the slip guard could operate the cock on the rear of the main train by pulling a cord. Latterly with the vacuum brake an appliance joining the two brake hose-pipes together automatically sealed the vacuum on the main train as the hoses parted, while cocks were provided for sealing the air or vacuum on the slip coach manually.

As the express approached the slipping station, the slip guard would begin to make preparations. First came the sealing of the air or vacuum of the brakes; if this was not done, when the interconnecting brake hose-pipes came apart automatically both sections of the train would come to a stand, as railway brakes are designed to come on automatically if a fault occurs in air or vacuum supply. Next would follow the light application of the slip guard's hand-brake, and then, at a distance from the station varying with the speed of the train, gradients and other factors, he would pull the lever releasing the hinge of the coupling hook. A bell on the front of the slip coach was provided to enable the guard to give warning of approach to any permanent way men or others who might step unthinkingly onto the track after the passage of the express. The slip would be brought to rest at the platform using the hand-brake or the continuous brake operating on air or vacuum in the coach reservoir.

As just mentioned, the distance from a station at which

384

a slip was detached varied with local conditions, and demanded in some cases very fine judgment. One of the most unsuitable stations in the entire country for such a practice was Accrington, on the Lancashire & Yorkshire Railway, at the foot of a 1 in 40 descent, and round a curve so sharp that a man had to be stationed at a point on the platform where he could see both ends in order to signal to the driver that the slip really had come off his train; in fact, at the low speed at which the train (the 16.25 from Salford to Colne) was able to travel, the slip was not detached until the train was actually running alongside the platform.

Much the same thing happened at Reading, on the Great Western, where the speed of up trains slipping coaches had to be reduced so that they could take the loop off the up main line to reach the platform. The GWR installed a special distant signal at Reading Main West Junction to show drivers of the slip-coach expresses that were going to run through the platform loop to slip that the track was clear back on to the main line at the far end of the station.

A limit was usually set to the number of coaches which could be slipped at any one time, but occasionally it extended to quite substantial portions of the expresses concerned. In the years before the 1914-18 war, during the summer season the Great Western 11.50 from Paddington to Torbay slipped at Taunton a complete four-coach train, restaurant car included, for Ilfracombe. Even more striking were the Great Western expresses which carried two or more slip portions, and most notable of all, of

384 A coupled slip coach showing pipe connections and chains to keep them clear of the track. *British Rail*

385 Detail of the special hinged slip coupling hook. *British Rail*

course, the Cornish Riviera Express. For many years the Riviera slipped two coaches at Westbury for Weymouth, one each for both Minehead and Ilfracombe at Taunton, and one or two at Exeter for Torbay (or later for Kingsbridge). Thus for the first 95 miles of the run six coaches were depending on the leading slip coupling; while beyond Exeter, without the express having made any intermediate stop, it was reduced to little over half the weight with which it left Paddington.

Another GWR express with three slip portions before reaching its first stop (Birmingham) was the 16.00 from Paddington to Birkenhead, which dropped slip coaches at Bicester, Banbury and Leamington; yet a third was the 18.10 to Birmingham, but in that case the first two slips, at Bicester and Banbury, were separated from the third, at Lapworth, by a stop at Leamington.

So that signalmen and others could check that slip portions had not broken away from the main train during a journey, standard tail signals were devised. On the rear of a single slip portion there was carried a pair of lamps, red and white, made conspicuous in the daytime by being encircled with red and white discs; the lamps were carried side by side. If the train was to detach two slips in succession, however, the rear one would carry similar coloured lamps and discs one above the other. For the rare cases of three slips on the one train, the rear slip carried a triangle of disc-encircled lamps, two red and one white. Including the main train, therefore, a three-slip train would start the journey with no fewer than eight tail-lamps!

After the opening of the shortened Great Western route to Birmingham, via Bicester, so that most of the down expresses could compete on level terms with the London & North Western two-hour Euston-Birmingham service, it was necessary for the GWR also to make the run non-stop. Slip coaches made it possible to serve both Banbury and Leamington with the Birmingham trains, but in the up direction, with passengers wanting to board the train rather than alight, the same places could only be connected with London by stopping the expresses. The result was that in general all the up GWR times in steam days were longer than those in the down direction.

Reference has been made already to the argument against the practice of slipping coaches that each slip required to have its own guard. There were other disadvantages also. One of considerable importance was that when a slip-fitted coach was marshalled in a corridor train, its blank leading end interrupted the through corridor. To the end of its slipping days, the Great Western Railway never varied its practice in that respect, but just before the outbreak of the 1914-18 war the London & North Western Railway built the first vestibuled slip coaches in the country, mainly so that passengers in the coach to be slipped (at Coventry) should be able to obtain meals and refreshments. But passengers had to be careful to get back into their slip coach before the gangways were disconnected and the coach was detached! At about the same time the Midland Railway also invested in a few vestibuled slip coaches, but no other railway followed suit.

One remarkable slip coach working that certainly did not last until later years was found in the Great Western timetables from 1866 to 1868. A through broad-gauge morning train from Windsor to the Metropolitan line dropped a slip coach at Westbourne Park, destined for Paddington. The coach continued under its own momentum behind the main train until sufficient distance had opened out between the two for the Bishops Road signalman to shift the points between the two. The slip coach then drifted into its Paddington arrival platform, where it was due three minutes after the main train had stopped at Bishops Road. The only advantage to passengers in the slip was that their coach stopped opposite the cab rank, but why they could not be expected to walk over the bridge from Bishops Road is an unexplained mystery!

In the heyday of slipping practically every railway in Great Britain and Ireland operated a certain number of slips, even down to and including the 15in-gauge Ravenglass & Eskdale, on which between 1921 and 1924 a down train from Ravenglass to Dalegarth slipped a coach at Irton Road by the simple expedient of the guard of the main train leaning over the back of the rear open coach and pulling the pin out of the coupling!

By the middle 1930s slip coaches had almost disappeared from British metals save on the Great Western Railway, which still operated 29 of them. One or two even came back into use after the 1939-45 war, including the Westbury slip of the Cornish Riviera Limited. But their operating economics worsened and the end was inevitable; it came about on September 9, 1960, when the last slip coach in Britain was detached at Bicester from the 17.10 from Paddington to Wolverhampton.

So closed a fascinating chapter in British railway history. One or two Continental railways experimented with slip coaches, notably the Western Railway of France in 1934 at Motteville and Bréauté-Beuzeville from a Saturdays-only Paris - Le Havre non-stop express, but all such experiments were short-lived, and the practice is very unlikely to be revived.

British Stations

THE EARLY British railway company directors knew that passenger stations in the larger towns enhanced the company's 'image', and all the more if the premises incorporated the company's headquarters or other offices. Pleasing, dignified and solid buildings also suggested reliability in what was soon to prove an age of mushroom concerns in the Railway Mania of the 1840s.

The station buildings of the first Liverpool & Manchester Railway terminus at Crown Street, Liverpool, were a solid structure and the company lavished money on the celebrated Moorish Arch (shown in so many early prints) across the cutting. The L&MR Manchester terminus at Liverpool Road, part of which remains today, likewise is a solid structure of good design. They were far eclipsed, however, by the Euston terminus (1837) of the London & Birmingham, now, including the world-famous Doric Arch entrance to the forecourt, totally demolished. The site is covered by the new Euston — a structure for which few have much enthusiasm. Although intended to be functional, it is not really modern architecture and many users complain that it is inconvenient. Largely because of lack of common sense in local planning, British Railways was prevented from building a tower block of offices over the terminus, which would have earned money from letting and at the same time eased London street congestion by affording work-places for many commuters who travel to and from Euston by train.

The original plan for Euston, soon abandoned, was for London & Bristol Railway trains to use a structure to the west of the site, matching the London & Birmingham buildings and trainshed. Other glories of Euston were the Great Hall and the adjacent spacious L&BR (and later London & North Western) headquarters offices. They were — and rightly — believed to epitomise the railway. That did not stop the L&NWR later in the century — and rather uncharacteristically — from blocking the view of the Doric Arch from the Euston Road by building its hotel block — in a bid for extra revenue.

The Euston buildings, like most station buildings of the 1840s and 1850s, were in one or other of the classical styles, or composite of several, or an adaptation of a classical style to the English (or Scottish) idiom. The standard was high. Exploring railways throughout Great Britain, you can still find remnants of 'Early Railway' style station architecture of 1830-60. Some are incorporated in later, often shoddier, buildings; some form parts of freight depots or have been converted into warehouses or offices.

The 1830-60 period was one of good architecture: Southwark (now part of London Bridge), Brighton, Chester Central with its fine frontage, the magnificent Newcastle Central and two London termini — Kings Cross (1852) and Fenchurch Street (as rebuilt in 1853). Kings Cross combines the fine engineering of the twin train-sheds with the splendid façade and the dignified, particularly British, architecture of the station buildings. Fenchurch Street façade is at present marred by a canopy in front, but work is now well under way in clearing the mess and building a new booking hall which will be pleasing in a modest steel-and-glass way and low enough and positioned to set off the façade to advantage. Fenchurch Street facade is at present marred by a canopy of later date, but one may hope that some day the original elegant canopy over the pavement will be restored. The elegant frontage at Cambridge has been restored (but Oxford station was a mean structure until its recent rebuilding; it is now modest and well-mannered).

386 London Kings Cross (1852), illustrating the particularly British architecture of the period. *British Transport Museum/B Sharpe*

387 The world-famous Euston entrance (1837), now no more. *A Wood collection*

388 Fenchurch Street platforms after the rebuilding in 1853, probably about 1900. *Ian Allan Library*

389 The new Euston (1968). *I Krause*

390 Main entrance of the new Waterloo station when it was opened by Queen Mary in March 1922. *Topical Press Agency*

391 Waterloo station approaches in the 1960s. *I Krause*

The Gothic revival was at first mainly an epidemic affecting ecclesiastical and allied (school, for instance) buildings largely because it was associated with pious and charitable uses. When it caught on with railway stations it did so like wildfire. An early example is Bristol Temple Meads, with its trainshed with Gothic beam roof. The greatest Gothic station of them all is Gilbert Scott's St Pancras, opened in 1869, with associated hotel (now offices) and the great span of the trainshed. St Pancras is a complete monument, even to the wooden panelling in the booking hall, let alone the 'gas-pipe Gothic' marble shafts of pillars in the hotel and the elaborate window tracery. Even Somerstown freight depot, across the road to the west, tries to conform. No wonder that preservationists fear that St Pancras might share the fate of the old Euston. It seems unlikely, for plans for combining St Pancras and Kings Cross have proved to be impracticable from the engineering aspect; the amount of traffic along the old Midland line is still increasing, demolition of the trainshed and massive hotel block would be difficult and costly, the Government is aware of the aesthetic significance and there is pressure for retention on environmental grounds.

The latter half of the century saw Gothic station buildings spawning everywhere, mostly in bastard styles much inferior to St Pancras. Even wayside stations, such as an early one in the eighteen-fifties at Battle on the South Eastern line to Hastings, were Gothic in contrast to the dignified yellow-brick architecture of any Great Northern stations, medium and small. As though a compliment to St Pancras, Glasgow St Enoch, the Glasgow & South Western terminus of the joint Midland and G&SWR Anglo-Scottish route, has (or had) a Gothic air. Many other Scottish stations, though not the more recent, have Gothic overtones, and some, like Perth, the former Dundee West and Stirling, suggest 'Scottish Baronial'. Even timber buildings, such as the early wayside station buildings of the South Eastern, can have charm or, at least, good manners. The corrugated iron that began to be used in new stations, especially on light railways in the 1890s, has always been an abomination.

The uninspiring blocks that front Charing Cross and Cannon Street (or what remains of it) date from the 1860s. Also of that era are the London Chatham & Dover's St Pauls (now Blackfriars, being reconstructed, and recently still bearing on its façade the names of Continental destinations that could be reached by LC&DR boat trains and steamers). From that time onwards, architects began to adopt French Renaissance and a variety of styles for stations, although the new trend overlapped the slow decline of the Gothic revival. A heterogeneous variety includes, in London, the two Victorias, the London & Brighton terminus and, cheek by jowl, the 'South Eastern & Chatham and Great Western' erection of the early 20th century, monument to an uneasy railway partnership that never came to fruition, apart from a Victoria to Birmingam Snow Hill GWR express and a few local trains.

By the end of the century railway boards had begun to feel that 'there is no money in passenger stations'. That is why the Great Central's turn-of-the-century Marylebone terminus is a mean building, not atoned for by the huge Hotel Great Central, today the headquarters of British Railways. Even so, during the closing years of the last century and the Edwardian era some big (though perhaps not beautiful or even pleasing) buildings for big stations were completed: Glasgow Central for example — a remarkable instance of participation by the Caledonian Railway in urban development — to the benefit of the railway passenger and railwayman, perhaps rather than the generality of citizens and visitors to Glasgow. It was one of the first to include offices and shops for letting.

There were also Birmingham Snow Hill, Cardiff General and Aberdeen Joint, the GCR stations at Leicester

and Nottingham and Dover Marine, and the start on the meanest of all big British stations — the rebuilt Waterloo. Only pictures can give an idea of the variety of styles. The architects employed by the railways had lost their ability to design anything distinctive. There is no really outstanding architecture in any large British passenger station designed since St Pancras — which is odd, when one bears in mind many admirable public buildings of the period (or several

overlapping periods as far as trends were concerned) built for purposes other than railway.

In fact, St Pancras was the last of the 'great' stations. There were many smaller structures that were distinctive in their way. You need only to travel by train over branch lines still open, or walk over or drive to lines that are closed, to see a variety of styles. The habit of lodging the station master (as he then was, however small the station) on the premises gave the architects scope in designing 'station houses'. Unstaffed stations as opposed to the halts and mere platforms that began to be erected in the Edwardian era hardly existed. On many lines in rural Sussex (some long since closed to passenger and some even to freight traffic) there is an enormous variety of station buildings and platform canopies, varying in respect not only of the date of design, but also of the standard practice that varied from time to time on the railway concerned; London & Brighton, South Eastern, London & South Western, even Kent & East Sussex and Hundred of Manhood & Selsey Tramway, and their successors.

Much farther north there are differences even in wayside stations of the old Highland Railway, illustrating the history of its expansion. There are varieties everywhere: stations straddling streets and on piers, and buried in

392 Gothic-style London St Pancras (1869), last of the really great British stations to be built. *G P Cooper*

393 Elegant frontage at Cambridge (early 1850s), here pictured in 1908. *Ian Allan Library*

394 Victorian Gothic Bristol Temple Meads station in 1967. *P J Fowler*

396 Typical style of the 1930s – Southampton Central. *Topical Press Agency*

395 A fine example of expansive Victorian Gothic – Carlisle Citadel. *British Transport Museum/B Sharpe*

397 A suggestion of 'Scottish baronial' at Stirling. *P J Sharpe*

398 York station in 1971. *M Esau*

394

396

397

depressions like Edinburgh Waverley. A good setting can add charm even to the straggling buildings of old Folkestone Harbour station, or Wemyss Bay (transfer between train and Clyde steamer), or Aviemore with its mountain background, or the bald little maritime terminus at Kyle of Lochalsh, or Kingswear with its landing stage or the scores of stations in unexciting but lovely settings in East Anglia and Somersetshire, or more striking scenery in Devon.

Emphasis hitherto has been on the architecture of the buildings. In the early days of railways the low platforms — or even simply the ground when there were no platforms — were regarded simply as an adjunct to the buildings. The buildings mattered, rather as the buildings mattered more than the yard in the coaching inn, which was the nearest thing to a station that had previously been known. Then came the high platform of carriage floor level, or a little below. Platforms have been a major factor in the design of stations. They necessitate footbridges and pedestrian subways, and should be roofed at least in part where there is no overall roof. Footbridges and 'umbrella' and other types of platform roof alter almost the whole look of stations. How many country stations are characterised by the type (open or roofed) of footbridge? The designs of platform canopy are legion, and one species of railway connoisseur specialises in classifying and identifying canopy styles.

There are 'split stations' with separate platforms for diverging lines and there was long a 'double-split' at Ashchurch near Cheltenham, where Midland Railway branches to Tewkesbury and Evesham diverged west and east respectively from the Bristol to Birmingham main line in the centre. Ambergate in Derbyshire was once a triangular station, with up and down platforms for each of three double-track lines forming the triangle where the Midland's former Manchester (now only to Matlock) line branched off from the main line from Derby to Sheffield. Only the Derby to Matlock line platforms are now used, and the others by now are wholly or partially unusable or demolished.

Platforms are solid and therefore expensive to build and remove. This has affected the whole layout of many large stations, where growth has been piecemeal and conditioned by platform layouts. Examples are the old Euston, where the only solution in rebuilding was to make a clean sweep, and Kings Cross, where at least the platform numbering has been rationalised. The only really rational principle of platform arrangement is in the trainshed at St Pancras, where the strongly-built 'train' floor over the cellars beneath allows the platforms, built largely of timber, to be remodelled relatively easily. The wooden platforms at Charing Cross and Cannon Street were relatively easily altered when those termini were rebuilt.

The type of traction affects the design of a station and the comfort of the passenger. It is perhaps surprising that in steam days more attention was not paid to ventilation, whether in stations underground or adjacent to tunnels. Birmingham New Street, in a depression but conveniently near the centre of the city, with tunnels adjoining, long had a reputation for smokiness. In these days of electric and diesel traction the absence of smoke since rebuilding New Street is no compensation for the low roof, with massive supports and staircases, over the sharply curved platforms, in contrast to the old, more spacious overall roof. New Street, however, sprang from small beginnings, and railway managements of later years are not to be blamed for the site. The same is true of London Liverpool Street, Glasgow Queen Street, Liverpool Lime Street and other big stations in cramped sites below ground level. Even Nottingham Victoria, now closed, a turn-of-the-

century creation on the Great Central extension to London, is between two tunnels, although much land was acquired for the many platforms, while traffic never grew to anything approaching the capacity of the station.

Curves, as stated, can be inconvenient. Even so, they have an aesthetic value. There is something magnificent in the curve of the trainshed at York, a fine example of civil engineering, of which the station buildings and hotel are unworthy. Newcastle Central combines such structural beauty with the classical architecture of the buildings and the hotel. The combination of curved platform and Victorian Gothic at Bristol Temple Meads sets off the designs of the diesel locomotives and passenger vehicles as trains run in and out. At Runcorn the sharp curve affords good views of electrically hauled expresses between Euston and Liverpool, with the arch of the girder bridge over the Mersey in the background.

Runcorn is a good example of BR engineers making the best of a bad job. It was necessary to renew the over-age station buildings, but the curve could not be removed. This does not matter, for the day expresses stop at Runcorn because it is the railhead not only for the town in its own right, and for part of Cheshire, but also for a large part of South West Lancashire more easily reached by road from Runcorn than by continuing by train into Liverpool Lime Street. Consequently BR has provided a great deal of car parking space.

Apart from Euston, there has not been much building of large stations since the 1939-45 war. What has been done — for instance at Sunderland, Harrogate, Stafford and Manchester Piccadilly and at smaller stations such as Harlow and Chichester and some on the Glasgow electrified suburban lines — is pleasing. A striking example of new techniques is the use of timber at Manchester Oxford Road. The standard has certainly risen since the decade before 1939, which saw some ungainly structures. What an opportunity was missed — not by the architect, whose scope was limited — at the Southampton Ocean Terminal, opened after the war and already starting to outlive its usefulness! Even the architect of the new Euston was restricted. There are plans for a new office block to replace the existing building at Liverpool Lime Street. The local planners would like to have part of the original trainshed visible from the square in front of the station — and some even would deplore demolition of the existing building because it is a monument of the great age of railways.

Running a Station

BRITISH RAILWAYS Board Chairman, Richard Marsh, commented after only a short time in office that the railway seemed to engage in almost every activity beside the running of trains. Certainly today's area manager, the man running a station, is deeply involved in the handling of an almost bewildering variety of functions that few other industrial managers would be called on to exercise.

Perhaps, however, the relatively new term 'area manager' is still a trifle confusing to those outside railway circles; after all the man in charge is still so often referred to as 'the station master'. This old title has vanished as surely as has the steam engine from home rails.

The old SM was certainly a vital cog in the railway but he was essentially an operating man. His realm was usually limited to a single station; he might have many staff but much of the commercial work was in the hands of departments of equal status, with whom he had to liaise but could not control. The system worked well enough when the railway was content to deal with small quantities at a multitude of calling points, and there was no doubt either that fine social qualities of the old style SM reaped local dividends for his company. But the fast-paced present century demanded a different and more specialised man-in-charge with wider horizons, especially when the nationalised system was obliged by statute to operate on orthodox commercial lines providing only those 'services' capable of paying their way. Beeching's reshaping came and not least nor last to be remoulded was the station master. Transitionally the title was changed to station manager and the new post covered groups of stations, but with very much the same duties as the previous incumbents. As the railway network consolidated, thinning to a more viable size to provide a more specific and sleeker service, local control was revamped to today's form.

Enter the area manager, whose function extends well beyond the platform ramps and whose working day is 24 hours. He occupies a key position in the railway structure. Visualise two ordinary domestic filler funnels placed spout to spout. The area manager is situated at their conjunction. Above, the well of the upper funnel represents the departments of the Divisional Manager's Office, the office to which the AM is directly responsible. Its demands are channelled through the AM who translates the orders into practice, using his workforce. The process is reversible. Ideas created at area level are offered up for divisional approval. But in either case it is the area manager through whom all the multitude of functions are cleared, prepared and executed.

How does one run a station? It's as good a question as how many beans make five? For the old style SM (let it be mentioned that quite a few present-day area managers

399 (facing page) London St Pancras station. *I Krause*

400 Lincoln area manager, Mr Bill Homer, talking to one of his station supervisors. *I Krause*

401 Lincoln Central station, with area manager's office in the tower. *I Krause*

were station masters of the previous organisation) many of his duties could be culled from the railway's rule books and procedural manuals. Today's AM can put his hand to no thick neatly indexed manual entitled 'Teach Yourself How to Run a Station'! Indeed, he must possess all the railway working knowledge and man management ability that SM's had, but additionally acumen for public relations, commercial expertise, salesmanship, and work study practice. Even the rudiments of catering, building construction and the law, will be needed at some stage. Most important, however, is an ever receptive, imaginative, searching and understanding mind.

Then by what yardstick can a well-run station be judged if the task is so amorphous? Take the following true incident, mundane as it is:

'Morning sir', greets a smiling porter, '10p for parking the car, please.'

'Actually I'm here on business — to see the area manager,' comes the reply.

'That's OK then,' is his response. 'We've a special spot for "railway" cars, but you're welcome to leave it where it is.'

'Thanks,' says the driver climbing out, and before he can ask the obvious question, the porter (railman in today's parlance) is answering it.

'Area Manager's Office is through that door, but I think you'll find him down the end of platform one with some divisional men.'

What's that got to do with running a station, pray? It demonstrates in microcosm that this was a good station. The railman was alert to his duties and the revenue value of his job, for he'd been at the car window only polite moments from its stopping. He'd not queried the exemption to the charge nor been officious in insisting the car be moved to the proper spot. Moreover he'd flattered the driver by putting value on his time with helpful instructions on where the visitor could swiftly locate the area manager, and to the observant shown that he, the porter, was interested in the happenings at the station enough to know the movements of its most important functionary. In brief, a first-class front-of-house man.

So the running of a station is as simple as the choosing of the car park attendant? Of course not, but the example does show one of the essentials of a good manager — the ability to weld a large number of men, undertaking a multitude of various tasks, into an enthusiastic lively team. Being word perfect on operating regulations does not run a railway, even less so a station or area. It is true the foregoing dictum can apply to any sizeable business, but the bandspread of railway functions involved makes running a station or area exceedingly complex. Remembering that no two stations, no two areas are alike, nor any two days similar, how does the local 'Mr Railway' order his working day?

Bill Homer has his office high in Lincoln Central's grey nineteenth-century tower. For him there are no 'official' hours such as the 325 railwaymen of all grades working in the Lincoln area enjoy. Though it is unlikely he will actually be at his desk much before 9.30 in the morning, that does not mean his day starts then. In fact, it is more than probable that the area manager has been afoot since 06.00 — perhaps to discuss with a night-shift man some particular problem or to check the departure of the 07.20 London passenger train from St Marks.

Correspondence will be the desk job of the day and it will equal in quantity as many rail topics as W. H. Auden's poem 'Night Mail' relates. Matters arising follows. Complying with directives from HQ (for him that is the divisional manager's office at Doncaster) will find him passing on instructions to supervisors and assistants. The latter, together with the chief clerk, will be present for the next item of the day, the morning conference. These four are Mr Homer's right-hand men. The chief clerk smooths the routine of general administration, the assistant area managers each handle either the operating, commercial or signalling works and stores functions. But do not run away with the idea that being a station chief is merely a matter of doling out work. The morning conference is a report-back and intelligence session, since even routine is spelt with a capital R for an area that encompasses two main city stations — St Marks and Central — plus the rail routes stretching to just north of Market Rasen, to the south stopping short of Sleaford, as far as the River Trent in the west and eastwards to Bardney. With the exception of Lincoln's motive power depot, that means all the rail installations as well; five stations, 27 signal boxes, a marshalling yard, 63 route-miles of track, five junctions and 13 manned crossings.

There is good reason why an area manager has assistants. To become too deeply concerned in every day-to-day activity would divert the vital team-leader function. He must be free to 'concentrate where the work is'.

Where the work is this morning lies not on rail property. Straightforward intelligence work shows a local engineering firm has secured an overseas contract. Materials will be needed and the product must be transported. The commercial assistant has already visited the firm, assessed its needs and found its people receptive; yet he judges a top-level visit would benefit. The morning

discussion elicits extra useful facts and at its close the area manager is on his way to follow up the initiative and conclude, with the help of costs from divisional HQ, a bargain. On the way back time is probably taken to pay courtesy calls on other customers. Showing the flag and maintaining contact is essential to rail sales welfare.

Once more back at the station office, the AM takes time for a quick round of the environs, a visit to the booking office — a tactful word to the buffet staff (not on his payroll) that their dustbins are hampering the postmen collecting mails, a quick greeting to the bookstall manager — a tenant of the railway and a customer too.

An AM does not have to be out of his office long before the work begins to stack up. Tomorrow's workday is changed for a start. There is a message to attend an HQ meeting covering the details of a new timetable. The local press have also been on the 'phone. 'What about this rumour of a line closure?' — they are asking, — 'Will the AM comment?' Although press questions are a divisional HQ function the area manager is, of course, acquainted with local editors; their papers have the ability to publicise the good works of the railway as well as the occasional shortcomings. In the same way he will probably be a member of the local Chamber of Commerce and perhaps on some local committees, according to individual interests.

'Absolute honesty and absolute integrity', is the way Mr Homer defines his relations with customers, press and staff. The latter must be able to rely on each member of his staff. Given this and the prime object of railway endeavour, the customer is certain to receive the high quality of service the manager seeks to attain. Management has an obligation to control and minimise insecurity and there is internally no greater insecurity as doubt, as 'not knowing'. That is why, when 14.30 shows on the station clock, the AM is getting together with his Local Departmental Committee; it is made up of local staff representatives and management and is part of the railway's envied consultation procedure — trouble-shooting at the human relations level it could be termed.

On today's agenda is a plan to concentrate the handling of freight traffic at one point in the area. Two weeks' agreed notice has been circulated of the meeting, and the atmosphere is relaxed because the AM, like his men, is still an employee. At Lincoln it happens that he is the 'team leader' and although in past years the number of jobs has been reduced, the humane manner in which relocation of staff has been handled has avoided direct redundancies. There is, then, confidence in him that the proposals of today are no attack upon railwaymen's livelihood, but are to strengthen the viability of the railway. LDC meetings throw up no losers or winners; it is consultation at its best — where *force majeur* has no place. The area manager has mapped out a number of alternative plans which could achieve the desired end. Now he seeks the views of his staff; suggestions and ideas from them could well materially add strength to the course eventually chosen.

One of Lincoln's yards is on the return route to the office. HQ has queried the persistent late running of one particular freight train and, while the matter is in the hands of the operating assistant, it is a good pretext not only to maintain acquaintance with ground level work, but also to keep contact with the area's staff wherever they are. Mr Homer reckons to use 15 per cent of his time 'seeing and being seen' in all parts of his section. This is more than a social relations exercise since every man with interest in his job will conjure ideas. The area manager is in the position to take them up, and with benefit to the industry, let alone industrial relations.

The AM's day is not yet over. That HQ meeting must be prepared for. It is important and the fruition of many

402 Signals in the Lincoln area are controlled from the older type of mechanical lever frames.

403 Level crossings also are manually controlled.

404 Parcels trolleys at Lincoln.

405 General view of the west yard.

406 Handling freight in the west yard. *All I Krause*

404

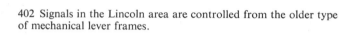

405

months' HQ planning work for the introduction of new services. It will mean extra through trains and the upgrading of an unstaffed station's status. It is dark when the office is finally shunned and the AM is the last to leave. Even now his route home might not be direct — a detour to an isolated signalbox — to check and sign the train register — could be on the itinerary, or he might reserve the visit for the early hours of the morning. The railway runs 24 hours a day — so must its senior men.

The need for the man running the station to know everyone's job to the last detail is not essential, although it is certainly necessary for him to possess more than bare facts. On safety regulations — and checking personally on signalboxes is part of them — no latitude is allowed. Periodically the station chief gets a grilling on rules and regulations from a divisional officer. To fall short of perfection is to risk suspension.

The difference between mediocrity and success can hang upon the AM's contribution to the following day's meeting with divisional men and fellow area managers. He and he alone has the complete detail of his section at his fingertips. The new service is a through one — long distance. What of seat reservations and car hire? Is advertising to be mounted and how shall it be supported? How will catering and staffing be arranged? The AM might not have direct responsibility for some of those functions, but his public will judge him first if quality of service is lacking. Some time is taken with schedules and there is a general urging of improved speeds. Speed sells rail travel and the AMs know that given it, new traffic can be gained. There are also the details of that station to attend to — the one now re-established on the Inter-City map — and it is not just a simple matter of re-opening the booking office. Facilities for staff and customers must be refurbished and improved to the railway's higher standards. Even if the building is Victorian the service

must be of the hour, and so must the railwaymen who operate it.

If the past day and a half has been partly peripatetic, Mr Homer nevertheless spends a fair time behind a desk. He plans his time though and roughly allots 10 per cent to public and railway correspondence; 25 per cent to staff consultation and relations; 10 per cent to commercial projects; 10 per cent upon report and intelligence work to be used by superior offices; 10 per cent in financial and budget control; and 15 per cent on maintaining contact with all parts of the area and its staff. Any of these headings can find the lights burning late in that grey tower office at the station.

There are a good many other things an energetic station chief may turn his hand to. They might seem trivial sidelines to the bystander, yet they are team moulders and morale boosters too. A new cleaning product can be bought for the carriage cleaners to try out — their job is not an altogether easy one. There is also the true instance of the AM who found that due to lack of catering staff the local league football team would go hungry on its away match rail journey at a holiday time. The team got its steaks though — served and cooked by the AM and an aide! The quality of service had been threatened — the man in charge took charge.

In this chapter Lincoln has been used as a 'for instance', but the running of a station has a parallel though much varied theme throughout the system. There is no primer, no textbook, to running a station. Experience counts, yet while a station can work, go through the motions, to succeed — and that means pleasing the customer and making a profit — it depends strongly upon the vision, drive and enthusiasm of its chief. The story of running a station is really the story of the man who has charge of it. He must write his own textbook.

407

408

407 Rather less organised than current preparations for train departures, an impression of a Prussian State Railway station of the mid 1800s. *DB Film Archiv*

408 Typical BR booking office scene. *I Krause*

409 Policeman or 'Bobby' who worked at the lineside and regulated the passage of trains on a time-interval basis. *British Transport Museum*

SIGNALLING

Early Days of Railway Signalling

PICTURES IN this section sum up the great change that has taken place in the work of the railway signalman. Today, he is seated in front of a few rows of buttons or switches and able to see from track diagrams in front of him the position and identification of every train under his control. Signalboxes are no longer concerned just with a few miles of track and their signals. Now they are control rooms often covering many miles with as many signals and points all under the eyes and control of only a few signalmen as were once worked by many individual signalmen in separate boxes.

A modern train control centre (signalbox is no longer an appropriate title) can cover train movements over greater distances than was possible with the old cabins with levers connected to the signals by wires, whose length for practical purposes was usually not much longer than half a mile. Until the widespread introduction of power-operated signals, the railways of Britain were guarded by signal cabins spaced at least every five miles and on lines with heavy traffic, particularly in the vicinity of large stations and junctions, the cabins were sometimes within a few hundred yards of each other. Pulling and pushing the heavy signal and point levers for 12 hours or more at a stretch, the old-time signalman's lot was arduous.

Signals in the very early days of the railway generally were given by flags, lanterns and hand and arm signals. 'Policemen' stationed at intervals alongside the track were responsible for the safety of trains by signalling the time which had elapsed since the preceding train had passed his position. For many years in Britain signalmen were called 'Bobbies' because their original duty was to police the line. However, the first passenger steam railway, the Liverpool and Manchester, installed rotating 'disc' signals within four years of its opening in 1830 and on the LSWR disc signals were introduced in 1840.

As train speeds increased it was found that a man with a flag or lantern standing at track level could not be seen in time by the driver of an approaching train and means were sought to improve signalling by erecting rotatable masts with shaped boards. Although the boards were not all disc-shaped (actual shape varied according to the railway company) 'disc' is a convenient group description of this type of signal to distinguish them from the semaphores which came later.

One alternative tried in 1840, but not perpetuated in Britain, was a ball hoisted to the top of a mast to indicate when the line was clear. In North America this type of signal was used for many years and from its use came the expression 'highball' to indicate proceed.

Brunel's Great Western disc-and-crossbar signals, first used in 1838, were of exceptional size, sometimes sixty feet above the ground with the crossbar eight feet or more long; some remained in use until the 1890s. In the stop position the crossbar was presented. If the line was clear

410 Hole-in-the-wall signal box at Victoria on the London, Chatham & Dover Railway. *British Transport Museum*

411 Early signals, left to right: Wood's crossbar c1840; GWR ball 1837; LSWR rotating disc c1840; horizontal axis double disc 1846. *Science Museum London*

the disc was displayed by turning the post through 90 degrees. For many years these signals, and similar types on other lines, were operated by the policemen moving a lever at the base of the pole. Control by a lever at a distance through wires did not come into use for some years. It is said that a policeman at Watford on the LNWR in 1846 devised the first system of operating a signal at a distance. He used a weight on the signal and a wire running to his hut.

The discs on rotatable posts were gradually superseded by the semaphore signals which were to become a distinctive feature of the British railway. The first semaphore signal, supposedly derived from the signal arms used by ships of the Royal Navy (but more likely derived from the Chappé land relay chain) was installed by C. H. Gregory on the London and Croydon railway in 1841. At first the semaphore arms could be set to three different positions: the arm horizontal to indicate 'stop'; at 45 degrees to show 'caution' and vertical, concealed in the slotted post, 'all clear'. Although in general these indications, or aspects, replicated the displaced policemen's arm signals, there was little standardisation between individual railways, nor indeed any need for it in early years, of signal aspects and their interpretation.

An essential part of a signalling system is communication between signal cabins. Despatching trains on the time-interval system had to be abandoned gradually as traffic and speeds increased above certain low levels, and the electric telegraph was introduced into railway operation to provide the answer. However, the single-needle telegraph, in which letters were represented by the

deflection of the needle, could not be adopted extensively for railway use in the 1840s because the greater number of station masters and signalmen could neither read nor write. This situation was emphasised when I. K. Brunel gave evidence on railway safety before a Parliamentary Select Committee in 1841. The NER adopted the 'speaking' telegraph in 1846, although even until as late as 1851 illiteracy among staff restricted its usefulness as a means of communication between stations and signalmen. However, in that year C. V. Walker, of the SER, introduced the single-stroke bell telegraph system using a simple code of bell strokes which could be learnt easily by the signalmen. For example: one stroke — 'attention'; two — 'train entering section' and so on.

Around 1850 there was significant progress in block telegraph systems, notably by Edward Tyer who simplified the equipment and reduced the number of wires and batteries required to operate it. He also anticipated the modern track-circuit by developing a treadle rail with electrical contacts for announcing the position of trains.

In 1861 he invented the step-by-step 'alphabetical' telegraph for communicating between signalboxes. This was the precursor of the train describers with which signalmen could supplement the single/block bell code by 'describing' each train forward to the next box. For example, in addition to 'offering' and getting 'accepted' from the next signalbox and advising 'train entering section', the describer could be used to pass details of a train, eg 'Up fast parcels train for branch line'.

The single-needle telegraph came into use alongside the block-bell telegraph as a method for passing traffic

412 Maker's catalogue illustration of signal types used on the Great Western Railway. *British Transport Museum*

413 Old disc-and-crossbar signal on the Somerset and Dorset Joint Railway at Spetisbury. *British Rail*

412

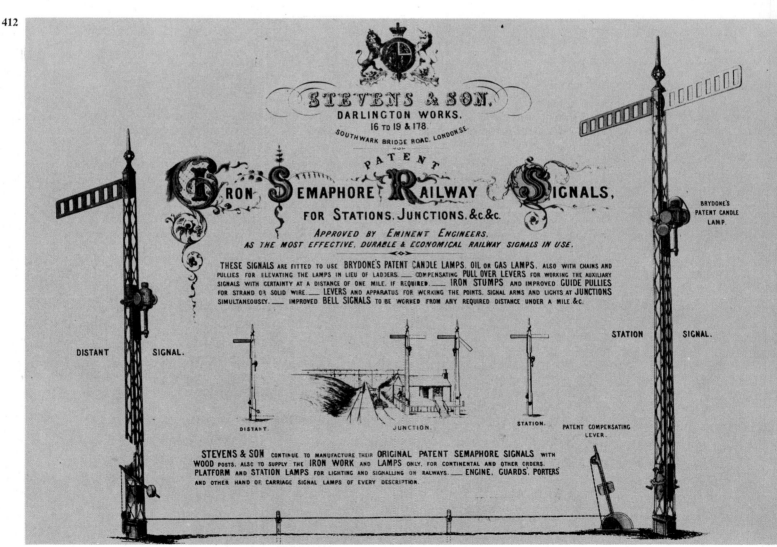

information and public messages. It survived into the era of the all-electric area-control signal box as it was an ideal system for broadcasting information without unduly distracting the signalman. Signalmen could 'listen with one ear' to the clicking telegraph needle at the same time concentrating on the track diagrams, the signal indicator lamps and the signal levers.

During the 1870s more and more signal and point levers were being concentrated in frames at one point so that they could be interlocked with each other to prevent the signalmen displaying signals which conflicted with the position of the points. Instead of signalmen who operated the signal levers and pointsmen who stood at the point levers beside the track, all were brought under the control of one man in a signal cabin. This became the standard British arrangement and one which was encouraged by legislation administered by the Board of Trade.

It was not, however, adopted in other parts of the world even when there were traffic conditions sometimes as complicated as those of this country. To this day in some countries, the control of the block sections between stations is the responsibility of the station master while the points and signals in the station are under the control of an official in another office. In general, though, outside Britain the same intensive operating conditions did not exist and simpler forms of signalling could be used with safety.

In the 1890s the three-position semaphore went out of favour because, for one reason, it was not easy to arrange the mechanism so that the arm was accurately set. Sometimes the arm took up a position between stop and caution. It was replaced by the two-position signal with the arm falling vertically into the slot in the post, as before, to indicate 'clear'. However, the semaphore arm moving into a slotted post had the serious drawback of occasionally becoming frozen in the 'off' position by ice or snow. Such a 'failure to danger' could hardly be considered satisfactory although in the signalling systems accepted in some countries to this day fail-safe practices have yet to be enforced.

In the UK the lesson was learned early enough. At Abbots Rippon in 1876 the signalman acted correctly and set the signals for the trains passing through his section. In driving snow and freezing air temperature, the southbound Flying Scotsman was rapidly overhauling a slow freight train on the same line. Blinded by snow, the driver of the freight overran the stop signals at Holme, where the signalman intended to shunt the freight into a siding out of the way of the Scotsman, which was only 16 minutes away. It was not until the freight train had run past two more signal cabins, which were not on the telegraph line and therefore were unaware of the developing situation, that the signalman at Abbots Rippon, advised by the telegraph, stopped the train and instructed its driver to back into the siding.

The signalman to the north of Abbots Rippon had correctly set his signals to danger behind the departing freight train and would keep them 'on' until he received the bell code, 'train out of section' from Abbots Rippon. Within a few minutes the block bell told him that the Scotsman was approaching his signals. To his surprise it

414 Old crossbar-and-light signal to protect level crossing at Barnoldswick, still in use when this picture was taken in 1955. *R F Roberts*

415 Disc-type signal as used on the broad-gauge Great Western Railway. *British Transport Museum*

413

414

415

did not slacken speed but swept past and disappeared to the south, lost in the swirling snow. At Abbots Rippon it crashed into the side of the freight train which had not completely cleared the main line. The driver of the express had seemingly ignored the distant signal for Abbots Rippon; the lever for which and that for the home signal were both in the 'on' position. The disaster was worsened because of poor communications and the appalling weather conditions, which prevented a northbound express from being stopped before it crashed into the wreckage.

The driver of the Flying Scotsman had been lured into danger by signals giving a false indication that the line was clear. The signalmen concerned had acted correctly but the signal arms were frozen in the clear position by snow packed in the slots in which the arms moved. The balance weights designed to pull the arm to the stop position in the event of a broken wire could not overcome the resistance of the frozen arm and the pull of wires weighed down by frozen snow.

Abbots Rippon highlighted inadequacies in the signals and their equipment of the 1870s and the difficulties of drivers and signalmen working in adverse conditions. However, as had happened before and since, the report of the Board of Trade Inspector on the accident contained recommendations intended not only to avoid a recurrence but to improve the safety of the railways generally. Among them was the abandonment of the type of semaphore signal which fell to 'clear' into a slot in the signal post.

Even more important however was the abandonment of the principle of keeping signals normally in the 'off' position and putting them to danger after a train had passed. (In France and some other countries this method of working signals remains in use even now.) Instead, in British railway practice, the signals were to remain normally in the 'on' position and were to be cleared only after the necessary bell signals had been exchanged and the line proved clear.

Had that been the practice at Abbots Rippon then the signal arms might have frozen in the danger position which, while inconveniencing operations, would have been a 'fail-safe' method. Another outcome of that historic accident was the adoption by the Great Northern and by some other lines, of the balanced or somersault signal designed to be unaffected by such things as the weight of snow.

Safety of train movements had been the subject of a number of Governmental regulations which were introduced successively from 1839 onward. The Board of Trade and its inspectors were empowered to investigate operating practices and the provision of satisfactory methods and equipment for the safety of railway passengers. However, it was in the Railway Regulations Act of 1889 that the Board of Trade finally consolidated and codified regulations and orders applying to all British railways. The regulation covered the adoption of the absolute block system of working for all passenger lines, ie one train only in a section at a time; the interlocking of all points and signals on passenger lines; and the adoption of continuous brakes, operated by air or vacuum, on all passenger rolling stock.

Signals proliferated as railway companies complied with the Board of Trade requirements that all passenger train movements had to be under the control and protection of signals interlocked with the points and with other signals which might conflict. Even every exit from little-used sidings had to have the appropriate shunting signals to govern movements. There were of course variations in the way each company arranged and operated its signals. On some lines there was a separate signal for all possible moves; on others only the minimum to satisfy Board of Trade regulations.

416

417

416 Inside the London & North Western box at Willesden around the turn of the century, showing block telegraph instruments on the right. *Ian Allan Library*

417 (inset) Old crows-nest signalbox at Waterloo station on the London and South Western Railway. *British Transport Museum*

418 Extract from signalman's bell code book as posted in signalboxes as a constant reminder.
British Transport Museum/B Sharpe

419 Three-position upper-quadrant semaphore signals at Victoria station in the 1920s. *Ian Allan Library*

MIDLAND & GREAT NORTHERN JOINT RAILWAY.

G.O. 246.

BELL OR GONG SIGNALS

(As provided in the Block Telegraph or Electric Train Tablet Regulations).

	EMERGENCY BELL OR GONG CODE.		
12	OBSTRUCTION—DANGER	6	6
17	STOP AND EXAMINE TRAIN	7	7
19	TRAIN PASSED WITHOUT TAIL LAMP	9	9
20	TRAIN DIVIDED	10	5-5
22	VEHICLES RUNNING AWAY ON WRONG LINE	12	2-5-5
22	VEHICLES RUNNING AWAY (SINGLE LINES ONLY)	12	2-5-5
23	VEHICLES RUNNING AWAY ON RIGHT LINE	14	4-5-5

Traffic Manager's Office, King's Lynn, January, 1905.

JNO. J. PETRIE,
Traffic Manager.

418

419

Signalling 1890-1949

THE DEVELOPMENT of the electric telegraph in early Victorian times and its adoption by the railways laid the foundation of modern railway signalling, yet it took 60 years of haphazard railway operation and many accidents before it was made compulsory. Some railways adopted a primitive form of telegraph for sending messages about trains running over dangerous sections of line - tunnels, for example - as early as the late 1840s. But the equipment was cumbersome and messages were spelt out letter by letter. Soon the railways adapted telegraph instruments into a simpler form to show the state of the line between two stations merely by the position of the telegraph needle supplemented by bell code signals so that signalmen could advise each other of the movement of trains.

Some of the most progressive railways quickly realised the advantages of the telegraph system for it meant that signalmen had a positive indication of whether the section of line they controlled was occupied by a train or not, a far better state of affairs than the old time-interval system in which signalmen had no means of communication between one station and the next. The sections of line, which generally ran from one signalbox to the next, were known as block sections, and the method of controlling trains by the electric telegraph became known as the block system. The principal rule was that there should not be more than one train in a block section on one line at one time and signalmen were able to advise each other as trains passed into and out of each block section by the electric telegraph

420 Reconstruction of a signalbox of the Great Eastern Railway, showing a power frame in the foreground and 1884 single-line tablet instrument. *Science Museum London*

421 Complex of mechanical interlocking in the London Bridge box of the LBSCR in the early 1900s, as the box was being phased out of service when the line was electrified. *British Transport Museum*

422 Taking over a token for single-track section security at Smallbrook Junction on the Isle of Wight Ryde-Ventnor line in 1965. *P H Rigg*

and bells.

A system was evolved whereby a signalman, before he could clear his signals for a train, 'offered' it by bell code to the next signalbox ahead and if the block section was clear the train was 'accepted' by repetition of the bell code back to the offering signalbox. As the train passed the first box the signalman sent the 'train entering section' bell signal to the box ahead, and when it arrived or passed the signalman there sent back the 'train out of section' bell signal. The block indicator needle, worked by the signalman at the exit end of the block section and electrically repeated at the entry end box, was used to show the state of the line and whether a train had been accepted or was actually in the section. This system remains in use today on lines still controlled by old-style mechanical signalboxes.

Some railways were slow to adopt the block system but it was finally ordained by Parliament in the Regulation of Railways Act 1889 that it should be installed compulsorily. This Act also required that all signals and points controlled from one signalbox should be interlocked with each other at the lever frame so that conflicting indications could not be given. This meant that a signal could not be cleared unless the points were correctly set, and at junctions two signals from different lines leading to a conflicting route could not be cleared at the same time.

Facing points, that is points giving a direct running move from one track to another, were avoided wherever possible except, of course, at route junctions or large stations; at small country stations facing crossovers from a

line in one direction on to the line in the opposite direction were almost unknown. Indeed, this sort of crossover was nearly always provided as a trailing connection so that if a train had to cross to the opposite line it had to run beyond the points, stop, then reverse back through the crossover. By this means, the risk of head-on collision by trains being accidentally diverted on to the opposite line was virtually eliminated.

Signals themselves by that time were almost entirely of the two-position semaphore pattern which denoted stop with the arm horizontal and clear with the arm lowered at 45 degrees. In the danger position at night they showed a red light and in the clear position a white light. Arms were generally painted red with a white vertical stripe near the left hand end; distant signals, that is the advance warning signals which repeated the indication of the next stop signals ahead, had a vee notch cut out of the left hand end. Signal arms on most lines were by then pivoting outside the post instead of within a slotted post, but some railways adopted the somersault arm which was formed of a centrally balanced arm coupled to a separate glass spectacle casting designed to defeat the unbalancing action of a snow build-up. A number of accidents had been caused because snow had affected the working of normal semaphore arms and caused them to show a false clear indication.

Other safety devices included facing point locks in which a bolt positively locked the point blades fully home in their normal and reverse positions so that there was no danger

424

425

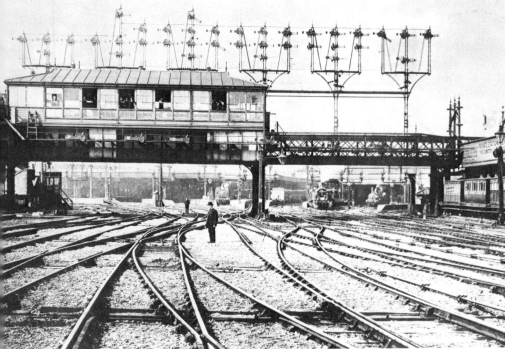

423

426

427

428

423 The massive array of semaphore signals needed to control the approaches to Waterloo station as it was between about 1892 and 1900. *British Transport Museum*

424 Picture from *Sphere* of September 1911 of a signalbox using pneumatic power to work signals. *Illustrated London News*

425 Old semaphore and new four-aspect colour-light signals side by side between Holborn and Elephant & Castle, SR, in preparation for the changeover in 1925. *Topical Press Agency*

426 Instrument for electric train staff system of early pattern for safe working of single-track lines. *Ian Allan Library*

427 A fairly modern key token instrument used for security of single-track lines. *British Rail*

428 Standard 1930s form of station layout diagram and telegraph instruments in Dunbar West manual signalbox on the East Coast main line. *G Ogilvie*

of a point blade standing away from a rail and causing a derailment. The point lock bolt was connected to a steel bar longer than the space between any two pairs of wheels on locomotives and coaches laid against the inside edge of the rail approaching and through the points. Before the points could be moved they had to be unbolted by a point lock lever in the signalbox, during which operation the bar, called the fouling bar, rose up to rail level. If a train was standing or passing over the fouling bar the wheel flanges prevented the bar from being lifted and in turn the points from being unlocked and moved.

On single lines it was thought necessary to have something more than the block system to prevent head-on collisions and the staff system was used. At first this consisted of a large wooden staff, one for each block section, and the driver of every train passing through the block section had to carry the staff as his authority to be on the single line. As there was only one staff for each section it followed that if everyone obeyed the rules there could be no collision. The basic system proved inflexible because ideally it meant that trains ran alternately in each direction and this did not always happen in practice.

From it was developed the staff and ticket system in which if several trains had to follow each other in the same direction over the single line the drivers of all but the last train were shown the staff but given a written ticket to proceed, while the last train of the group carried the staff. The tickets were kept in locked boxes opened by a key on the staff. Even this system was cumbersome, although it

survived on one or two lines until recent times; its place was taken on many single lines by the electric staff instrument or its similar but smaller related systems — the tablet and key token. The signalboxes at each end of a single line section were equipped with electrically interlocked staff instruments with several staffs in the system. Electric locks were fitted to the two instruments so that only one staff could be taken out of either instrument at one time, thus again ensuring the security of the single line.

With the virtual standardisation of the two-position semaphore signal and the abandonment of the old three-position type which, at night, showed red for danger, green for caution and white for clear, the green light was gradually adopted for the clear indication instead of white; white could be confused with ordinary lineside lighting, and particularly gas lights, then being adopted more widely in towns and on stations.

By 1900 the wonders and use of electricity were becoming known. The early years of the present century saw the introduction of track circuits, in which a weak electric current was passed through an insulated section of the running rails and when short-circuited by the wheels of a train occupying the line could be made to operate electro-magnetic relays, which in turn were employed to illuminate lights of signalbox track diagrams or to operate locks on signal levers.

Electricity was also used to power electric motors connected to points or signals which could be controlled a greater distance away from a signalbox than by mechanical means. Indeed there was (and is) an absolute limit of 350yds on the mechanical operation of points by rodding from a signalbox and the practical limit for a wire-worked signal was about three-quarters of a mile.

The earliest application of automatic signalling in Great Britain was on the Liverpool Overhead Railway in 1893 where electrically worked semaphore signals were placed to danger by an arm on the back of a passing train striking a lever on a contact box fixed on the lineside. As the train progressed, the operation of the striker arms altered the electrical connections to place the signals immediately protecting the train to danger and cleared the signals at the previous station to allow another train to proceed.

During the next 20 years, which saw the construction of most of the deep-level underground lines in London, improvements in signals and signalling systems were evolved gradually. At first some of the tube lines used the normal block system with signal cabins at each station controlling miniature semaphore signals illuminated by oil or gas lighting. Later, electricity was used for signal lights, still retaining a moving arm or vane containing coloured glass, but eventually the colour-light signal, which employed separate bulbs for each colour indication and had no moving parts, was adopted. Track circuits were gradually introduced to allow automatic operation of signals, which permitted the closure of many signalboxes at intermediate stations where no points existed.

Mainline railways also took advantage of power operation in somx new signalling installations; in 1898 the London & North Western introduced electric working of signals and points in the Crewe area. The lever frames no longer needed to be fitted with the long levers necessary for mechanical operation to obtain adequate movement of wire or rodding, and instead short levers, still with mechanical interlocking, were used to operate electrical contacts which transmitted the current to the signal and point-operating equipment. In 1902 the London & South Western Railway introduced automatic signalling, controlled by track circuits, with semaphore arms powered by low-pressure compressed air through electro-pneumatic valves, on its main line between Woking and Basingstoke.

429 First of the route lever signalling systems in Britain, at Newport East, using power-assisted signal and points operation. *British Rail*

430 Early power frame, train describer telegraphs and indicator lights at London Bridge station. *Ian Allan Library*

431 Colourful plate of early power signal company, forbear of the present British Westinghouse company. *York Railway Museum/B Sharpe*

432 Ramp in the track and control valve on a suburban diesel train set of the Great Western-type aws. *British Rail*

433 Early electric train-describer instrument of the middle 1920s. *Ian Allan Library*

430

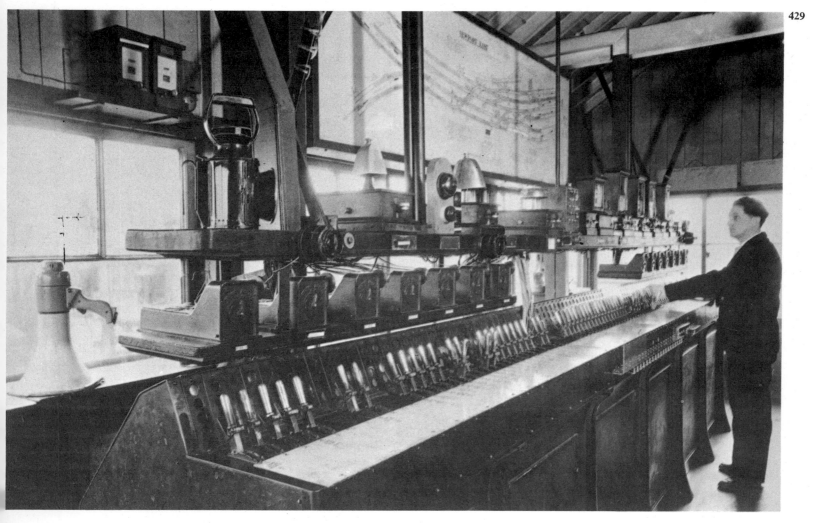

H & B R
SAXBY & FARMER L^D
RAILWAY
SIGNAL ENGINEERS

LONDON CHIPPENHAM
&

SGE

The track circuit was also gradually adopted to provide better protection in mechanically signalled areas controlled by normal block working, for it could be used to prevent a signalman clearing a signal leading to a section of line already occupied by a train.

Other allied safety devices similar in effect, if not in principle, were also used, including the local and block system. This pre-dated the track circuit and was used extensively on some lines in Southern England and in North East London. It employed treadles situated along the rail edge which were depressed by the wheel flanges of a passing train and used to actuate or release locks in signalbox equipment. Generally the system provided complete locking between the block instruments and the signals in such a way that a train had to pass the signals at one signalbox, and the signals had to be restored to danger behind it, before the block instrument for the section the train had just left could be released and cleared for a second train. In turn, the signals at the previous station could not be cleared for a second train until the block instrument for that particular section was put in the clear position. In this period also the telephone had been perfected and was installed widely for giving information on train running to supplement the block system and the needle telegraph still employed in its original form for sending general train messages.

In the years before and after the First World War more

changes became apparent in signals, particularly distant signals. One or two railways had begun to install three-position signals again but this time the arms worked in the upper quadrant, that is to say, from the horizontal danger position they were raised to 45 degrees for caution and upwards vertically for clear. In the caution position at night they showed a yellow light which conflicted with the normal caution indication of two-position distant signals which on most railways still showed red; gradually, however, some companies adopted yellow for the night-time indication of a distant caution and at the same time painted the arm yellow with a black vee stripe.

Indeed, because of the possible confusion between the two types of signal, the growing introduction of colour-light signals and automatic signalling, and the possible need for additional signal indications, a signal engineers' committee was set up in 1922 to examine signalling needs for the future. It advised against the adoption of the three-position semaphore and found that the normal two-position semaphore would be adequate for ordinary working. However, in closely signalled areas with a frequent service the committee recommended the adoption of the four-aspect colour-light system using red for danger, one yellow for caution, double-yellow for preliminary caution, and green for clear.

The Great Central Railway was the first to adopt

434 Standard BR upper-quadrant signal – and an illustration of how signals can be obscured by other trackside furniture. *A D Deayton*

435 Lower-quadrant signal on the Dundee/Kingsmuir branch line in Scotland. *A D Deayton*

436 (facing page) Working the heavy levers of a busy mechanical signalbox was an arduous job. *B A Reeves*

434

435

automatic colour-light signalling out of doors (as distinct from the underground lines in tunnel) in 1923, and two years later the first re-signalling schemes on the Southern Railway's South East London approaches embodying the four-aspect colour-light system were introduced. The final abandonment of the three-position semaphore left the way open for the adoption of the upper-quadrant two-position semaphore which was raised to 45 degrees for the clear position. The upper-quadrant type of signal was of lighter construction than the lower-quadrant, since it returned by gravity to danger instead of being weighted to ensure that the arm returned to the horizontal position. both when the lever was put back to normal in the lever frame or in the event of a broken wire. As a point of later railway history the upper-quadrant signal did not completely oust the lower-quadrant type, for the Great Western Railway continued to use the lower-quadrant semaphore, and indeed its successor, the Western Region of British Railways, still does where it retains mechanical signalling, and even on other lines isolated lower-quadrant signals survive in one or two places. The recommendations of the committee were so far reaching that there has been no radical change in signalling indications in Britain from then until the present time, nor is there likely to be while lineside signals exist.

The 1920s and 1930s saw the gradual extension of colour-light signalling but still largely worked by signalboxes controlling limited areas. While the old mechanical limits no longer applied, the power signalboxes of that period still controlled signals and points by individual miniature levers — one lever per function — and control areas were generally not much more than a mile or so from the signalbox. Sometimes lengths of automatic signalling intervened between adjacent signalboxes. In 1927 the Great Western took signalling control a stage further by the adoption of route levers at Newport (Monmouthshire). In this system, the levers controlling the signals (which were electrically operated semaphores) also set the points to which the signal applied in one operation. The movement of the miniature lever by the signalman was in stages: first to a check-lock position as the equipment proved that the line was free to be used and that no other conflicting move had been set (this was achieved by track circuits and normal interlocking), then to a position which operated the points, and, finally, when they had been proved in the correct position, the lever movement was completed which cleared the signal.

During the 1930s the LNER introduced the first all-electric signalbox control panels which laid the foundations for present-day power signalling. Instead of being controlled by levers, signal and point movements were initiated by thumb switches. The turning of a switch on the signalman's control desk, like the Great Western's system at Newport, proved the section of line free for use, operated the points and cleared the signal, from one signal to the next; in this case, however, the signals were colour-lights. By now the locking between the signalman's control switches was achieved electrically by relays instead of mechanical locks. This system, known as the OCS (one control switch) pattern was adopted more extensively in British signalling during the next 20 years.

437 Self-balancing somersault signals needing lower operating power in use on the Great Northern line in 1952. The one on the right is just returning to danger. *Ian Allan Library*

438 Clear position on a three-position semaphore, as still in use in a few places on BR. *British Rail*

439 Gantry with mixed semaphore and colour-light signals, both with route indication. *Science Museum London*

437

438

439

The Big Power Box

THE FIRST, and undoubtedly irregular, signal to be given by lights to show whether the line was clear was recorded in the 1840s. It is said to have been given by a lighted candle placed in a window of a house beside the line if the way was clear, and if the light was not there the line was blocked.

The first true signals to be given solely by lights were on the pioneer London Underground railways, built just before and after the turn of the century. At first a single light source gave the indications by a moving arm containing coloured glass spectacles which passed in front of it; later the true colour-light, with a separate bulb for each indication illuminated coloured glass lenses which magnified the light. Indeed the lenses were designed to concentrate the light into a beam directed towards the driver of an approaching train. It was this feature which later made colour-light signals out of doors so useful in fog, for the diffused lights can usually be seen from a distance in front of the signal during fog, even though the signal post itself is invisible.

The first automatic signalling system was installed on the Liverpool Overhead Railway in the 1890s and by the turn of the century electrically operated semaphore signals and points had been introduced by one or two mainline railways, for example the LNWR at Crewe on the main line from Euston to the North. Track circuits were evolved during the first 20 years of this century, and most of the ingredients were thus present for the introduction of power signalling on a more widespread scale after the First World War. The Southern Railway was the foremost exponent of power signalling during the 1920s and '30s with new installations at all of its London terminus stations.

In these early power signalling schemes points and signals were controlled from lever frames having small levers no more than about 6-9in high; interlocking between levers, to ensure that signals could not be cleared unless points were correctly set or that conflicting signals could not be given, was at first achieved mechanically in exactly the same way as the levers in a normal mechanical signal-box. Later, miniature lever frames used by the Southern Railway employed electric locks between levers but the principle was the same and the lever could not be operated unless it was free to be used.

The signalling at Newport, Monmouthshire, was modernised in 1927, but there the electrically operated semaphore signals were controlled from levers which served more than one function; as they were pulled the lever was checked in two intermediate positions while the equipment first proved that the line on which the train was to be signalled was clear and that no other signal leading to the same route was already clear, and second, that the points were switched to the correct position. Finally, the signalman pulled the lever to the fully over position which cleared the signal.

This equipment was known as route lever operation since the movement of a single lever set up a complete route from one signal to the next. At that time, however, no overall advantage could be seen in its more widespread adoption and during the following decade nearly all new power signalling schemes on the Great Western and Southern Railways used miniature levers having only one

440 Colour-light signals with signal cabin behind at London Waterloo station. *Westinghouse Brake & Signal Co Ltd*

441

SIGNAL SUCCESS

Colour-light electric signals speed the handling of trains. The British Railways Modernisation Plan provides for a considerable extension to this type of signalling which works automatically or is controlled from all-electric signal boxes.

441 Cuneo painting used in a British Railways modernisation plan advertisement depicting colour-light signalling.
British Transport Museum/B Sharpe

442

443

function per lever. A feature of most of the SR lever frames was the repeater lights behind the levers which showed the poition of points by the letter N (normal) or R (reverse). Signals were indicated by the lights repeating the aspect shown on the signal itself.

The signalbox track diagrams had also come to life by this time. In mechanical boxes without any track circuiting the signalman had a display of the lines he controlled, with points and signals shown in their geographical positions and bearing a number alongside corresponding to the lever numbers which operated them. When track circuits were installed the presence of a train on the section of line concerned was indicated either by red lights being illuminated on the track diagram on the section concerned or by other forms of indicator, such as a needle pointer which swung towards a label 'line clear' or 'line blocked' depending on whether there was a train there.

Sometimes track circuits were used only for indication purposes but usually they also operated locks on other signal levers leading to that section of line. In power signalling areas, however, all lines were usually track-circuited and the track circuits were not only indicated on the signalman's track diagram but were used to place signals to danger automatically as trains passed them. This was an added safety feature which made sure that there was a red signal behind a train even if the signalman forgot about it. The signal would clear for a second time only when the first train passed beyond the next signal ahead so that the track circuit became free, and also after the signalman had put the lever back to the 'danger' position and pulled it clear again.

On some sections of line the signals worked automatically and were not controlled by signal levers. This was achieved solely by track circuits; some small signalboxes at local stations, which only needed to work points perhaps once or twice a day, for example to let a goods train in or out of a yard, could be closed at other times and a special lever operated, before the signalman went home, which set the signals to work automatically. When the signalbox was open, however, the signals would be controlled by the levers.

There was usually none of the offering and accepting routine described previously for mechanical signalboxes between power signalboxes, and signalmen were normally warned of the approach of a train by the track circuit lights as the train entered the control area. However, the signalman needed to know the identity of the train and this was advised to him by a train describer. The early train describers were in the form of a clock face with a single hand which pointed at different descriptions on labels around the face. The describers were worked by electric impulses from signalbox to signalbox. As signalbox control areas became more complex, it was sometimes possible for a signalbox to supervise an area long enough for the signalman to have two or even three trains approaching him on the same line at a safe distance, and train describers in use by the end of the 1930s were able to display first, second or third train approaching by means of lights illuminated against a written description.

In 1935 the LNER introduced a new signalling scheme at Thirsk on the East Coast main line in which the colour-light signals were controlled from thumb switches on the signalman's track diagram. It was not a very large installation and the signalman could sit at a desk with the control console in front of him. Each switch set up the route to a particular line, checking that the line concerned was free, changing the points if necessary, and clearing the signal.

Interlocking between switches was achieved electrically by relays rather than by electric or mechanical locks. Briefly, a relay is a piece of equipment containing an electro-magnet. If the magnet has an electric current

442 New panel indications and lever identity plates installed in Victoria Eastern signalbox in 1939. *Ian Allan Library*

443 Panel for entrance/exit type of control at Portsmouth SR, in which the control buttons are on the route diagram itself. *British Rail*

444 Three-aspect colour-light main signals, with call-on and shunting signals, installed at Glasgow St Enoch in 1933. *Ian Allan Library*

444

passing through it is energised and attracts a metal arm towards it. The arm is linked to a series of other electrical contacts which by the movement of the arm can be opened or closed, thus making or breaking other electrical circuits. When the relay is de-energised, that is with no electric current passing through the magnet, the arm drops away changing the position of the connected contacts. A series of these relays linked together between track circuits and signal operating switches can thus be used to pass electric current to signals and points, or to prevent the passage of electric current if the conditions are not right. The system is called relay interlocking and forms the basis of today's railway signalling.

The LNER pioneered the thumb switch type of signalling control panel known as the OCS (one control switch) system. Just before the Second World War this company introduced a small signalling panel in a rather out-of-the-way place in the Liverpool Dock area at Brunswick, which might have seemed insignificant at the time, for it controlled only a very short section of line, but

445

446

445 Typical intermediate-period installation, at Gloucester Road, SR, with one lever per function, electro-mechanical interlocking and signal indications behind levers.
Westinghouse Brake & Signal Co Ltd

446 Typical control panel in a modern big power box, at Derby, LMR. *Westinghouse Brake & Signal Co Ltd*

447 Another modern LMR control panel, at Wolverhampton. *British Rail*

it proved to be the pioneer of the standard method of signalling today. Instead of using a thumb switch for each route controlled by a signal as in the OCS system (for example, if the signal concerned led to four different lines then four separate switches were provided) the new panel employed one switch only, called the entrance switch, situated on the diagram alongside the signal to which it applied. A second switch, known as the exit, was placed further along each of the lines could be reached from that signal. The operation of the two switches set up the route between them culminating with the clearance of the signal.

Signalling development made little progress during and after the Second World War and the first of the post-war resignalling schemes on the LMS and Southern Railways and their successors, the London Midland and Southern Regions of British Railways, followed established methods using miniature lever frames. At York, however, the LNER was much bolder and introduced what at that time was the world's largest signalling scheme controlled by an OCS route-relay-interlocking system. Indeed, the LNER never looked back and used this type of control for a number of its resignalling schemes of the 1950s. At the same time the entrance/exit type of panel was also being developed and was used for one or two installations in the early 1950s. By that time, too, the signalman was being assisted on the more complex layouts by rows of white

lights along the track diagram in front of him showing which routes had been set and signals cleared, a feature first seen at Northallerton in 1939. The white lights turned to red as the track concerned was occupied by a train.

The areas supervised by power signalboxes were gradually becoming larger but were still limited to the immediate station area and perhaps a mile or so on each side. During the mid-1950s two developments were perfected which changed the whole course of British signalling: first, the design of much smaller relays which allowed more equipment to be housed together in a signalbox of moderate size; and second, and most important, an electronic development whereby a number of electrical circuits could be converted into electronic impulse signals and sent over the same pair of wires to be decoded at the far end into individual circuits again for the operation of specific signalling equipment.

The developments opened the way for the remote control of signalling several miles away from a signalbox and it was thus possible to think in terms of a signalling control area 30 or 40 miles long instead of 3 or 4 miles. This would not have been possible because of the cost if each electric circuit to individual signals and points had to be carried over separate pairs of wires. Moreover, it meant that many intermediate signalboxes could be closed and their function taken over by one central signalbox. Many

447

of the signals could be arranged to work automatically from track circuits, although their indications were shown on the track diagram of the supervising signalbox so that the signalman had a continuous picture of train working throughout the area.

The new principles of larger control areas were introduced on a moderate scale with the LMR electrification in 1959 between Manchester and Crewe and during the following few years new signalboxes with more extensive control areas were brought in by the dozen, mostly for electrification extensions: Barking, Tilbury, Pitsea and Southend on the Fenchurch Street - Shoeburyness line; Hither Green, Orpington, Sevenoaks, Tonbridge, Ashford and Folkestone on the London - Dover main line; and the extensive Euston, Willesden, Watford, Bletchley, Rugby, Birmingham and Wolverhampton boxes on the LM electric lines.

Each new signalbox seemed to set more records for the number of signals and points that it controlled and the number of miles of track it supervised. The Western Region also put in hand similar schemes so that today the vital routes between London, Swindon, Bristol and Taunton, also to South Wales, and the important cross-country route via Gloucester to Birmingham and onwards through the London Midland Region to Derby and Nottingham, are controlled by no more than about a dozen signalboxes. One at Bristol, completed early in 1972, looks after 117 route miles of line.

All these boxes employ the entrance/exit type of control, some retaining an entrance switch and an exit button, but others employing solely push buttons, most of which serve as the exit button from one section and the entrance button to the next section ahead and thus have to be pushed twice, once for each function. It is fascinating to watch the signalman setting the route through a complex area merely by pushing buttons. White lights on the diagram trace the route which has been set, signal lights on the diagram change from red to green and then as the train passes a series of red lights is seen weaving itself along the route that has been set. The train itself may be many miles from the signalbox and indeed the signalmen in these modern power boxes rarely see the trains they are signalling.

New forms of train describer have been developed because obviously much more information is wanted than the old first, second, third train approaching describers could give. There may be as many as 20 or 30 trains on the diagram at one time and a new system was adopted in which code figures and letters denote the class of train, its destination and train number or route. This is the code that is carried on the front of nearly all BR trains and is generally displayed as a figure, letter and two figures.

The train code is displayed on the signalman's track diagram, for in each signal section there is space on the line diagram for the code to be shown. It is reproduced either on a miniature cathode ray (television) tube no more than an inch or so in diameter or by electro-mechanical counters, and sometimes by other means. As the train runs through the layout its presence on the signalbox diagram is shown not only by the moving row of red lights but also by the code number, which steps from one signal display to the next, and so on through the layout, keeping pace with the red lights. The codes are set up by the signalman at the starting station either operating push buttons or dialling on a telephone-type dial, after which the electronic equipment makes sure that the code is passed from one

display to the next. When it leaves the control area of one signalbox it is automatically transferred to the incoming display of the next signalbox ahead.

While railway discipline was essential in the safe working of trains, and numerous safety devices were adopted to try and prevent signalmen's errors, from the earliest days accidents could be caused by a driver running past a signal at danger into collision with another train. Almost from the start of the London Underground system this was recognised as a considerable danger in the confined tunnels and mechanical train stops were provided at stop signals. The automatic stopping device (automatic train stop or ATS) consisted of small arms close to rail level which, when the signal was at danger, were raised into such a position as to engage with an arm suspended from the train. If a train passed a signal at danger the trip arm on the train was knocked back and opened a valve which applied the brakes automatically.

On mainline railways this system was not satisfactory because of the different speeds and weights of train. A few railways experimented with automatic warning systems (AWS) and automatic stop systems but the only one that came to fruition to any extent in the 1930s and '40s was that of the Great Western Railway. This system employed a sloping ramp about 40ft long between e rails; it engaged a oe under the locomotive which was lifted as it passed over the ramp. Ramps were placed near distant signals; if the signal was clear an electric current was passed into the ramp and through the shoe to equipment on the locomotive which rang a bell in the driver's cab. If the signal was at caution there was no electric current and the raising of the shoe by the dead ramp caused a horn to sound in the driver's cab which the driver had to acknowledge by pressing a plunger. If he did not do that the brakes were applied automatically. Despite recommendations that some such form of protection should be used on all railways, it remained virtually unique to the Great Western until the end of the 1930s. It also provided the Great Western with a remarkable safety record.

On the Fenchurch Street - Shoeburyness line the LMS experimented with a form of automatic warning system but unlike the Great Western pattern it involved no physical contact between the locomotive and track equipment. Instead it employed magnets, a permanent magnet to initiate an indication at a distant signal, followed by an electro-magnet which was energised if the signal was clear and opposed the warning which would be given by the permanent magnet. If the signal was at caution the electro-magnet was not energised and the permanent magnet acted on the locomotive equipment which caused a horn to sound a long blast in the driver's cab; if it was not acknowledged by the driver pressing a button, the brakes were applied automatically.

During the 1950s British Railways developed a form of AWS which combined the best features of both the GW and LMS types, using magnets to operate the system and the GW horn and bell indications in the cab. They were supplemented by a visual indicator to show a driver whether he had passed a clear signal or whether he had cancelled a warning indication. This system has gradually been installed during the last 20 years and is now standard on practically all BR main lines. It is also used on lines with multiple-aspect signals but cannot distinguish between double yellow, yellow or red, all of which will give a caution indication in the cab. Because of that, and the need for faster trains to have a more positive indication, a new form of AWS is being developed based on the existing system but with added refinements which will show the indication of the last signal passed.

More comprehensive, however, are the experiments now being conducted with full cab signalling, even possibly embodying some form of automatic control of train speed, in readiness for the 150mph trains of the future. It employs either conductor wires laid between the track or uses the running rails to carry coded impulse signals which are detected by equipment on the train. All sorts of information can be fed into the train equipment by the codes as well as signal aspects, including line conditions, for example gradients, permanent speed restrictions or similar physical features which might affect speed; the data can be assessed by train-borne equipment to show the driver continuously the maximum permissible speed at which the train may run and, if it is exceeded, apply the brakes automatically.

The driverless train might sound remote but already automatic trains are running on the London Underground and a few other of the world's railways. The Victoria Line tube trains have a man in the front cab but once he has opened and shut the doors at stations and pressed a start button the train accelerates and runs automatically; its speed is regulated and the train is stopped at stations by equipment picking up coded signals from the track. If it closes up towards a train ahead the equipment will automatically slow it down and if necessary stop it. When the line is again free it will restart automatically.

Points and signals at junctions on the Victoria Line, including the coded impulses to the train equipment, are controlled automatically by programme machines. These consist of rolls of paper with punched holes rather like a pianola roll. The punched holes contain details of each train on the line, the route which it is to take and the time at which it is due to pass. Feeler arms make contact through the punched holes to initiate the operation of signals and points. As each train passes so the roll steps forward for the next train and the next programmed route is prepared automatically. If a train is late the equipment is able to store the details and when the train eventually arrives its route will be set for it.

The whole of the Victoria Line and other London Transport railway routes are controlled in this fashion with the programme machines supervised from a control centre where the traffic controller and the signalman look after the entire line. Normally the signalman does not intervene except in an emergency or if equipment fails. When an item fails in all British signalling it does not mean that trains are allowed to proceed uncontrolled; if any component does not carry out its proper function the signals will always show or go to red and trains will come to a normal stop. Throughout most of the history of British signalling the equipment has been designed on fail-safe principles.

In the 80 or so years since the Regulation of Railways Act was passed in 1889, signal engineers in particular and railways generally have been working towards making railways the safest form of travelling. It might seem sometimes that new developments have been adopted rather slowly, but in an area where the loads of meeting or passing vehicles might be 1,000 passengers or more the functions of new equipment have to be proved safe beyond all doubt.

448 Four-aspect colour-light signals, approaching Old Oak Common, with light indications covering three routes diverging to the right. *British Transport Films*

449 Section of the control panel at Wilmslow, of the one-control-switch (OCS) type.

450 Modern electric point-operating machine on British Railways.

451 Equipment room to provide power for the operation of a modern area control signalbox.
All Westinghouse Brake & Signal Co Ltd

449

450

451

THE RAILWAYS AND ADVERTISING

The Railway's Public Face

THE LONG-STANDING love affair between the British and their railways originates in very many ways from careful design, cunning graphics and striking use of colour. In the mid-sixteenth century, the painter Hans Holbein roused Henry VIII's interest in the ugly Anne of Cleves by emphasising the magnificent dress in which she sat for him; three hundred years later, early designers did just as much for railways.

In the 1970s, bright conformity and clarity are the prime criteria of design, echoing speed, efficiency and comfort,

452 Old SECR notice warning cabdrivers to be on good behaviour. *British Transport Museum/B Sharpe*

453 and 455 Crests of the North Staffordshire and the Manchester, South Junction and Altrincham Railways.

454 Scene typical of the advertisements decorating railway stations in the early days. *P Mackertich*

456 BR Travelcentre at Euston. *British Rail*

457 Neat and functional treatment by British Railways of Dudley Port station, between Birmingham and Wolverhampton. *British Rail*

456

457

the vital aspects of modern travel. However, in early railway days, such considerations had no relevance. The important task then was to make rail travel an accepted part of everyday life, at a time when the horse had for centuries held a monopoly of motive power, and the rural quietude of Britain was as yet unshattered.

It was a task greatly complicated by the inherent ugliness of the basic material. As early as 1828, Robert Stephenson realised that there was not much visual appeal in an iron monster breathing fire, smoke and cinders, for in that year, he wrote to a colleague that he had already begun discussions with his famous father on the problem of reducing 'the size and ugliness of our travelling engines'.

One solution was to divert the eye with brilliant colour schemes. Stephenson's *Rocket* of 1829, for example, was painted bright yellow and black with a white chimney and polished brass mountings, while its rival, *Novelty,* sported blue frames and wheels, and a glossy copper boiler casing. Another disguise was a cloak of classical grandeur, and one result, as seen in Stephenson's *Planet* of 1830, was a

smoke-stack resembling a column from the Athenaeum of Ancient Greece. Likewise, E. B. Wilson & Co of Leeds virtually made a hallmark of matching sets of classic dome and safety valve.

This sort of 'window-dressing' formed part of an obvious but well-considered effort to exploit not only current taste, but current emotion as well. Designers were very much aware that they lived in an age that prized individual enterprise, loved ornate grandeur and responded with spirit when appeals were made to tradition. Early station designers, faced with similar problems, found similar solutions, and lavished magnificence on the mundane to such an extent that few, if any, of their creations actually resembled what they were.

For example, the great Doric portico at Euston, with its lodges flanking it on either side, could easily have been the scene of some Ancient Roman triumph. The classic porticos and colonnades of Curzon Street, Birmingham, built in 1838, and the station at Tithebarn Street,

Liverpool, opened in 1850, strongly resembled some of the grand country houses which had been status symbols for the eighteenth-century aristocracy.

Religion, a great preoccupation in Victorian times, was invoked in William Tress's Gothic station at Battle, Sussex (1852), with its air of a venerable country church. And holy connotations were even more apparent in the booking hall at St Pancras which, with its great arched roof and pew-like ticket offices, was highly reminiscent of a cathedral. In such settings, the new-fangled form of travel assumed a more beneficent and more dependable aspect.

It was an impression reinforced by the presence of the top-hatted tail-coated guards who graced station platforms in the 1850s, as well as by the colourful posters which, by 1851, were already making maximum use of all that was most decorative in lettering and layout.

Added to the great care taken over the appearance of locomotives and carriages, many of which bore majestic names like *Samson, Goliath* and *Venus,* details like this soon made rail travel a visually exciting adventure. It all disguised the fact that, with the possible exception of first-class travel, early journeys by rail could be exceedingly uncomfortable, draughty, dirty, cold, tiring, and frightening to those of a nervous disposition. However, the attempt was so successful that the Victorians took railways to their hearts, conceiving an affection for this revolution in transport that has proved unique in the history of industry. Henry VIII's unfortunate fourth wife was never so lucky.

In design terms, the Victorians' infatuation showed itself in all sorts of ways. On country stations, the loved one was embellished with small gardens, in which the name was picked out in different coloured flowers. Baskets of blooms were hung from platform verandahs that were edged with delicate valances, and the cast-iron pillars and brackets supporting station roofs were often worked in a fine and intricate tracery. It was, however, at major junctions that the full magnificence of railway design was displayed in a brilliant panoply of colour.

From mid-century onwards, the beautiful liveries of various companies vied with each other at the platforms in ways basically no different from knights and chargers in medieval lists. Engines of the Caledonian Railway, for instance, glowed a deep Prussian blue, lined out in black and white, with frames decorated in crimson. The North British Railway used the rich livery designed by William Stroudley and also seen on the Brighton line — a warm golden ochre edged by a wide band of green, and between them fine lines of red, black and white. Much later, in 1899, S. W. Johnson's 4-2-2 No 2601 *Princess of Wales* graced the Midland Railway in all the splendour of its crimson-lake livery and yellow linings.

The nameplate and number lettering on engines was hardly less elaborate. Names and numerals were often painted in gold leaf, shaded and countershaded to give them extra depth and richness. A final touch of elegance was lent by elaborate crests, devices and coats-of-arms, the grandeur of which had nothing to do with the importance or extent of the line they advertised. The Manchester, South Junction and Altrincham Railway Company, for example, possessed a coat-of-arms which owed a great deal to the decorative arts of Renaissance Italy. The seal-like device chosen by the North Staffordshire Railway Company might have well graced some important royal document in medieval times, and medieval heraldry was also an evident influence on the shield with three lions in relief that was the mark of the East Lancashire Railway.

However, as in so many love affairs, good looks alone cannot hold perpetual fascination, and by the early years of this century, other factors had begun to jade former passions. In much more than the matter of railway design, the 1914-18 war dissipated many of the more fanciful and high-blown of Victorian notions, and did much to temper with raw realism a pride that had too often neared arrogance. Opulence and splendour began to seem empty to a generation scarred to the soul by horror of a kind that had never before intruded on the public conscience.

The austerity of war also had its effect in quietening popular taste for grandeur, and in 1922, when the railways were merged into four main companies, the former need to advertise was considerably reduced.

However, the most cogent of all reasons for the change which took place in railway design after the war was the search for more power, more speed and more efficiency. The importance of this was emphasised in the 1930s, with the rise of a powerful rival — the motor car. The railways also had to face competition from electric tramcars, and taken together, all this made the science of rail travel more important than the art.

One effect was a general saddening in the appearance of stations, and not much imagination to spare for detail. Certainly, streamlining of engines and rolling stock, even if for purely practical purposes, gave both a certain simple elegance, but simplicity as applied to stations lacked all appeal. The stern granite face of Aberdeen Joint station,

458 One of British Rail's most modern passenger stations, the concourse at London Euston. *British Rail*

459 Platform canopy in the modern idiom at Oxford. *British Rail*

460 Restrained railway information and publicity in the waiting room at Bristol Parkway. *British Rail*

458

built in 1915, was impressive but daunting, and Waterloo, built in 1922, seemed spacious but struck many as impersonal. Becontree station, also built in 1922, had an entrance like some fearsome institution, while Heathway, a contemporary sation on the London Midland & Scottish Railway, possessed a platform of the utmost dreariness, redolent of a spartan military barracks.

Vistas like this naturally drained stations of all their former vibrant spirit, as bleak inhospitable stone, bare brickwork and cold concrete replaced the imaginative use of materials the Victorians had lavished on their predecessors. There were, of course, exceptions where more careful design employed the new materials of the age with more flair, and better concealed their essential starkness. For example, at Otterington station on the London & North Eastern Railway, built in 1933, varied use was made of brickwork and tiling, and although the platform itself seemed an uninspired slab, the overall design had a certain homeliness, set off as it was by two chimneys on the main roof.

More impressively, Malden Manor on the Southern Railway, which opened in 1938, was given that cheerfully rounded look so characteristic of architecture at that time. Outside, its expanses of concrete were relieved by skilful angling of the various blocks, while the platform awnings inside had a split-level look and the symmetrical sculpture of the platform supports and ceiling retained a good deal of eye appeal while remaining strictly contemporary. Malden Manor was not the only SR station to interpret the designs of the 1930s in bold imaginative style. The plain tastefully sculptured surface and radiused corner were also features at Surbiton, Horsham, Chessington North, Chessington South and Woking. However, the outbreak

of war in 1939 scuttled all hopes of a wider renaissance, and from the austerity of the war and its utilitarian aftermath, railways emerged with a sadly dog-eared appearance.

Even in the early 1950s, too many stations were too unwelcoming, with their jumble of kiosks, their clutches of unsightly litter bins, rows of vulgar vending machines and riot of posters drained of impact by bad siting. In such unattractive places, the remaining vestiges of former gloss and glory naturally vanished. The pejorative impression was underlined by the vigorous post-war development of the airlines, with their resplendent liveries, imaginative motifs and readily recognisable house-styles, all of them features which the railways had pioneered but forgotten.

At the same time, the private motor car was a hotter rival than ever before, and in 1955, when the government was at last able to sanction a £1,200-million modernisation plan, railways had a distinctly second-rate image in the public mind. Again, there were the inevitable exceptions. The stark bold lines and plain spacious sweep of post-war Coventry station earned it the title of 'the finest new station built in Britain this century' and a contemporary design at Harlow Town made adventurous use of both modern building materials and modern building styles.

Even so, the overall picture was so depressing that there was clearly a great need for the Design Panel which the British Transport Commission created as one of the first results of the decision to modernise. The panel, whose task was 'to advise on the best means of obtaining a high standard of appearance and amenity in the design of equipment', first met on August 8, 1956, with the design of new diesel and electric locomotives as its first priority.

Consequently, stations had to wait for the panel's

attentions, but its eventual effect on them was salutary. Through its minor station improvements scheme, the panel inspired a general clean-up, brighter colour schemes, better balance between information signs and poster displays and better integration of platform amenities. It was basically no more than a face-lift, and until the decision, in 1962, to incorporate all regions of British Railways, it was not possible to take the ultimate step in attracting the disaffected public.

The psychological merits of a corporate image, with a recognisable symbol, a name style and distinguishing colours, had already been amply demonstrated by British European Airways, the giant Shell Oil Company and, in the mid-1930s, by London Transport. By contrast, British Railways before 1962 was a very poor relation in the graphics stakes.

At the time of nationalisation in 1948, the liveries of engines and rolling stock embraced various shades of green, blue, black, 'chocolate and cream', 'plum and spilt milk', crimson, medium blue lined in black and white, and green with an orange and black lining. The untidy range of hues was reduced by the adoption of six regional colours, with maroon, orange, green, brown, dark blue and light blue employed for the background to station name signs and the covers of regional timetables. Identification was not, however, pushed to its logical conclusion, for the trains themselves often failed to match. In the North Eastern Region, for instance, electric trains in Newcastle were painted Southern Railway green instead of their proper regional colour, orange, and some locomotives were GWR green or LNWR black.

The plan which aimed to eliminate the last remaining anomalies, and make the public visually aware of railways as an entity, was BR's corporate identity programme, launched in January 1965. With its house colours of blue, grey and red, brilliant yellow as a warning colour, and its double-arrow symbol creating at one and the same time an impression of movement and homogeneity, the programme represented a complete break with the graphics patterns of the past. It helped and is helping to make possible a more-positive approach to 'selling' rail travel in an age when public consciousness is everywhere beseiged by advertising.

Equally, the need for British Rail to be tastefully but firmly obtrusive is emphasised by the modern trend towards integrating stations within commercial development blocks. This has, by its very nature, robbed the railways of their isolation, and in some ways of their individuality as a service. The corporate identity could do much to counter this by stressing unity and on platforms themselves, this is most obviously achieved by having train colours matching those on various station signs.

Another important aid to unity and individuality lies in the adoption of the plain sanserif Rail Alphabet now used not only on station signs, but also on locational and direction signs, notices, street direction and road traffic signs. The unique but modern character of the alphabet is also a valuable aid to instant recognition, and has an assuringly efficient air which previous more-patrician forms of lettering lack in modern eyes. In addition, its high legibility, the great care taken in suitable siting and lighting, and the use of pictograms, go a long way towards ensuring that finding one's way about a station today takes a minimum of time.

Though, naturally, much remains to be done, British Rail's refurbished image has already imprinted itself on the public mind in a vigorous and forward-looking fashion. This is no small achievement for a venerable industry which barely two decades ago was transport's Cinderella and which faces in the aeroplane and car, rivals which possess a more overt glamour. Cinderella, after all, only had the Ugly Sisters.

461 Announcements by two railways of special trains serving non-railway events.

462 A Midland Railway poster lauding the attractions of Blackpool.

463 One of the famous LMS advertisements commissioned from noted Royal Academicians, 'Speed' by Sir Bertram MacKennal. *All British Transport Museum/B Sharpe*

Railways and Publicity

ADVERTISING AND PUBLICITY material put out by railways over the past 150 years makes interesting material for studies from several angles — the development of technique in the art of printing; appreciation of art and in particular of the art of typography; and, rather slowly, realisation of what makes effective appeal. There are many facets; posters, pamphlets, brochures, book marks, lantern slides, full-scale books, and cine film have all had attention. This aspect of railway work may be divided into three: factual information about the services offered — and over considerable periods, of the services *not* offered; prestige and development publicity; and use of the railway to advertise other people's wares.

On the factual information side, the railways followed the tradition of stage-coach proprietors and canal companies which had established a style of combining timetables with slogans indicating their superior charms. One, opposite the writer on the office wall, reads thus: 'CHEAP travelling from the Kings Arms and Commercial Inns, Kendal; coaches leave the above inns every morning at SIX o'clock through Lancaster and Preston to Liverpool and Manchester in nine hours certain at very reduced fares. NB — Passengers travelling by these Coaches arrive in Liverool in time for the Steam Packet to Dublin and in Manchester in time for coaches to London in 22 hours, being only one night out on the road.' The date is 1833 and apart from numerous changes of type size and heavy underscorings of the salient points, there are half-a-dozen type faces used, including Ultra Bodoni, which was hailed by the advertising profession as the very

MS SPEED

BY SIR BERTRAM MACKENNAL. R.A.

L·N·E·R
Our Centenary
1825-1925

"LOCOMOTION" driven by George Stephenson

464 Design executed by Fred Taylor for the LNER centenary.

465 Another LNER poster illustrating the development of eating facilities on trains over the years.

466 An early example of 'knocking copy' by the LNER, with due apology to the Southern.

467 Colourful LNER poster advertising travel for one penny per mile, issued nearly a century after an Act of Parliament stipulated that fare, *inter alia*, for rail travel.
All British Transport Museum/B Sharpe

latest in quite recent years.

By contrast canal notices about facilities, thefts of goods and the like were usually much more restrained in choice of type and thus much more effective. Curiously, many late nineteenth-century canal announcements were in the form this century has conditioned us to expect in the way of Russian deviationists' confessions. In 1886 the Lancaster Canal published 'a Public Apology' from an unfortunate boatman who had wasted water at a lock and again, 'a Submission', from three boys aged about 15 who 'having been caught bathing in the Preston and Lancaster Canal and being threatened with Prosecution, do agree to make this Public Submission, pay all expenses, and Promise not to offend again, in consequence of Legal Proceedings being stayed'.

The printing of the Surrey Iron Railway's toll sheet at its opening in 1804 showed not only that the direction of the world's first public railway understood per-ton-mile statistics but that the benefit of using few sizes of type and minimising the distraction of wildly varying styles of type was accepted.

Both typographically and in spirit, the Stockton & Darlington Railway's handbill of September 19, 1825, announcing the order of proceedings on its opening day, six days hence, was a very modern-looking document, which could have set a precedent, but unfortunately does not appear to have projected its influence very far ahead. The Liverpool & Manchester issued a combined rail and coach timetable in 1831, but the bill setting out the timetable in 1835 under the heading 'Travelling by the Liverpool and Manchester Railway' showed nine trains, of which four were first class and five second class, in each direction on weekdays, with variations on Tuesdays and Saturdays; there were four trains on Sundays. The traveller had to guess whether times were am or pm. The fares table included charges for four-wheeled and two-wheeled carriages and included the tariff for horses; one at 10 shillings, two at 18 shillings the pair and the bargain rate for a three-horse customer of 22 shillings. The

utilitarian message was driven home in utilitarian print.

With the Railway Mania and keen competition for public patronage, a sort of Dark Age of this type of public advertisement was entered, put out either by the railways, sponsors of excursions or the rival organisers of fly-boats who tried to persuade would-be patrons of the rapidity of their services. All were terribly cluttered up with information. A 'grand railway trip to Liverpool', organised by the Independent Order of Odd Fellows in 1842 in aid of a 'Widows' and Orphans' Institution' has 19 lines of assorted type and despite being ostensibly an excursion starting at crack of dawn on a Monday and returning on Wednesday evening, gives only the second-class *single* ticket price from Birmingham.

Another, replete with detail of an excursion to Hull on a Sunday produced a caricature notice from Sabbatarian interests stating that the participants in such an un-Godly proceeding would be 'hauled to Hell'. At that time a great many railways either did not work on Sunday or did not start trains between 10.00 and 16.00 hours on that day. Even into modern times churches near the Bow depot of the North London were stiff at Matins with NL enginemen and supervisors who were not booked for duty during the Sunday morning church interval.

Keeping to the factual style of information, the Great Eastern in 1887 pioneered with a list of seaside and country hotels and furnished lodgings; the idea seems to have spread rapidly, but most imitators found it impossible to refrain from using some longwinded all-embracing title, such as *List of Lodgings at Seaside and Holiday Resorts, amid Hill and Dale in Wild Wales on the Cambrian Railways.* After reading the front cover the eager holidaymaker was probably too out-of-breath and exhausted to open the book. The Great Eastern holiday list had a briefer title, but it was overlaid by three disparate holiday scenes, one on top of the other, surmounted by the company's coat-of-arms. The Midland and the South Eastern & Chatham guides had the date on the cover, thus preventing the unsuspecting user from writing letters fruitlessly to someone who had gone out of business; the Vale of Glamorgan and Barry Railways issued a booklet under the simple title *Holiday Haunts,* later used by the Great Western after grouping. A typical piece of railway propaganda of the turn of the century period was the London & North Western brochure to publicise its new route to Buxton: *Dovedale as it will be seen from the North Western Company's New Railway from Buxton to Ashbourne.*

The spate of railway publications seems to have put a term on the privately published guides to railway scenery. There were series by George Measom, published by W. H. Smith & Son, imitated in the eighteen-seventies by *Guides to the Great Railways of England* by Morton and, in the next decade, the more limited series by Cassell. For the most part they were worthy but dull publications listing the delights of the countryside about railway routes; we had to wait until this century was well advanced for books of the calibre of *The Euston to Crew Companion.* In those halcyon days the printing of the railway-produced guides publicising resorts and the holiday accommodation available cost an estimated 5p each in modern terms and about three million of them were sold for something under 1½p; a similar loss was made on the publicising of services in the timetables, issued two or more times a year in some cases, and another costly source of publicity was the issue of series of postcards of railway engines, trains and ships — a business that was in all probability also handled at less than cost.

The development of printing processes so that coloured lithography on a large scale became possible produced the pictorial poster, however. The lush period of development was between 1895 and 1914 and in those years attempts

were made to push practically every aspect of railway trading as far as passengers were concerned. On the freight side, the illusion of monopoly still remained with railway managements well into the lorry age. At the beginning of this century the modest-sized Lancashire & Yorkshire Railway was spending about £7,000 a year on poster printing. The railways did not appear to use outside poster sites to any extent, so that at that time they were preaching to the converted who were already on railway premises for some purpose.

Artist Gunn Gwennet, commenting in 1900 on railway posters, thought the railways did not get value for money from their posters, partly because too many relied on bald announcements in type and largely because the pictures in the others were inferior as works of art. Not only should the picture used be considered for its quality as a work of art, but it should be both bold and simple; to be well-drawn was vital. A Gunn Gwennet drawing of a girl sitting on a trunk in a railway station was used by the London, Brighton & South Coast Railway as an advertisement for Bexhill-on-Sea. Neither picture nor text conjured up a vision of the sea or Sussex and a clutter of type on one side referred to times of trains and on the other to the fact that a new and luxurious hotel on the sea front was now open.

This failure to tell a simple story long dogged the British railway poster. By contrast Tanconville did one for the PLM which had the one word 'Cannes' at the top of a seductive view of the Mediterranean coast. PLM added its initials in a minor key on the other side and some circular tour particulars appeared at bottom left, partially obscured by a fishing net on the beach. This could have been improved by omitting all the details of cheap

465

466

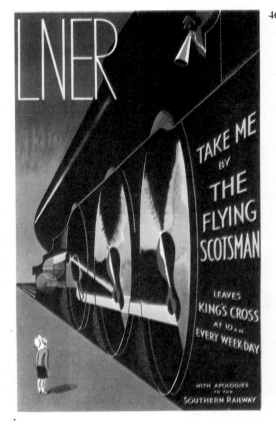

467

facilities, which were in next-to-unreadable print anyway. 'Monaco', by Hugo d'Alesi, also for the PLM, was not so effective because of an inset view of Thermes Valentia surrounded by roses and some messy printing in five styles in six lines which told one about sea bathing, summer and winter, return tickets, circular tour tickets and reduced rates for families. The idea of using established artists was slow to grow with railway publicity committees in Britain.

A typical poster issued by a railway in 1903 was the Cheshire Lines 'Summer Holidays in the Isle of Man' effort; name of railway and title was draped across the poster under the Cheshire Lines Committee's badge in type that looked as if the draughtsman had made it up as he went along. A map showed the Isle of Man and the Lancashire coast, with Lancashire firmly occupied by the three-legged arms of Man. Scrolls carried the legend 'The popular express route via Liverpool' with 'Double service' adrift between their folds. A jumble of prominent lettering imparted the information 'to Douglas and Ramsey for 1 day, weekend, 11 days and tourists' tickets for 2 months', set out on nine different levels. There were 16 other lines of information, the name of the manager, the location of his office and that crowning stupidity 'For full particulars see small bills.'

A Blackpool and the Lakes excursion was advertised by the Furness Railway and had the merit that most of the type was at least in level readable lines. Two girls on a ship's deck sharpened a reference to the fast steamer *Lady Margaret* and PS *Lady Evelyn*. A London & South Western poster of the period advertised the London to Paris service via Southampton and Havre with four vignettes of scenes and wording worked into the loops and whorls surrounding them. Another example of cramming, although not so tasteless, was a Midland & South Western Junction double-crown spread about 'Cheltenham The Garden Town' which included four scenes, nine lines of commendation and two lines advising the potential customers to look at the company's timetables and notices.

The North Staffordshire Railway, another example of a small railway with a lot to say, claimed to afford 'tourists, excursionists, pleasure and picnic parties access to the following places celebrated for scenery of Rock, Wood, Water and Dale' and this wordy introduction was followed by 15 names, six pictures and a map as well as a commendation of 'Stoke-on-Trent and the Neighbouring Pottery Towns' and four other lines of information including the admonition to 'see Company's Time Tables'. More sense was shown by the North Eastern with the one-word heading 'Northumbria' to a splendid painting of Bamburgh Castle and a left-hand strip of the arms of seven towns in Northumberland. The twenty words of large text called attention to castles, coast and Roman wall.

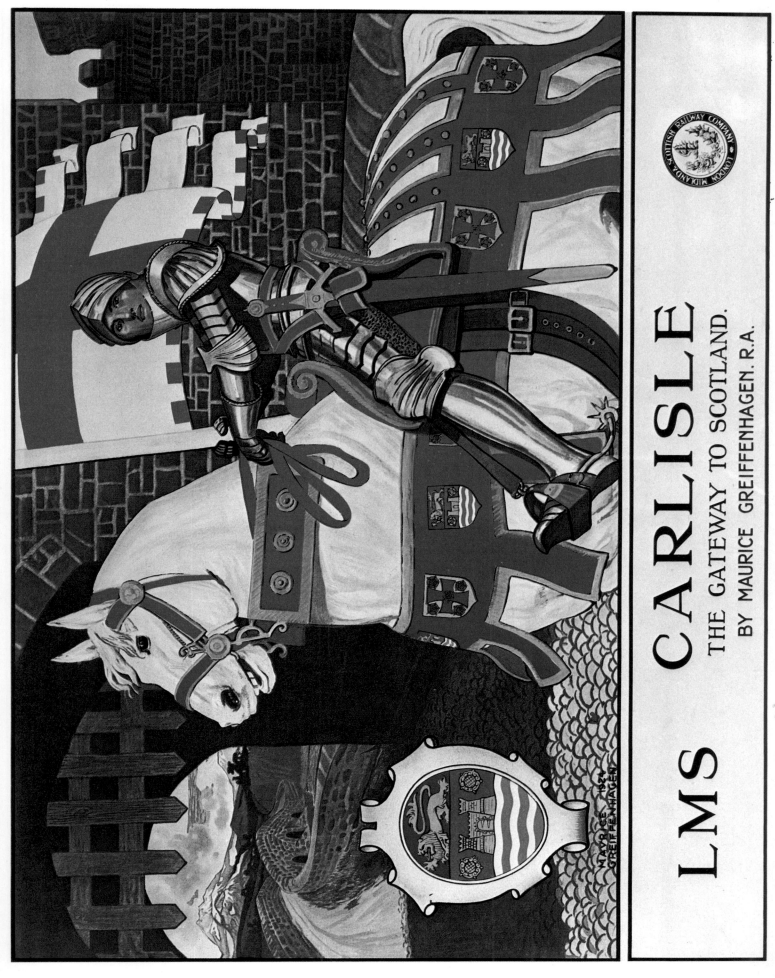

468 Another LNER promotion of one of the resorts served by its main lines.

469 LMS Poster 'Carlisle: The Gateway to Scotland' by Maurice Greiffenhagen RA.

470 (overleaf) GWR 'Cornish Riviera' poster of the early 1900s.
All British Transport Museum/B Sharpe

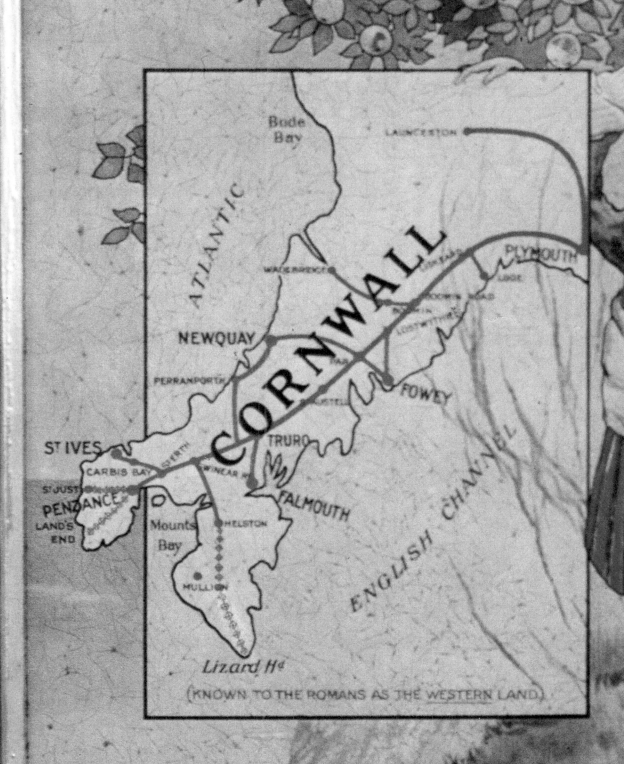

ERN RAILWAY
COUNTRY FIRST

(KNOWN TO THE GREEKS AS THE WESTERN LAND.)

TWEEN

AND ITALY
E, CLIMATE & NATURAL BEAUTIES.

LMS STIRLING
BY SIR D. Y. CAMERON. R.A.

471 One of the series of LMS posters by well-known artists, 'Stirling' by Sir D Y Cameron, RA.
British Transport Museum/B Sharpe

472 A London & North Eastern Railway advertisement of the between-the-wars period. *British Transport Museum/B Sharpe*

473 Rail travel advertising brought right up to date for BR's Inter-City services. *British Rail*

ADVERTISER'S LICENCE, as seen in the florid Edwardian Great Western Railway poster reproduced here, characterised advertising by railways, no less than other commercial activities, from the early days. Until the railway's virtual monopoly of freight transport by land began to be endangered between the world wars, most advertising — and certainly posters — was for passenger business. Not until the end of the last century did the development of efficient and reasonably cheap colour printing, combined with cut-throat competition with other railways (and sometimes steamers) for passenger traffic, initiate the great age of railway posters that lasted until 1914.

The railways did not make as much use of enamelled metal sheet to publicise their own services and facilities as did the traders and manufacturers whose products were vividly proclaimed on the metal sheets that covered almost every flat surface in busy British and American passenger stations, although occasional examples, such as London Underground metal poster maps, have been found. The 1880s saw the first realisation of the possibilities of renting space in premises, and the railways were the first big undertakings to have such space to rent.

Some railway picture posters were unashamedly commercial, but well-designed, well-executed and gay and decorative for all that. From the 1890s one or two French railway companies commissioned colour posters from recognised artists. Among them is said to have been Toulouse Lautrec (who certainly produced playbills) but no railway poster by him seems to exist. At all events the nationalised French Railways has continued the practice, including posters by Utrillo in 1953 and quite recently an outstanding series by Salvador Dali.

Standards on railways everywhere were high — not only in Britain, on the Continent and in North America, but also in India, Argentina and elsewhere. The main object was to stimulate travel to (usually) a holiday resort, or to use the advertiser's rail or combined rail and shipping route for holiday or business travel. There were posters depicting simply natural scenery and/or local fauna or historical buildings. Some were enlivened by quasi-classical female figures who tended, as the new century opened, to give way first to girls in 'folklorique' costumes and later to those in the fashion of the day, including the magnificent and alluring Gibson Girls — and much railway advertising in the past half-century has featured their daughters and granddaughters. The pre-1914 decade saw the evolution of the humorous poster, including Hassall's well-known 'Skegness is SO Bracing' for the Great Northern. Also featured were the interiors (made to look unnaturally commodious) of sleeping cars, Pullmans and other vehicles.

A feature during the age of railway competition was the railway system map, in which the advertiser's lines, shown bold, were straight compared with the spidery delineation of competitors' routes; and every city that could conceivably be considered as served by the advertiser was shown as being on that railway. Nor did the artist shrink from distorting nature, as in th GWR poster of Cornwall reproduced overleaf, though some evidence supporting the claim of Cornwall's likeness to Italy, culled from the Ian Allan picture library, is reproduced on page

After the war of 1914-18, in which a great deal of advertising effort in belligerent countries was directed to conditioning the public to wartime travel, the Edwardian trends continued in the form of excellent scenic posters, notably a series commissioned by the London Midland & Scottish Railway from eminent artists. Humorous themes multiplied. There were prestige posters that extolled train punctuality and suggested matey accord between passengers and railwaymen. In the late 1930s the Southern Railway produced a series of highly artistic designs advocating, for example, travel in the autumn. The advertising of freight services began in earnest, notably of the advantages of rail-served factory sites, at about the same time.

Apart from fares bargains and special trains, passenger advertising today tends to feature travel comfort, catering and other amenities of rail travel. To a great extent the railways seem to have given up the struggle for holiday traffic, in the light of air and road competition, though many excellent scenic posters continue to be issued by the French, Swiss and some other European railways. The present growth of Motorail accompanied-car services could well usher in a fresh round of colourful railway advertising.

472

473

GUIDE FREE FROM INFORMATION BUREAU BRIDLINGTON OR ANY L·N·E·R AGENCY

Inter-City makes the going easy
(and the coming back)

A Chapter of Accidents

474

ACCIDENTS will happen, so the proverb runs, even in the best regulated families. To this rule railways, despite all their costly and elaborate safety precautions, are no exception. And when there is a casualty like a derailment or a collision, such is the energy stored up in the mass of a weighty train travelling at speed that the consequences can be disastrous, not only in damage to or destruction of rolling stock, but also in terms of human life and injury. Some of the most terrible railway accidents in British history have been due to relatively simple causes, and of them the Quintinshill collision of May 22, 1915, was the most fearful in its consequences in British history.

Quintinshill signalbox is 1½ miles north of Gretna Junction, on the former Caledonian main line from Carlisle to Glasgow; it had no special features other than down and up loops into which trains could be diverted if it was desired to clear the main line. Every morning an 'all stations' slow left Carlisle at 06.10 for Beattock, the timekeeping of which was important, as it connected at Beattock with the Tinto, an express carrying commuters from Moffat and the Clyde valley to Glasgow. Normally

this should have followed from Carlisle the 23.45 and 24.00 sleeping car expresses from Euston, but if they were running late, as frequently happened, the practice was to start the 06.10 from Carlisle on time, and to shunt it where necessary to let one of the sleepers by. On this particular morning the 23.45 was half-an-hour behind time, so the 06.10 was started on time, and was to be held at Quintinshill. It so happened that both the reception lines there were occupied by freight trains, and the only track on to which the slow train could be shunted was the up main line.

Now the signalman at Quintinshill was due to be relieved at 6 o'clock in the morning, but the practice had arisen, completely unauthorised, that if the 06.10 was to be shunted at Quintinshill the relieving signalman would travel on it from Gretna to Quintinshill and so be saved a 1½ mile walk. So that his late arrival might not be noticed by the authorities, what should have been entries in the signalbox register from 06.00 onwards were made by the night signalman on scraps of paper, and copied into the book by the relieving man after his arrival.

While he was catching up on the entries on the morning
in question, the night signalman was reading the
newspaper the relieving man had brought with him,
the signalman at the next box to the north (who had not
received from Quintinshill a 'blocking back' bell signal, as
should have done, to advise that the up main line at
Quintinshill was occupied) offered to Quintinshill an up
troop train, which was approaching at speed. Distracted
by chatter in the box and by his work with the register, and
entirely without looking out of the signalbox window at
the train standing on the up line, the relieving signalman
accepted the troop special, and pulled off all his up line
signals. He had meantime pulled off all his down line
signals for the sleeper from Euston.

The troop train driver had no chance. An overbridge
concealed from his sight the standing train until, at 70
miles an hour, he was almost on to it. The effect of the
impact was such that the 213-yard length of his 21-vehicle
train was reduced to a heap of matchwood only 67 yards
long. Into this wreckage a few moments later there
ploughed the double-headed 13-coach down sleeping car
express, also travelling at a mile-a-minute. Most of the
coaches were of wooden construction, there was gas
escaping from the coach storage cylinders, and with live
coals in the fireboxes of four engines, fire was
inevitable; it raged for a whole day and burned out a total
of 15 vehicles.

In this holocaust there perished no fewer than 227
persons, mostly officers and men of the Royal Scots. Both
signalmen were subsequently tried and convicted for
manslaughter, and sentenced to lengthy terms of
imprisonment, but this could in no way atone for the
dreadful havoc caused by their gross dereliction of duty.
With modern signalling, interlocking, AWS (automatic
warning system) and track-circuiting, such a catastrophe
is of course virtually impossible.

About 37 years later, on October 8, 1952, another
disastrous accident involving three trains took place, at
Harrow & Wealdstone; in this case the real reason for what
happened was never fully established. An up outer
suburban train was standing in the station at the up fast
line platform picking up passengers, and fully protected in
the rear by home and outer home semaphore signals and
by a colour-light distant signal a mile away at Headstone
Lane. The morning was misty, but could not be described
as fog. Suddenly there appeared through the mist a night
sleeping car express from Perth, headed by the Pacific
locomotive *City of Glasgow*, running one and a half hours
behind time, which crashed at full speed into the standing
local train. At that very moment the heavy 07.55 express from
Euston to Liverpool and Manchester, double-headed by
the Jubilee class 4-6-0 *Windward Islands* and the Pacific
Princess Anne, was approaching Harrow at 60mph
without the remotest chance of being stopped, and crashed
into the already considerable wreckage.

Since Quintinshill no such frightful a pile of wrecked
locomotives and coaches has ever been seen to equal that
which was spread all over Wealdstone station on that
tragic morning. The disaster cost 112 lives. As the driver of
the first express was killed, the reason why he failed to
stop, or even to reduce speed, was never established; the
only possible explanation was that he might have been
dozing or asleep. If that was so, the AWS horn might
have awakened him in time, but at that date there was no
AWS on the LMS main line.

The third most serious disaster in British railway
history, measured by the number of casualties, was
December 4, 1957, at Lewisham, on the Southern Region,
and was due primarily to a driver overrunning signals at
danger in a foggy evening, and the 16.56 express from
Cannon Street to Ramsgate was following a suburban
train to Hayes on the fast line from New Cross. The engine

474 and 475 Scenes from the 1952 Harrow & Wealdstone station
three-train crash. *Conway Picture Library*

475

of the express was *Spitfire*, one of the original Bulleid light
Pacifics, which never had a good reputation for lookout
from the footplate, especially with drifting exhaust in thick
weather. Anyway, just beyond St John's the driver passed
a double-yellow and then a single-yellow signal, both
colour-lights, without any reduction of speed, and only
when the train was passing the next signal at red did he
take action.

But it was too late; a few moments later he ran into the
back of the stationary suburban train. And as fate would
have it, the collision took place under the Nunhead
flyover, carrying away the columns supporting the
overhead girders, which came crashing down on to the
wreckage. It was a most unfortunate location and
undoubtedly contributed to the heavy death toll of 90
persons. Here again AWS would probably have prevented
the collision, and shortly after the accident Southern
Region started to instal this most valuable safeguard
against the overrunning of signals.

While many railway accidents have been due to drivers
passing signals at danger, or to derailments resulting from
excessive speeds on curves, there have been others resulting
from happenings of a completely unprecedented kind.
Two such occurred within a mile of one another near
Weedon, on the main line out of Euston, though separated
in time by 36 years. The first was on August 14, 1915, in
London & North Western days, and the second on
September 21, 1951, on what had then become the London
Midland Region of British Railways. The trouble which

resulted in the 1915 accident began with the George V class 4—? *Wolfhound,* at the head of ?? 08.45 from Birmingham to Euston. The driver was ?? ?ing round his engine at the Rugby stop when he noticed that a split pin was missing from the washer which secured the right-hand coupling-rod to the crank-pin of the driving axle.

A fitter was on the platform, and so that the train might not be delayed he extracted the corresponding pin from a neighbouring engine which was shunting, and transferred it to *Wolfhound;* he maintained that he opened the two ends of ?? in out properly, but evidently he failed to do so. For as *Wolfhound* was approaching Weedon at 70mph the fireman saw something strike the ballast on the right ?? of the engine, throwing a mass of stones up into the ?? engine then began lurching violently from side to ?? but the driver managed to bring the train to a stand with the engine just inside Stowe Hill tunnel.

What had happened was that the pin had worked out of it ?hole and five miles later the washer had become unscrewed and dropped off (both were found later where they had fallen on to the track). Then the coupling-rod itself had broken loose at one end, with its 10ft of length flailing round. The first impact with the ballast bent the rod considerably and after that, at about seven-yard intervals, with every impact the sleepers of the down main line were disturbed, pushing the rails of the down track as much as seven inches out of line. Once again, by sheer misfortune, the second portion of the down Irish Mail was just approaching at full speed, and both its locomotives, with their 15 coaches, were derailed, ten passengers being killed. The remarkable feature of this accident was that the defective engine and its train escaped unscathed, while another express left the track.

In the 1951 accident the train involved was the 08.20 from Liverpool to Euston, with Pacific No 46207 *Princess Arthur of Connaught* hauling a formation of 15 coaches. At precisely the same point as that at which *Wolfhound's* coupling-rod came off its pin, the Pacific's leading bogie came off the rails, derailing to the right. Because of tyre wear the two bogie axles had earlier been transposed, but the fitter who did the work had not left the axleboxes ?er ?? to move up and down in the horns. The leading pair of wheels had therefore been relieved of their share of the engine's weight, and had lifted off the track as the engine was rounding a left-hand curve.

The extraordinary thing is that the locomotive travelled on for ?ull mile without the crew suspecting that anything was wrong, mainly because this section of the line had been relaid a short time previously with heavy flat-bottom rails without chairs, so that the derailed wheels encountered no obstructions. With the bogie off the rails, t ?? went through Stowe Hill tunnel in which the ?? ?ded to set up a resistance to movement of the ballast. But once out of the tunnel and on to bull-head track the derailed wheels started hitting the rail chairs, which soon caused distortion of the track; once the driver ?sed that something was wrong he evidently applied the brakes but it was too late. The locomotive derailed and went down the embankment, followed by eleven of the fourteen coaches, 15 people losing their lives.

It might be imagined that a serious accident could hardly be caused by anything as innocent as a platform barrow, but on two occasions barrows have caused disastrous derailments. One such was on August 2, 1898, at Wellingborough, on the Midland main line. Some boys were playing about on the down platform with a porter's barrow when it ran away, down the slight slope of the platform, and fell on the track just as the 18.30 Manchester express from St Pancras, composed of some of the latest vestibuled stock, was approaching at full speed. The leading bogie wheels of 4-4-0 locomotive No 1743 picked up the barrow and carried it as far as the

points at the north end of the station, where derailment occurred, with the loss of six lives.

A much bigger barrow was involved in the derailment of an up Liverpool express at Wembley on October 2, 1940. The heavy barrow, loaded with parcels, was being taken across the line from the up slow to the up fast platform by three men, and had nearly reached the top of the fast platform ramp when one of them slipped; the weight of the barrow then overpowered the other two, neither of whom was very strong, and ran back down the ramp. The men did all they could to stop it, but unsuccessfully, and finally it skewed round and stopped with one corner fouling the up main line, just as the Liverpool train was approaching at speed. The bogie of the Patriot class 4-6-0 *Stephenson* caught the barrow, and at the crossover roads immediately beyond the engine derailed and turned over most of the coaches following it. Eleven lives were lost, and the tragedy in this case was that the train was running very late; had it been on time there would have been no accident.

Fouling of another kind was responsible for a serious accident on February 11, 1942, at Beighton, on the Great Central main line just south of Sheffield. Three days earlier seven steel plates, each 9ft 6in long and 8ft 7in wide, had been loaded at Frodingham steelworks on to a 20-ton LNER plate wagon, itself 8ft 4½in wide inside. Had the plates been 8ft 9in wide or more, they would have been loaded on edge in wagons fitted with trestles and secured by binding chains, but at this intermediate width it was regarded as safe to load them with one edge on the floor of the wagon, and the other supported on packing-pieces to come just above the wagon side, over which they slightly projected. Shortly before eight o'clock in the evening of the day of the accident the wagon reached Holbrook sidings, and in some marshalling operations more than usually hard impact caused the load to shift so that the top plate, though unnoticed in the blackout, projected nearly three feet over the wagon side. As ill-luck would have it, the wagon was standing in a siding which had a clearance of only just over seven feet from the adjacent main line, instead of the standard nine feet.

The next train that passed on the main line was a freight, which was not fouled, but after that came a troop special of 13 coaches and two vans, carrying 400 soldiers and sailors. The 4-6-0 engine got by, and then three coaches with no more damage than the loss of door handles. But the fourth coach caught the plate and swung it round that it cut to a depth of 6ft into the side of the sixth and succeeding coaches. But for the fact that the sixth and seventh coaches had their corridors on the near side, the casualties might have been greater, but as it was 14 of the men in the special lost their lives. Subsequent experiments showed how easily plates loaded in that manner could be shifted on impact, and the practice was stopped.

Such have been some of the totally unexpected happenings that can cause a railway disaster; fortunately, viewed in the context of the millions of passenger-miles run, they can be classed as very rare.

476 Workers shoring up a collapsed flyover in the St Johns, Lewisham accident, December 1957. *Conway Picture Library*

477 Recovering a derailed locomotive after the accident at Hither Green in February 1960. *D Cobbe*

478 and 479 Pictures of the Liverpool-London express crash at Weedon, September 1951. *Conway Picture Library*

480 A railway crane starting to clear a pile-up of locomotives and wagons at Linton Junction, Nottingham in December 1971. *J Hooke*

476

477

478

479

480

481

482

Railways and the General Strike

ACCORDING TO THE first issue of the *British Worker,* the Trades Union Council newspaper issued during the General Strike of 1926, 'the strike early laid its paralysing hand on the great railway station at Carlisle, where seven important lines converge, forming a railway hub second in importance to none in the country. Within a few hours the usually animated platforms were deserted and desolate. Passengers arriving early in the morning could get no farther by train, but some were able to proceed in hired motorcars to Glasgow or Edinburgh, paying as much as £25 a time.' The stoppage of rail transport was complete.

The origins of the General Strike are complex and need not greatly concern us here. Suffice it to say that what had started out as an internal dispute within the sorely troubled coal industry had gradually snowballed into a full-scale confrontation between the TUC on one side and the government on the other. Neither party had intervened willingly but both found themselves obliged to do so by a variety of moral, legal and political pressures brought to bear upon them. But in one important respect their positions differed. The government had long prepared for a national labour stoppage. The TUC had not. Although the idea of a general strike had gained a certain currency among advanced and militant political left-wingers, it had never been taken seriously by the actual union leadership. When they found themselves in charge of one, therefore, they were almost paralysed by their own trepidation and hamstrung by their lack of foresight.

Government preparations had included arrangements for an emergency transport system organised by road commissioners and local haulage committees. The political and economic significance of maintaining communications had been grasped from the outset. The TUC also took the point but simply assumed that a railway stoppage would paralyse the country. The role of motorised transport had been completely underestimated. In the event it was to

prove the government's most decisive weapon. Drivers were recruited by the thousand, largely from ex-officers and undergraduates and mostly through the offices of the officially inspired Organisation for the Maintenance of Supplies. It was to become only gradually apparent, however, that their contribution would inevitably lead to the failure of the strike.

Initially, at least, the unions could congratulate themselves on a magnificent display of labour solidarity. On the London Midland & Scottish Railway, for instance, only 207 out of more than 15,000 engine-drivers reported for work on the first day of the strike. The proportion of firemen was even smaller, 62 out of 14,000. More than forty per cent of the salaried staff came out as well. As a result, passenger services were a mere 3.8 per cent of normal on May 5. On the last full day of the strike, May 11, they were still only 12.2 per cent. Freight services were even worse hit, one per cent worked at the start of the strike and three per cent at the end. The Great Western and the Southern systems fared a little better, reaching nearly 20 per cent of normal on passenger services by the end of the strike. Nationally speaking, the railways were all but totally paralysed for the first four days of the strike. On the fifth day the *British Gazette*, the government counterpart of the *British Worker,* was proud to announce that nearly three thousand trains had run the previous day. It omitted to state that that was less than ten per cent of normal. The Underground fared rather better, achieving 71 out of a normal 315 trains.

In retrospect, the General Strike has attracted its fair share of myths. It was remarkably non-violent, considering the numbers involved and the depths of emotion stirred by the issue at stake, but there were nevertheless more than 5,000 arrests for violence and sedition, as well as serious rioting in many industrial towns in the north of England and Scotland. To suggest that the whole affair was entirely peaceful would be absurd, but the myth survives. So also does the legend of the volunteers who are supposed to have mastered the complexities of railway operation overnight. For weeks after the strike the newspapers printed pictures of eager young men, clad in gaudy sweaters and plus-four suits, loading mail-bags or manning signal boxes, while middle-aged businessmen fulfilled a life-time's ambition and lived out their fantasies as begrimed and sweaty footplatemen.

But driving an engine calls for greater skill than driving a car. It was one thing to allow medical students to career around in buses to the delight of their friends and the terror of their luckless passengers, it was quite another to turn them loose on the railways. Reading complex signals or threading one's way through a tangled mass of track and points called for a lifetime's experience and expertise and to maintain a head of steam on a gradient was a matter of fine judgment, as many of the volunteers were to learn the hard way. Just as the short-lived antics of burly university sportsmen at the docks had afforded free amusement for the dockers, who watched them with genial contempt, so the fumbling and hesitancy of the volunteer railwaymen gave the strikers some occasion for mirth. The *Westminster Worker,* a strike-bulletin issued locally in the central London area, dryly announced to its readers that 'We understand that luncheon cars are to be put on trains running between Westminster and Blackfriars.'

Some of the volunteers' escapades seem to have been positively hair-raising. It was, apparently, not uncommon for drivers who had 'taken a wrong turning', simply to reverse up to where they thought they had gone wrong and start again. More often, however, it was a case of continuous stop-go. An American journalist reported the following incident to Hamilton Fyfe, editor of the *British Worker:*

He travelled from Warwick Avenue tube station to Baker Street. The first hitch was a stop in the tunnel, which put all the lights out. When the alarm caused by that had subsided, the train crawled along until Baker Street was reached. There, the American, who was standing on the platform of the car next to the locomotive, heard an agonised voice calling to the conductor: 'I say, Bill, I can't start the darned thing. Give me the instructions.' The conductor handed him a clip of leaflets; in a few minutes a buzzing sound from the locomotive began suddenly and as suddenly ended. Then the voice again: 'Bill, I've touched the wrong handle and the brake's gone fut. Send for the chief engineer . . .'

Baker Street is also immortalised in the recollections of a young girl drama student who wrote the following account of her journey home to her mother:

'There, everybody carries your luggage and is awfully nice. It is perfectly mad to hear, instead of " 'Arrer 'n' Uxbridge'', a beautiful Oxford voice crying "Harrow and Uxbridge train''. Ticket collectors say thank you very much; one guard of a train due to depart, an immaculate youth in plus-fours, waved a green flag. Nothing happened. He waved again and blew a whistle, then said to the driver in injured tones, "I say, you might *go.*'' It's all very jolly and such an improvement on the ordinary humdrum state of things.'

Maintenance, of course, was sadly neglected. It was unglamorous, attracted few volunteers and was poorly organised. As the strike lasted only nine days, however, the neglect never became a factor of major importance. If the experiences of one volunteer platelayer are anything to go by though, things might well have become serious had the stoppage lasted much longer. 'We spent one day in a dreary fen between March and Ely,' he recollected, 'shovelling granite chips between the metals. By the end of the day we were so blistered that there was no question of turning up again next day.' An undergraduate who later became headmaster of a well-known school had happier

481 A volunteer driver of a GWR lorry during the 1926 General Strike. *National Union of Railwaymen*

482 Students helping to sort mailbags during the General Strike. *Klugmann Collection*

483 The training of soldiers as railwaymen, as featured in the *Illustrated London News*, November 1913, partly for emergency employment on civil railways in the event of strikes and partly to improve army transport potential.

THE ILLUSTRATED LONDON NEWS, Nov. 28, 1913.—843

SUGGESTED BY FRANCE? BRITISH SOLDIERS AS RAILWAY-MEN. **483**

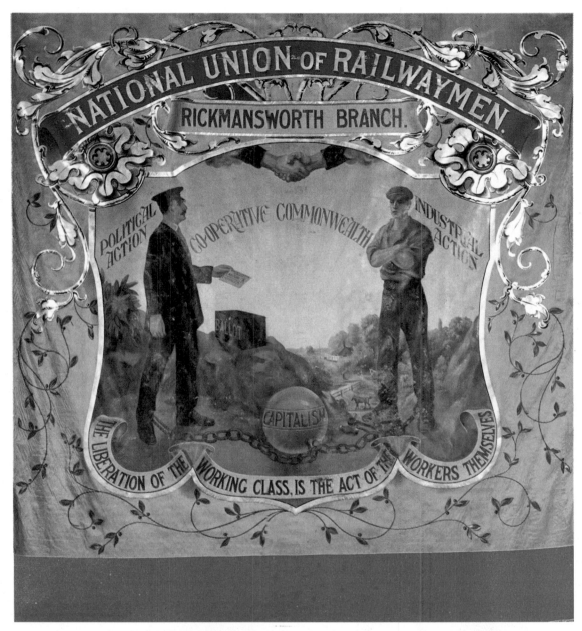

484 and 486 NUR banners in the John Gorman collection.

485 J H Thomas, general secretary of the NUR for many years,
including during the 1926 strike. *National Union of Railwaymen*

487 NUR members rally under their banners at a strike meeting.

memories to record of maintenance work on the Underground.

'Our work was done by gangs of four under a non-striking officer. We used to leave a cache of beer at each station. When we reached the end we waited on the platform for the train that had brought us to go home and for the current to be turned off, and then we collected the tools from a little shed a few yards down the tunnel. To begin with, we collected the tools without waiting for the current to be turned off, but after I had, on one occasion, slipped off the platform and landed astraddle of the live rail, we became more cautious. Current off, we proceeded, two down each tunnel, knocking in with a sledgehammer any of the wooden blocks which had fallen out or seemed likely to do so.

'This was easy enough — more unpleasant was greasing the check-rails, which involves use of the most appallingly stiff grease. One had a small bucketful of the stuff and a stick for smearing it on, but it was like trying to smear on a piece of indiarubber. However, every station was a resting-place, complete with beer. We finished about 3.30 or 4 o'clock in the morning and were taken to Earl's Court where a vast building was used by about 500 to 1,000 volunteers and where the canteen was run, to the best of my recollection, by glamorous debutantes.'

There were many minor accidents on the railways during the General Strike, but only one serious one and that the result of the single known instance of deliberate sabotage. Stone-throwing at trains was common enough and passengers learned to pass vulnerable stretches of line standing on the seats to avoid broken glass, but this could be accepted with relative good humour. Fortunately the single, and successful, case of sabotage, resulted in no fatalities. The lifting of a rail at Cramlington, near Newcastle, resulted in the derailment of the engine and one coach of the celebrated Flying Scotsman. Several passengers were taken to hospital for treatment.

On May 12, the return to work was ordered by the unions and the railways faced a special crisis of their own. The railway unions, whose support of the whole general strike undertaking had been considered vital, had in fact only decided to support it after much agonising hesitation. Union leaders realised that their men were in many cases more easily replaceable than the miners they were backing up and would, moreover, be obliged to bear in person the brunt of the public's displeasure. And the railway companies had made their attitude quite clear. The GWR, for instance, had warned its employees that their means of living and personal interests were involved and the LNER had issued a notice to the effect that striking railwaymen would be regarded as having acted in breach of contract. It was scarcely surprising, therefore, that the railway companies should have used the unions' surrender to the government as an opportunity for settling old scores by victimising activists.

The companies' attitude was, however, not without its ironic aspect, given the attitude of J H Thomas, leader of the National Union of Railwaymen. A dedicated social climber with the highest political ambitions, he had withdrawn the support of the railwaymen on a technicality when the miners had tried to force a showdown in 1921. In the last-minute negotiations before the outbreak of the General Strike he had played a leading part in the effort to find a face-saving formula for reconciliation. He was, by temperament, a man who shrank from conflict — he even gave his life-story the title of *A Life for Unity*. But it is hard to believe that he was not acting throughout with at least one eye to the future, determined to emerge with enhanced stature in the eyes of the establishment as a 'responsible' statesman of labour. As spokesman for the TUC negotiating team, he had addressed the union delegates assembled in the Memorial Hall to pledge their support for strike action if need be. 'I have never in my life,' he said, 'begged and pleaded for peace as I have begged and pleaded today.' It was probably true, but not in the sense in which his audience understood it.

Thomas continued to press for a resumption of negotiations throughout the nine days and was, indeed, largely responsible for the unions' abject capitulation. All the more ironic, therefore, that it should be the railwaymen who faced the most ferocious anti-union backlash in the aftermath of the strike. The conditions on which they were to be re-employed were as follows:

1. Those employees of the railway companies who have gone out on strike to be taken back to work as soon as traffic officers and work can be found for them. The principle to be followed in reinstating to be seniority in each grade at each station, depot or office.

2. The trade unions admit that in calling a strike they committed a wrongful act against the companies, and agree that the companies do not by reinstatement surrender their legal rights to claim damages arising out of the strike from strikers and others responsible.

3. The unions undertake (a) not again to instruct their members to strike without previous negotiation with the company; (b) to give no support of any kind to their members to take any unauthorised action; and (c) not to encourage supervisory employees in the special class to take part in any strike.

4. The companies intimate that, arising out of the strike it might be necessary to remove certain persons to other positions, but no such persons' salaries or wages will be reduced.

The last provision covered companies demoting signalmen to station porters and the unions had no choice but to accept. Among the many concessions they were obliged to make was the suspension of the 'guaranteed week' which assured their members of a basic wage. Even so, about 45,000 men, nearly a quarter of the membership of the NUR, had not been re-employed by October, nearly six months after the end of the strike.

Analysing the failure of the General Strike in the *Observer,* J L Garvin, the famous columnist, asserted that the defeat of the TUC had been inevitable from the outset, 'Because its whole system of thought is stupid and out of date and years behind the progress of modern science and mechanism. Nearly twelve months ago, when the plan was threatened in earnest, we told Socialist Labour what would happen. We agreed with them that transport was the key, but we told them that in an age of motor traffic multiplying year by year on every road, they can never seize that key.'

A motor car manufacturer put it more simply in an interview with the *Daily Mail,* 'motoring has once and for all knocked the possibility of a serious transport strike on the head. With half a million capable motor drivers in the country it is an anachronism.'

487

Railways at War

THE GREAT WAR of 1914-18 marked a turning-point in the history of Britain's railways, as in so many of her institutions. The pride and self-assurance of the Edwardian era were never to be recaptured. In 1914 the Regulation of Forces Act, passed in 1871 in the shadow of Prussia's railway-borne victory over France, put the railways of Britain under state control for the first time in their history. Henceforth they were to be operated as a single unifed system under the direction of a Railway Executive Committee presided over by the President of the Board of Trade. But it was still far from nationalisation. The membership of the Railway Executive Committee was entirely composed of the general managers of the eleven largest railway companies and the companies were

guaranteed the same profits as they had made in 1913, a year which, incidentally, had been rather prosperous. Thus the system of state control which was adopted was one in which railways were run *for* the government but not *by* the government.

The wartime tasks imposed on the British railway system were immense. The flow of traffic was greatly intensified at the very time that 30 per cent of the railway labour force was recruited into the army and the diversion of railway manufacturing capacity to munitions production made it almost impossible to obtain new rolling-stock. Maintenance and investment were seriously neglected, with significant consequences in the post-war period. In retrospect this seems an incredibly short-sighted policy;

but, given the task to hand, it was probably inevitable.

To grasp the overall picture is difficult and a more accurate impression may be gained by looking at the work of one or two vital lines. Consider, for example, the strains imposed on the London & South Western Railway, the main supply-route for British forces on the Continent, or on the Highland Railway, which performed the same function for Scapa Flow and Cromarty Firth, two of the Grand Fleet's most important bases. Admittedly the London & South Western, which served Aldershot and Salisbury plain, had long military experience to fall back on, but it had never before faced the problem of funnelling literally millions of men, converging along five main routes, into the single port of Southampton, which was the main point of embarkation for the Western Front. More than 20,000,000 soldiers were transported by the London & South Western in the course of the war, an average of

13,000 every day.

No less remarkable was the achievement of the Highland Railway, for it was peculiarly ill-adapted to the needs of war. Before 1914 heavy traffic on the line had been confined to a three-month summer tourist season; three-quarters of its length was only single track and there were few sidings or loops. Within a year a third of its locomotives were to be out of service and another third badly in need of repair; but still the line somehow kept the traffic flowing and remained a vital, if tenuous, link in a chain of communication which maintained the naval shield on which Britain's national security depended.

In the autumn of 1914 the generals, and the public, had anticipated a 'war of movement' which would be 'over by Christmas'. It was expected that the pattern of the Franco-Prussian war would be repeated - a massive deployment of troops by railway followed by a single, bloody and decisive

488 War poster on behalf of the four main-line companies by Reginald Mayes. *British Transport Museum/B Sharpe*

489 Scene of troops entraining at Victoria station during the 1914-18 war, from a painting by Richard Jack, RA. *British Transport Museum/B Sharpe*

490 German prisoners of the British entraining at Salonika in 1916. *Illustrated London News*

491 Women working in the Underground Railway's Ealing repair shop in 1916. *Conway Picture Library*

489

490

491

battle on the frontiers. The stabilisation of more than a hundred miles of trench fortifications created a novel situation in which railways were to play a new role as the need to supply forward positions, and, later, to stockpile ammunition and stores for major offensives, led to the extemporisation of a tactical railway network behind the lines. Communications problems, revealed starkly during the Somme offensive of 1916, led to an official decision to set up an organised system of light railways, which was rapidly extended in 1917 and 1918; from the main system trench tramways, utilising men and horses for motive power, proliferated as feeder lines. By the end of hostilities the army's Railway Operating Division had a total strength of 18,400 men organised in 67 companies. In all 76,000 troops and 48,000 men in labour service units were employed in running and safeguarding this largely new network of 800-odd miles, a network which necessarily came to bulk large in Allied strategic thinking.

According to the official war history the decision of Marshal Foch, the supreme co-ordinator of the Allied counter-offensive of 1918, to grant the Germans an armistice, was largely determined by the realisation that the Allied advance was about to run out of reach of its railheads. If it had not been so, of course, Hitler and his followers would never have been able to argue so powerfully that the German army had never been defeated nor the homeland invaded. In view of the strategic and tactical importance of railways in that war, it was perhaps rather appropriate that the armistice which brought it to a close should have been signed in a railway carriage - which Hitler was to insist on using again to accept the surrender of France in 1940.

Railways were, of course, important in other theatres of war, and especially in the Middle East, where Colonel T. E. Lawrence's train-wrecking activities played a large part in disrupting the defence of the Ottoman Empire. In Salonika and East Africa, railway units also played their part in ensuring Allied victory, while, on the other side, German railwaymen struggled to maintain a vast network, stretching from the Baltic to the Bosphorous. In Russia the total collapse of the railway system, resulting in the cessation of supplies to the front or of food to the towns,

was a major factor in precipitating the outbreak of revolution. In Britain the situation was by no means so dramatic, but it was acute enough for the Liberal-Conservative government of the day to entertain a solution which in many circles would be branded as revolutionary, and even Bolshevik, in its inspiration — nationalisation.

State control of Britain's railways, which had been debated and dismissed as far back as the 1840s, had now been vindicated by the test of war. It had not only enabled the railways to meet the extraordinary demands made upon them, it had also enabled them to achieve a number of striking economies in operation through such schemes as the pooling of wagons or arrangments to eliminate unnecessary haulage of coal. The coal distribution rationalisation alone saved 700 million ton-miles a year after its introduction in 1917. As early as 1915 the Trades Union Council had passed a resolution calling upon the Government 'before relinquishing its present control to introduce legislation having for its object the effecting of complete national ownership of the railways.'

Sir Herbert Walker, general manager of the London and South Western and de facto head of the Railway Executive stated publicly that he did not 'think that our railways will ever again revert to the independent and foolish competitive system' of the pre-war period. Lloyd George himself intimated that nationalisation was seriously being considered by the government and, in December 1918, Churchill actually asserted that that was in fact the government's policy.

In 1919 a Bill was introduced to establish a Ministry of Ways and Communications with powers of compulsory purchase which would enable the state to acquire railways, docks and canals by Order in Council. But the times were not propitious for such a momentous step, despite the success of the wartime experiment. The spectre of Bolshevism was abroad; there was a general resentment against the continuation during peacetime of war controls and a desire to 'get back to normal' which swept away the whole apparatus of state control of industry, agriculture, finance and transport which had been constructed piecemeal in the course of the war. By the time the Bill emerged from Parliament the purchase clauses had been

"PERHAPS THIS'LL TEACH YOU TO STAY AT 'OME NEXT 'OLIDAY"

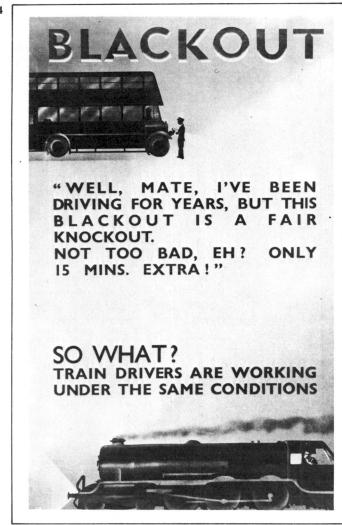

cut away and the proposed all-embracing Ministry of Ways and Communications reduced to a mere Ministry of Transport. Nationalisation was finally rejected in the summer of 1920 in favour of a compromise measure of rationalisation which was embodied in the Railways Act of 1921.

The 1921 Act was to play a major part in determining the future development of the railways. The 120 companies of the pre-war era were reduced to four main groups — the London & North Eastern, the London, Midland & Scottish, the Great Western and the Southern. The reorganisation would, it was hoped, enable the railways to achieve new economies of scale in operation. The public interest would be protected by a Railway Rates Tribunal and an elaborate system of conciliation procedures designed to prevent stoppages like the national railway strike of 1919. Some competition would remain along the 'frontiers', and cities like Exeter, Leeds, Sheffield and Glasgow would be served by more than one group but, on the other hand, major industrial areas like South Wales and Lancashire would thenceforth depend entirely on the services of a single railway organisation.

Unfortunately the amalgamation scheme, though it looked like a step towards greater efficiency, had been determined largely by political pressures and according to political principles. The economic aspects of the problem had been pretty well ignored or were assumed to require no detailed examination. There was, therefore, no study made of the optimum or viable size for a railway unit and the maintenance of the shibboleth of private ownership, which blocked the dismantling of former companies, led to the creation of four groups which were extremely unequal in their size and capacities. The London & North Eastern, for instance, struggled with an unhappy legacy of uneconomic country branch lines and was to find itself dependent for most of its custom on a Tyneside plunged in the depths of industrial depression. The Southern, which had borne the brunt of the strain imposed by war, found itself faced with the need to accommodate a massive and expanding commuter belt around London. Thanks to the energy and vision of the indefatigable Sir Herbert Walker it found its salvation in a programme of electrification which brought

495

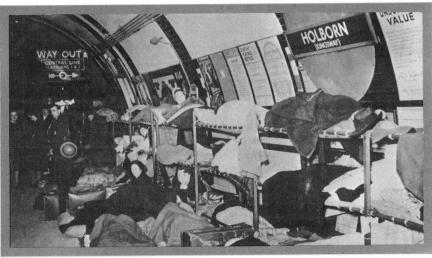

492 A Giles cartoon from the *Sunday Express* during the 1939-45 war. *Imperial War Museum*

493 A4 Pacific *Sir Ralph Wedgwood* well mangled by a German bomb at York locomotive depot in 1942. *British Rail*

494 Poster intended to soften complaints about driving conditions with masked lights in the 1939-45 war. *Imperial War Museum*

495 Londoners sheltering from bombs overnight in an Underground station. *London Transport Executive*

Portsmouth, Brighton and Chatham virtually into London's backyard.

The 1921 Railways Act imposed on the railway companies a new outlook which required great organisational and psychological readjustments, while regrettably maintaining a tradition of Parliamentary regulation that hamstrung the railways when they attempted to meet the challenge of motor transport, which had developed rapidly as a result of the war. Large-scale production of military vehicles, plus the protectionist McKenna duties, imposed in 1915 to economise on shipping space by limiting the importation of luxury goods like French and American cars, had created the facility in Britain to turn out large quantities of buses, lorries and cars. With their permanent way maintained at the expense of the taxpayer and with no statutory obligation to provide 'reasonable services' or to publish their freight rates, the road hauliers and bus companies were all set to cream off the profits of the best routes, leaving the railways to make what they could from such stricken customers as the coal and steel industries. Little wonder that by 1938 the railways were clamouring for a 'square deal'.

The outbreak of war in 1939 precluded any possibility of salvaging the lost fortunes of the railways and once again imposed upon them the massive strains of total war. In an age of air and motor transport and after nearly a quarter century of under-investment, the railways were still called upon to shoulder the major part of the burden. Not only did they have to cope with a vastly expanded volume of regular traffic, they also had to hold themselves ready to adapt the whole system to meet a national emergency at a moment's notice. The most spectacular exercise of the emergency machinery was, of course, Operation Dynamo, which was set in motion on May 26, 1940, to assist the evacuation of the troops from Dunkirk. The main problem was to get the men away from the South Coast ports to reception centres far inland as quickly as possible. Two thousand railway coaches were immediately pooled for the purpose and Redhill junction closed to act as a clearing-house. There was no time to organise a timetable and all train movement orders were therefore issued minute by minute over the telephone. Thanks to the skill of the railwaymen and the enthusiasm of thousands of volunteers, all of whom put in incredibly long hours, about 320,000 men aboard 620 trains were ferried away from the danger areas in a single hectic week.

Bombing was, of course, a new hazard to be overcome. It was particularly severe in the summer and autumn of 1940, when more than half of all the stoppages and delays caused by aerial action occurred, and again during the V2 attacks of 1944. The most concentrated damage was inflicted by saturation raids on dock areas, but direct hits on bridges also caused long delays and throughout the war unprotected trains seems to have been a temptation which few lone raiders could resist.

Stations suffered mixed fortunes. Dover naturally received considerable punishment while, far away, Middlesbrough was smashed by a stick of bombs. In London, St Pancras was badly damaged and nearby Kings Cross had part of Cubitt's famous roof blown away. Locomotives seem to have been remarkably tough; of the 484 which were hit only eight were a total write-off. Three thousand or so wagons and carriages were destroyed. Doubtless many more were causalites of marshalling in blackout conditions. Total damage has been estimated at £30,000,000, a figure which pales into insignificance beside the estimated £200,000,000-worth of arrears of maintenance.

Total war meant a total mobilisation of national resources and the mobilisation of the whole population. It meant diverting more than 100 locomotives, converted at Swindon from steam to diesel, to distant Persia to serve the Allied lifeline to Russia. It meant an LNER driver and fireman earning a George Cross apiece for driving an exploding ammunition train out of Soham station into open country. It meant shuttling 100,000 men through Southampton in the six days after D-day. Total war involving such extraordinary disruptions left Britain's railways in a disastrous state. Nationalisation became, therefore, not so much a political objective to be achieved as a vital prerequisite for post-war economic recovery.

Twice in the present century Britain's railways have been called upon to make heroic efforts and great sacrifices in the nation's defence. Many of their problems have been the direct result of the loyalty and devotion with which the call of duty was answered. An honoured place in Britain's transport system is the only fitting epitaph for such a record.

496 Middlesbrough station after an air raid in 1942 *British Rail*

THE LATEST PHASE-
BRITISH RAIL

497 No 92030 on an iron ore train south of Harbury tunnel in
October 1965. *D Huntriss*

499

500

498 British Rail ran out of steam in August 1968. This forlorn 8F 2-8-0 stands derelict at Rose Grove depot. *R Bastin*

499 Fast electric services on the LMR's Euston-Glasgow line. *British Rail*

500 The last vestige of pre-war standards of luxury on BR – the Brighton Belle, seen here diverted to London Bridge in April 1969. The train was withdrawn in 1972. *C J Gammell*

501

502 A Western Region class 52 diesel-hydraulic, all of which now have been withdrawn from service. *British Rail*

502

503

501 Unusual combination of 2HAP and 4CIG dc electric mu sets forming a Victoria-Portsmouth train on the SR mid-Sussex line. *British Transport Films*

503 BR experimental 4PEP sliding-door emu for high-density service, at Shepperton. *J A Bingham*

504 Arundel castle forming a backdrop to a SR 4CEP emu on the mid-Sussex line. *British Transport Films*

505 Prototype BR high-speed train (HST) with diesel-electric power cars at each end, designed for 125 mph. *British Transport Films*

506 Class 47 Brush diesel-electric No 1106 at Derby with a York-Poole train. *V Bamford*

507 A pair of BR-Sulzer Type 2 diesel-electrics on a car-delivery train at Skipton, Yorks. *R Lush*

504

222

505

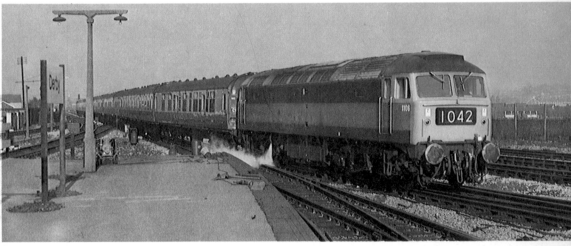

506

507

508

508 SR 4VEP third-rail electric mu approaching Vauxhall from Waterloo. *British Transport Films*

509 Prototype Advanced Passenger Train outside BR's Derby Research Centre. *British Rail*

509